Dick Goddard's Weather Guide AND Almanac

for NORTHEAST OHIO

GRAY & COMPANY, PUBLISHERS
CLEVELAND

A portion of the proceeds from the sale of this book will benefit animal charities in Northeast Ohio.

Gray & Company, Publishers
1588 E. 40th St., Cleveland, OH 44103
(216) 431-2665
www.grayco.com

Library of Congress Cataloging-in-Publication Data
Goddard, Dick
Dick Goddard's weather guide & almanac for northeast Ohio / by Dick Goddard.
Includes bibliographical references and index.
1. Ohio--Climate. 2. Almanac. 3. Weather forecasting. I. Title.
II. Title: Dick Goddard's weather guide and almanac for northeast Ohio
QC984.O3 G66 1998
551.69771—ddc21   98-40094   CIP

ISBN 1-886228-12-4

Printed in the United States of America
10 9 8 7 6 5 4 3 2

CONTENTS

INTRODUCTION

Almanacs traditionally cover a wide spectrum of subjects, not just the weather. While covering these, my goal is to keep you from being bored while you're learning something. Because my heroes include Mark Twain, Gary "Far Side" Larson, and Drew Carey (a fellow Kent Stater), I'm sure some hackles will be raised and a few sacred oxen will be gored by my words and illustrations.

We have a lot of weather in Northeast Ohio. So much weather that it often sticks out into other sections of Ohio, nearby states, and parts of Canada (thank you, Mr. Twain). While this almanac deals primarily with our particular weather, it, like most almanacs, also covers a smorgasbord of subjects from adiabatical expansion to Zubenelgenubi (it's a star).

This book should provide you with some basic information about Northeast Ohio weather that you can use every day. There are weather averages, daily temperature records, solar calendar data, some basic astronomy, some weather folklore, and features on a variety of topics, including the Ohio seasons, how weather works, remarkable Ohio storms, how Lake Erie affects our weather year round, and meteorology as a career.

Television weather forecasting is truly an American phenomenon, and I've devoted a major section to the subject. In Cleveland, as in all major television markets, of the dozen or so on-air forecasters only a few are actually qualified meteorologists. TV stations unabashedly, and without penalty, hang the title meteorologist on whoever does the job, even though that person's main weather experience might only consist of having been out in it. The truth is that none of us who present the weather could function without the basic services and information provided by the National Weather Service. Most of the TV and radio weatherpeople are "rip-and-read" performers who simply lift copy directly from a printer and parrot the forecasts of the government meteorologists.

Educators in the United States lament the fact that our high-school seniors rank very low in math, physics, and geography when compared to their peers in other countries. This book makes no pretense at higher education, but perhaps it will encourage a youngster or two towards a career in meteorology or some related science.

Ironically, computer chips are turning us into a nation of idiot savants. A friend of mine in a nearby state told me that he called a computer programmer in Salt Lake City for technical assistance and was asked, "Where's Michigan?" Since digital watches give us the time numerically, many have no idea what the hands and numbers on a clock signify. The terms clockwise and counterclockwise are a mystery.

It was Moose Paskert, my freshman football coach at Kent State University, who introduced me to the KISS philosophy ("Keep It Simple, Stupid"). In keeping with that, I've tried to write this book using nontechnical terms. I have eschewed both obfuscation and sesquipedalianism. There is, however, a reading list in the back of the book that will refer you to more detailed reading on many of the weather topics covered here.

The joy of watching the Northeast Ohio weather parade is that each day the marchers change. This book is for those who marvel at the ever-changing tapestry of the sky and the music of the weather— the syncopation of raindrops, the crash and rumble of thunder, and the discordant sound of the chilling Devil's Fiddle on a cold winter's night. These natural events, over which humankind has no real control, provide our common daily backdrop and dictate everything from the clothes we wear to the timing of our basic chores and travels. This book is as much a celebration of the weather in Northeast Ohio as it is a guide to it.

A PHILOSOPHY

A personal philosophy no doubt has no place in this book. But, since I'm playing the back nine—and it's my book—I'd like to share some thoughts I've accumulated while I was in the rough on the front side.

It was the old Notre Dame football coach Frank Leahy who said, "I'd rather be lucky than good." In the lottery of life I've drawn some lucky numbers. First off, I arranged to have the greatest parents and grandparents possible. None of them ever made it out of grade school, but they were honest, hard-working people who gave me lessons in life that you can never get from books. They did not burden me with superstitions and unproven beliefs (I'm an interdenominational skeptic—I believe that Humpty Dumpty was pushed).

Not having been born to the manor has been a true blessing. Growing up as an only child on a small farm in southern Summit

County taught me to appreciate things. It was in no way a hardscrabble life, but like most of the kids in my school I awakened on frigid winter mornings and put my feet down on an ice-cold hardwood floor. (My dad never did get the art of banking our coal furnace down to a science.)

Youngsters today complain about the modest pay they get for flipping hamburgers, but we have all served our time. Mine came during the two summers I spent as a teenager working on a nearby chicken ranch. For fifty cents an hour, six days a week, I filled reeking wheelbarrows full of chicken manure and then piloted them to ever-expanding golden pyramids that glistened and writhed in the hot sun.

It was at that point in my life that I decided against a career in solid-waste management. And I still don't eat chicken.

At one time I was dreaming about a baseball career. (I was one of about 20 kids—out of 200—to be asked back to a Brooklyn Dodger tryout camp; I didn't go back, which must have been a great relief to the Dodgers' third baseman, Spider Jorgensen.) But my heroes have long ceased to be people who sink 10-foot putts on the 18th hole or wide receivers who pull down the winning touchdown pass.

My dad is a real hero, and I treasure a letter I received a number of years ago praising the honesty of my father. Dad worked as a mechanic for a cross-country trucking company. It was during the heart of the Great Depression in the 1930s that my father found a billfold wedged under the seat of a truck cab. The wallet was promptly returned to the driver, with the hard-earned, and hard-to-come-by, money inside.

When I was growing up, Ohio highways were dotted with "Burma Shave" signs that passed along gentle wisdom and humor. While traveling life's highway I've found a number of signposts that have made the trip less bumpy. Here's a good one, and I've scattered others throughout the book.

> *Educating the mind without educating*
> *the heart is no education at all.*
> – ARISTOTLE

THE ART OF FORECASTING

How difficult is the job of forecasting the weather? Even a genius like Galileo, the 17th-century Italian astronomer, mathematician, and physicist, failed when it came to predicting the weather. "I can foretell the way of celestial bodies," said Galileo, "but I know nothing about the movement of a drop of water."

In 1845 the highly respected French physicist Dominique François Arago warned, "Never, no matter what the progress of science, will honest scientific men who have a regard for their professional reputation venture to predict the weather."

ADMIRAL FITZROY

The careers of British Admiral Robert FitzRoy and Professor Mark Harrington lend tragic support to Arago's admonition. In 1831 FitzRoy was a young officer in command of the HMS *Beagle*— and deeply interested in meteorology. His ship carried the equally young—and often seasick—naturalist Charles Darwin on the historic journey that eventually led to Darwin's epic treatise, *On the Origin of Species.* FitzRoy's superiors began to take note of his weather knowledge, and years later, on the recommendation of the Royal Society, he was named the first chief of the British Meteorological Office.

FitzRoy had the daunting—no, make that impossible—task of producing weather forecasts for the British navy with little more than a barometer and observations of the wind. Though he made a truly admirable effort, unforeseen storms regularly took their toll on the British navy and merchant marine. Criticism of FitzRoy's forecasting ability steadily mounted over the years—some accused him of sorcery—and he was badgered and bedeviled by members of the snooty Royal Society. Parliament and the *London Times* joined in the attack. With his reputation savaged, the public humiliation became too much, and before breakfast on April 20, 1865, Admiral FitzRoy took his own life by slitting his throat.

Professor Mark Harrington was appointed the first chief of the United States Weather Bureau in 1891, following the changeover from military to civilian control. Praised by many of his colleagues for his hard work and innovations, Harrington lasted as chief for just four years. Harassed by members of Congress, whose constituents blamed Harrington for failed forecasts, he was forced to resign in 1895. Harrington spent the last 18 years of his life in a mental institution.

Thirty-nine-year-old Willis Moore immediately succeeded Harrington in 1895 and managed to dodge political harpoons for 18 years. The tenacious Moore greatly expanded weather service to the general public and garnered headlines by declaring that good weather forecasters "are born, not made." Moore decided which meteorologists would be kept or fired based solely on their forecast accuracy. He admitted that under these stressful working conditions the national weather service had sent more men to the insane asylum than any other branch of government. Moore became infamous (to the delight of his critics) when his forecast of "clear" for President William Howard Taft's inaugural in 1909 came up a blizzard. Accused of mismanagement and fiscal irresponsibility, Moore was drummed out of office by President Woodrow Wilson in 1913.

THROUGH A CRYSTAL BALL DARKLY

To some folks Noah was the recipient of the first—and best—weather forecast. Ever since he built that gopher-wood ark and sailed away in the deluge, we have been trying to duplicate such expert forecasting ability.

The science of meteorology, particularly the business of forecasting, will forever vex mankind. Within this last century a number of atmospheric scientists were optimistic that the development of the supercomputer would be the silver bullet needed to produce reliable short- and long-range forecasts (we should always remember that optimism is the wonderful feeling of success we have before we really understand the problem). But chaos reigns in our atmosphere, and the day of the guaranteed weather forecast will very likely never dawn. Weather prognosticators will always be dealing in percentages, or estimates of probability. We will always be looking through a crystal ball, darkly.

The difficulty in predicting the weather is the fact that there is just so much of it. Our atmosphere is unbelievably complex and is in constant motion, both vertically and horizontally. One route to precise weather forecasting would be weather control, but therein lies a meteorological Catch-22. Seeding clouds to augment rain, for example, has achieved only modest success, and it is economically prohibitive. The threat of a lawsuit would be only a rainstorm away. Our

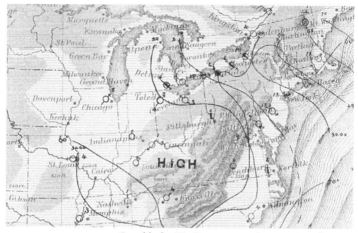

One of the first War Department weather maps, November 1870.

inability to control weather is no doubt fortunate: if any nation should gain such expertise, the weapon of flooding or making a rival country arid would be as fearful as any nuclear bomb.

In lieu of weather control, the best hope for success in long-range forecasting would seem to lie with the supercomputer and its ability to match current weather conditions to previous weather patterns (analogous forecasting). The difficulty here is that the predecessor of the National Weather Service was not established until 1870 (as a component of the War Department's Signal Corps), and complete weather records date only from the last few decades.

It's a meteorological truth that the further ahead the prediction, the less accurate it will likely be. In Northeast Ohio, where there is nonstop weather traffic, the 24-hour accuracy ranges between 80 and 90 percent, with the higher figure more common between late spring and mid-autumn. Two-day reliability runs between 70 and 80 percent, with the same seasonal variation. After the third day, unless there is an unusually persistent and dominant weather pattern, forecast accuracy falls another 5 to 10 percent. After four days weather predictions approach the 50-50 probability of outright guessing.

Surveys taken by television stations say that the public demands a five-day forecast. To many dedicated meteorologists, the five-day forecast is about as popular as a raspberry seed in a wisdom tooth. Such a forecast is predicated on the success of the previous day's estimate and because of this is subject to continual revision. (Like laws and sausages, you don't really want to know how five-day forecasts are made.)

Public acceptance of those who try to probe and predict the weather has been just as painfully slow as success in the art of forecasting. As recently as 1916 a congressman proposed that the United States Weather Bureau (now the National Weather Service) be abolished on the grounds that "a man using a sourwood stick can be more accurate." The National Weather Service has been a favorite, and easy, target for newspaper editorial writers. In the late 1800s, a daily journal used the forecasts of a 90-year-old

"HIM? HE HANDLES THE 5 DAY FORECASTS."

former scout for the legendary Kit Carson alongside the official Weather Bureau forecast. The scout's left leg had been severely injured some 60 years earlier and, claimed the old Indian fighter, was better than a real barometer. The leg was beating the government forecasts so badly that the Weather Bureau requested the newspaper stop the competition.

The location of the forecaster, of course, has a great deal to do with accuracy. Meteorologists in San Diego, or Yuma, Arizona, for example, with their cookie-cutter forecasts, can claim the highest accuracy rate in the United States. It's difficult to miss a forecast in places where the weather seldom changes. If you're a sensitive person with a thin epidermis, don't try forecasting in Northeast Ohio. (There have been a number of weatherpeople who have left the area

"FRANKLY, SENATOR, WE ARE ON THE VERGE OF A MAJOR BREAKTHROUGH."

because this weather didn't agree with them.) The essence of our weather is change, and what's here today is usually gone tomorrow (or tonight!). After several less-than-accurate forecasts I sometimes feel about as important to FOX 8 News as plot is to *Baywatch*.

Weather forecasting will always be as much art as science—with that large dollop of intuition thrown in. You're only as good as your last forecast, and there's the chance that we'll awaken to "six inches of partly cloudy" any morning. Forecasters can console themselves

HANG ON, HARRY... HERE COMES THE REVISED FORECAST!

by remembering that Babe Ruth struck out 1,330 times, but even when we are able to string together a modest series of successful predictions, we know that a failed forecast is right around the corner.

Mother Nature bats last.

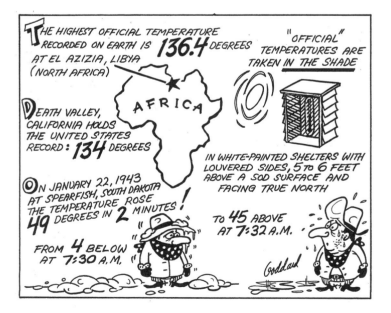

THE HIGHEST OFFICIAL TEMPERATURE RECORDED ON EARTH IS **136.4** DEGREES AT EL AZIZIA, LIBYA (NORTH AFRICA)

"OFFICIAL" TEMPERATURES ARE TAKEN *IN THE SHADE*

DEATH VALLEY, CALIFORNIA HOLDS THE UNITED STATES RECORD: **134** DEGREES

AFRICA

IN WHITE-PAINTED SHELTERS WITH LOUVERED SIDES, 5 TO 6 FEET ABOVE A SOD SURFACE AND FACING TRUE NORTH

ON JANUARY 22, 1943 AT SPEARFISH, SOUTH DAKOTA THE TEMPERATURE ROSE **49** DEGREES IN **2** MINUTES!

TO **45** ABOVE AT 7:32 A.M.

FROM **4** BELOW AT 7:30 A.M.

Goddard

WEATHER AVERAGES

Weather averages are like the average man . . . you'll probably never meet him. Abnormal weather *is* normal, and in Northeast Ohio it's frequently more abnormal—even extreme—than normal.

Weather norms are valuable, however, because they reveal definite climatological trends through the year. The official records are calculated by the National Weather Service for the most recent 30 years.

Sunrise and sunset tables are created by the Naval Observatory in Washington, D.C., and are based on the precise time that the rim of the sun is within one degree of the horizon. It is interesting to note that because of the bending of light rays (refraction) we actually see the sun before it is "up" and after it is "down." You will find that each year the times of sunrise and sunset will change slightly, one minute either way, on several days each year.

The water temperature of Lake Erie is taken from a submerged intake off Cleveland harbor at a depth of 35 feet.

CLEVELAND WEATHER EXTREMES

Highest temperature recorded in Cleveland:
104° F on June 25, 1988.

Coldest temperature recorded in Cleveland:
-20° F on January 19, 1994.

THE REASON FOR THE SEASONS

*Every day a new picture is painted and
framed, held up for half an hour, in such
lights as The Great Artist chooses,
and then withdrawn—and the curtain falls.*

– HENRY DAVID THOREAU

Our seasons are caused by the 23½-degree tilt of the earth as it spins in its counterclockwise orbit around the sun. There would be no winter, spring, summer, or autumn if it were not for this 365-day-plus cockeyed voyage.

In 23 hours, 56 minutes, and 4 seconds, the earth makes one complete revolution; this results in our cycle of night and day. If its axis were not canted, but straight up and down, the hours of daylight would always be the same for each latitude, and temperatures would vary little throughout the year. Because the earth is tilted, the length of daylight at the various latitudes between the North and South poles ranges from a few minutes to nearly 24 hours, depending on the latitude and the time of the year. At the equator, day and night are always of equal length; the pole that is tipped toward the sun receives 24 hours of daylight and the opposite pole is in continual darkness. Over the course of the year, each place on earth gets the identical amount of daylight.

The distance between the earth and sun averages 92.9 million miles, but the earth's 60-million-mile elliptical—not circular—path results in a 3-million-mile variance between its closest and farthest

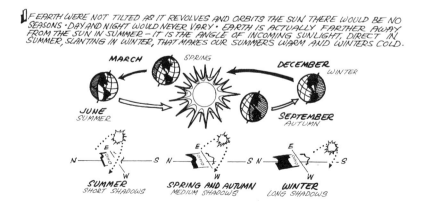

IF EARTH WERE NOT TILTED AS IT REVOLVES AND ORBITS THE SUN THERE WOULD BE NO SEASONS · DAY AND NIGHT WOULD NEVER VARY · EARTH IS ACTUALLY FARTHER AWAY FROM THE SUN IN SUMMER – IT IS THE ANGLE OF INCOMING SUNLIGHT, DIRECT IN SUMMER, SLANTING IN WINTER, THAT MAKES OUR SUMMERS WARM AND WINTERS COLD.

MARCH   SPRING   DECEMBER   WINTER

JUNE   SEPTEMBER
SUMMER   AUTUMN

SUMMER   SPRING AND AUTUMN   WINTER
SHORT SHADOWS   MEDIUM SHADOWS   LONG SHADOWS

approaches. This difference has little effect on seasonal temperature changes, however. In fact, in an interesting paradox, the earth is farther from the sun at the start of summer (aphelion is July 5) than it is at the start of winter (perihelion is January 3). It is the angle of the incoming sunlight—more direct in summer, more acute in winter—that makes our summers warm and our winters cold.

When the North Pole is angled toward the sun, the northern hemisphere has its summer and the southern hemisphere is in winter. Conversely, when the South Pole is angled toward the sun, it's winter up here and summer down there.

The starting dates of our seasons vary due to the earth's whirling, wobbling, nodding motions, the pull of gravity from other planets, and our faulty calendar. The summer solstice begins about June 21, when the midday sun is standing directly overhead at the tropic of Cancer, latitude 23° north. (Solstice is a Latin word meaning "to stand.") On this day the sun rises the highest and stays the longest. Around December 21, the sun is smack overhead at the tropic of Capricorn, latitude 23° south. This is the winter solstice, and the sun appears the lowest in our sky and stays the shortest time. About the 20th of March and the 22nd day of September, the sun is directly overhead at the equator. In March this position announces the vernal equinox; in September it proclaims the arrival of the autumnal equinox. (Equinox is a Latin word meaning "equal night.")

OHIO'S SEASONS

When we speak of "weather," we are talking about the current condition of temperature, precipitation, humidity, wind, air pressure, and cloudiness. The word "climate" describes the long-term tendency of the weather. To be succinct, climate is what you should have, weather is what you get.

Ohio's climate is considered to be continental, with moderate extremes of heat and cold, wetness and dryness. The extreme northern counties, especially those in the northeast corner of the state, experience a lake-effect influence due to the proximity of Lake Erie. Lake-effect weather, which is indigenous to only a few places on earth, results in remarkable differences in cloud cover, precipitation, and temperature over short distances.

While Ohio's summertime is warm and often humid, temperatures above 100 degrees are few and far between. On an average of five days each winter, Buckeye temperatures will dip below zero. Curiously, the Ohio annual average temperature is about 50° F, which is considered to be the mean surface temperature of the earth's atmosphere.

Land elevation in Ohio runs from 430 feet above sea level, at the joining of the Great Miami River and Ohio River in Hamilton County, to 1,550 feet above sea level just southeast of Bellefontaine in Logan County. The northwestern portion of Ohio is a flat lake plain that at one time was the bottom of glacial "Lake Maumee." The eastern counties of Ohio are in the Allegheny plateau, an unglaciated area with many hills that rise above 1,300 feet. This abrupt increase in elevation east and south of Cleveland is the major factor in creating the infamous and often heavy lake-effect snows of late autumn and early winter.

In official weather record keeping the months of March, April, and May are considered to be spring; June, July, and August are summer; September, October, and November are autumn; and December, January, and February make up winter. Of course, Clevelanders know that any day of any month in each season can have its little surprises—perhaps some chilling rain (and even a snowflake or two) in May, or balmy 70-degree readings in late January.

"WE WOULD LIKE TO THANK W.K. FOR BRINGING THAT TO OUR ATTENTION."

FARENHEIGHT/CELSIUS CONVERSION

°F	°C	°F	°C	°F	°C
-20	-29	27	-3	73	23
-19	-28	28	-2	74	23
-18	-28	29	-2	75	24
-17	-27	30	-1	76	24
-16	-27	31	-1	77	25
-15	-26	32	0	78	26
-14	-26	33	1	79	26
-13	-25	34	1	80	27
-12	-24	35	2	81	27
-11	-24	36	2	82	28
-10	-23	37	3	83	28
-9	-23	38	3	84	29
-8	-22	39	4	85	29
-7	-22	40	4	86	30
-6	-21	41	5	87	31
-5	-21	42	6	88	31
-4	-20	43	6	89	32
-3	-19	44	7	90	32
-2	-19	45	7	91	33
-1	-18	46	8	92	33
0	-18	47	8	93	34
1	-17	48	9	94	34
2	-17	49	9	95	35
3	-16	50	10	96	36
4	-16	51	11	97	36
5	-15	52	11	98	37
6	-14	53	12	99	37
7	-14	54	12	100	38
8	-13	55	13	101	38
9	-13	56	13	102	39
10	-12	57	14	103	39
11	-12	58	14	104	40
13	-11	59	15	105	41
14	-10	60	16	106	41
15	-9	61	16	107	42
16	-9	62	17	108	42
17	-8	63	17	109	43
18	-8	64	18	110	43
19	-7	65	18	111	44
20	-7	66	19	112	44
21	-6	67	19	113	45
22	-6	68	20	114	46
23	-5	69	21	115	46
24	-4	70	21	116	47
25	-4	71	22	117	47
26	-3	72	22	118	48

Winter

**SOME CALL THE OHIO WINTER
"INVIGORATING."
OTHERS PREFER THE WORD
"INTERMINABLE."**

At the time of the winter solstice in December, the sun appears at it lowest point on the horizon. In the northeast counties of the state, the shortened daylight combined with the heavy lake-effect cloudiness makes December the dimmest and darkest month of the year. On average, Greater Cleveland receives only 26 percent of possible sunshine during December.

The Erie Indians who lived along the lakeshore were frightened that the shortening days would lead to perpetual night, so they lit bonfires to coax the sun to stay in the sky. It worked for the Eries (as it does for us): curiously, just as winter began, the hours of daylight started to lengthen. Another paradox is that the sun reaches perihelion—its shortest distance from earth—on January 3. It is the sharp angle of the incoming winter sunlight that keeps the cold coming.

By early January, much of Ohio is usually a study in frozen motion as we are firmly locked into the season of silence.

Ohio's nighttime sky in December is ruled by the brilliant and brittle stars of the beautiful winter constellation Orion, the mighty hunter.

It was during the early morning hours of January 26, 1978, that the deepest and most powerful storm in Ohio weather history roared south-to-north across the state. This severe blizzard, literally a white hurricane, spawned a wind gust of 103 mph at the water intake crib just off Cleveland Harbor, and the air pressure fell to 28.28 inches of mercury, the lowest ever recorded in Ohio. The violent storm shut down the Ohio Turnpike for the first time in its history and stopped the United States postal delivery as well.

During the latter part of January the legendary thaw often pays a fleeting, but welcome, visit to Ohio. It's soon back to numb's-the-word, however, as the icy tyrant King Winter returns to use the state for his throne room.

**CLEVELAND'S WARMEST
AND COLDEST WINTERS
(BY MEDIAN TEMP)**

Warmest: 38.7° / 1931–32
Coldest: 19.8° / 1976–77

WINTER

CLEVELAND'S TOP 5 WETTEST AND DRIEST WINTERS (LIQUID)
Wettest
1) 14.95" / 1949–50
2) 13.84" / 1873–74
3) 13.22" / 1886–87
4) 13.08" / 1990–91
5) 12.81" / 1951–52
Driest
1) 3.27" / 1900–01
2) 3.32" / 1918–19
3) 3.64" / 1871–72
4) 3.65" / 1930–31
5) 3.96" / 1945–46

The coldest temperature ever recorded in Ohio was the -39° F reading (mercury freezes at -40°) at Milligan in Perry County south of Zanesville on February 10, 1899. An unofficial temperature of -44° was registered at Laceyville in Harrison County the same morning.

In the old days, farmers said that you'd make it through the rugged Ohio winter if you had "half your wood and half your hay" on the second day of February, Groundhog Day. Even though King Winter is still grinning at Ohio through icicle teeth as we honor the meteorological marmot, he is aware of the signs that signal the end of his reign. The archenemy of the ice tyrant is the sun, and in the late-winter Ohio sky the golden sphere rides a little higher each day and stays a little longer than it did the day before.

By mid-February, spring will have begun its inexorable march northward from the Gulf of Mexico. At a rate of 15 miles each day, the frost line pushes closer to Ohio. At each point it passes, the insects emerge from their wintering places and the migrant birds follow this food supply northward. Spring will soon be touching all growing things with the magic of rebirth.

If there were such a thing as a Hall of Infamy for Ohio's winters, these would have to be considered the most difficult in terms of cold, snow, or both: 1995–96; 1977–78; 1976–77; 1962–63; 1935–36; 1917–18; and 1898–99.

The Lake Erie water temperature continues its decline into the 30s during December, reaching its wintertime low of 33° F (it cannot go below that figure) by early January. The lake temperature holds at 33° throughout February.

MOST CONSECUTIVE DAYS WITH MEASURABLE SNOW ON THE GROUND IN CLEVELAND
73 days, Dec. 11, 1944–Feb. 21, 1945
65, Jan. 9, 1978–Mar. 14, 1978
64, Dec. 21, 1976–Feb. 22, 1977
63, Dec. 6, 1962–Feb. 6, 1963

WINTER GLOSSARY

Winter Storm Watch means that a storm is approaching. It could slide by and miss the area, so stay up on the latest advisory.

Winter Storm Warning means that a storm is imminent. Estimates of snowfall will be included in the warning.

Heavy Snow for most of Ohio is four inches or more in a 12-hour period, or six inches or more in a 24-hour period. In the snowy northern third of Ohio, heavy snow is considered to be six inches or more in a 12-hour period.

Snow in a forecast indicates the possibility of a steady fall with amounts of anywhere from one to three inches over the forecast period.

Flurries indicates relatively brief, intermittent periods of snow. The flurry may be light or heavy, but it passes quickly.

Snow Squalls are bursts of heavy snow accompanied by gusty winds. A squall can drop several inches of snow in one spot and leave nearby areas untouched.

Winter Weather Advisory alerts you to an important event such as freezing rain, sleet, blowing snow, strong winds, or fog but is below the level of a warning category.

WINTER ❄

Ohio snowfall averages

IN THE NORTHEAST OHIO SKY THIS SEASON

Our sky has twice as many bright stars in winter than in any other season. It's not because of cold, clear nights; it's simply because the earth is turned to its most favorable position for the viewing of stars.

Arguably the most beautiful constellation of them all, Orion— The Mighty Hunter—rules the frigid, brittle skies of winter. The red-orange superstar Betelgeuse (BET-el-jooz) is one of the largest known stars. (Sorry, kids, it isn't pronounced "beetle juice.") When fully expanded Betelgeuse may be 1,000 times as large as our sun. Blue-white Rigel (RYE-jel) is one of the brightest stars visible to us.

The three stars that make up the belt in the middle of Orion are Mintaka (min-TAK-ah), Alnilam (al-NIGH-lam), and Alnitak (al-nih-TAK).

Yapping at Orion's heels is Sirius, the Dog Star, the brightest star in our sky. To the upper right is cool-yellow Aldeberan (al-DEB-ah-ran) the ninth-brightest jewel in our heavens.

SUNSHINE %: 26
DRIEST MONTH: 0.71"/1958
WARMEST MONTH: 42.0°/1889
COLDEST MONTH: 19.2°/1989
LIQUID PCPN AVG.: 3.09"
RAINIEST DAY: 2.81"/1992
RAINIEST MONTH: 8.59"/1990
THUNDERY DAYS: 0
SNOWIEST DAY: 12.2"/1974
SNOWIEST MONTH: 30.3"/1962
LEAST SNOWFALL: Trace (most recently in 1931)
DAYS ONE INCH SNOW: 4

Northeast Ohioans have now entered the dark weather tunnel from which we will not emerge for many months. In dark December Greater Clevelanders will experience only 26 percent of possible sunshine. From now through January, Cleveland will rank with such places as Seattle, Washington, Portland, Oregon, and Syracuse, New York, as the nation's cloudiest cities. The sun (if seen) will reach its lowest point in the sky around December 21, the time of the winter solstice. It has taken 365 days for our small planet to complete its elliptical (not circular) orbit around the sun. Four hundred million years ago there were 400 days in a year, because our favorite planet was spinning much faster and days were shorter. It's been discovered that earth has nine separate movements as it wobbles, whirls, and nods while traveling at 1,100 miles per minute. While many Ohio animals are in their deep winter snooze, raccoons, opossums, and skunks may awaken to forage for food. If you started to feed the birds in autumn you must keep it up, since they now depend on you for a handout. Ohio's coldest Christmas was in 1983, with area high temperatures only around zero and a -50° wind chill; Ashtabula and Conneaut were snowbound.

DECEMBER

Day	Hi	Lo	Rec Hi	Rec Lo	Sunrise	Sunset	Lake°
1	43	29	65 / 1970	7 / 1929	7:34	4:59	45
2	42	29	70 / 1982	-5 / 1976	7:35	4:59	45
3	42	28	77 / 1982	-7 / 1976	7:36	4:59	45
4	41	28	70 / 1982	8 / 1871	7:37	4:58	44
5	41	28	67 / 1982	2 / 1871	7:38	4:58	44
6	40	27	68 / 1956	7 / 1977	7:39	4:58	44
7	40	27	66 / 1892	-5 / 1882	7:40	4:58	43
8	40	27	67 / 1966	-9 / 1882	7:40	4:58	43
9	39	27	62 / 1952	-5 / 1917	7:41	4:58	43
10	39	26	69 / 1971	-5 / 1958	7:42	4:58	42
11	39	26	64 / 1931	-2 / 1977	7:43	4:58	42
12	38	26	63 / 1949	-1 / 1962	7:44	4:58	41
13	38	25	65 / 1901	-3 / 1962	7:45	4:58	41
14	38	25	64 / 1901	0 / 1914	7:45	4:59	41
15	37	25	67 / 1971	-1 / 1958	7:46	4:59	40
16	37	24	64 / 1984	-9 / 1951	7:47	4:59	40
17	37	24	61 / 1984	-7 / 1989	7:48	4:59	40
18	37	24	62 / 1939	-5 / 1989	7:48	5:00	39
19	36	24	61 / 1939	-5 / 1884	7:49	5:00	39
20	36	23	62 / 1895	-4 / 1963	7:49	5:01	38
21	36	23	65 / 1967	-7 / 1972	7:50	5:01	38
22	36	23	64 / 1949	-15 / 1989	7:50	5:02	37
23	35	23	61 / 1933	-7 / 1960	7:51	5:02	37
24	35	22	65 / 1964	-10 / 1983	7:51	5:03	37
25	35	22	66 / 1982	-10 / 1983	7:52	5:03	37
26	35	22	64 / 1875	-8 / 1983	7:52	5:04	36
27	34	22	64 / 1936	-5 / 1944	7:52	5:05	36
28	34	21	68 / 1982	-3 / 1880	7:53	5:05	36
29	34	21	66 / 1889	-12 / 1880	7:53	5:06	36
30	34	21	63 / 1971	-12 / 1880	7:53	5:07	36
31	34	21	68 / 1875	-11 / 1880	7:53	5:08	36

Never think that you know all.
However highly you are appraised,
always have the courage to say to yourself,
I am ignorant.
– IVAN PAVLOV

FLAKY FACTS

The six-sided snowflake is actually a piece of ice. Indeed, the snowflake begins its life as a microscopic seed of ice no larger than the speck of dust (called the nucleus) on which it forms. The delicate ice-crystal jewel then grows by a process called sublimation: the transformation of a substance from an invisible vapor phase (in this case water vapor) to a solid phase without first becoming a liquid.

Snowflakes are six-sided because the water molecule—H_2O—has two atoms of hydrogen and one atom of oxygen. The molecule itself resembles a triangle with three equal sides. As the water molecule crystallizes, each new "bud" forms at an angle of 60 degrees from the hub of the triangle. This process continues until six molecular triangles are completed and a hexagon results.

While the snowflake crystal is always hexagonal, there are many forms it can take: prisms, needles, columns, plates, and stars. Prisms and needles form in temperatures between 18° F and 27° F; higher or lower temperatures produce columns, plates, and stars.

An average snowflake contains 10 quintillion (that's a 10 with 18 zeros after it) molecules of water, and in a run-of-the-mill snowstorm some one billion flakes fall.

Snow can be "wet" or "dry." The rule of thumb that one inch of rain equals 10 inches of snow is subject to wide variations. The ratio in wet snow may be 1 to 5, while in extremely dry snow the ratio may reach 1 to 40. The wetter the snow, the larger the snowflakes. Huge, saucer-sized crystals are the result of snowflakes that have grown by bumping into their neighbors on their way to earth. Snowflakes 15 inches across were once sighted at Fort Keough, Montana.

Light, very dry snow that resembles diamond dust as it glitters in the moonlight may have taken hours to

TOP 5 SNOWIEST AND LEAST SNOWY SEASONS

Snowiest
1) 101.1" / 1995–96
2) 100.5" / 1981–82
3) 90.1" / 1977–78
4) 88.5" / 1992–93
5) 80.9" / 1909–10

Least Snowy
1) 8.8" / 1918–19
2) 14.9" / 1889–90
3) 20.9" / 1890–91
4) 21.4" / 1931–32
5) 22.3" / 1894–95

WINTER

DEC

complete its journey. An indicator of just how light and dry snow can be is that livestock trapped by snow following a blizzard usually do not perish from exposure or starvation. The animals die from thirst because they are not able to lick enough life-sustaining moisture from the surrounding snow.

While the heaviest snow usually falls when temperatures are near freezing, it can never be too cold to snow. There is always a tiny amount of precipitable water vapor within our atmosphere.

FIRST COUSINS OF THE SNOWFLAKE

SNOW PELLETS are also known as soft hail or graupel. These small, white, opaque granules resemble tapioca and often shatter upon striking a hard surface. Snow pellets often precede snowflakes in the Northeast Ohio autumn.

SNOW GRAINS are white, opaque, ricelike particles of ice that neither bounce nor shatter.

ICE PELLETS are hard beads of clear or transparent ice (also called sleet). Ice pellets form when rain falls through cold air near the earth's surface; they rebound when hitting a hard surface.

> Earliest Measurable Snowfall:
> October 2, 1974 (0.1")
>
> Latest Measurable Snowfall: May 10,
> 1907 (0.2") and May 10, 1902 (0.6")

CLEVELAND'S 30 YEARS OF SNOWFALL (IN INCHES)

Season	Sep	Oct	Nov	Dec	Jan	Feb	Mar	Apr	May	TOTAL
1967–68	0	0.1	9.1	2.8	14.5	8.9	7.7	0.2	Tr	43.3
1968–69	0	Tr	6.8	8.3	5.8	5.6	9.0	1.5	Tr	37.0
1969–70	0	0.6	6.6	17.4	10.5	6.6	11.5	0.2	Tr	53.4
1970–71	Tr	Tr	5.2	6.0	8.6	14.3	16.6	0.7	0	51.4
1971–72	0		5.3	1.9	15.0	14.8	6.3	2.3	0	45.6
1972–73	0	5.5	7.8	15.2	9.8	20.4	8.3	0.9	0.6	68.5
1973–74	0	Tr	3.3	13.8	8.9	16.9	7.1	6.4	2.1	58.5
1974–75	0	1.6	5.3	24.1	9.7	9.9	15.2	1.2	0.0	67.0
1975–76	0	0	5.6	13.1	21.5	6.8	5.8	1.6	Tr	54.4
1976–77	Tr	1.6	8.9	16.3	21.1	9.6	4.2	1.7	0	63.4
1977–78	0	Tr	9.7	23.1	42.8	10.8	3.5	0.2	0	90.1
1978–79	0	0	1.9	2.5	15.1	16.0	2.4	0.4	0	38.3
1979–80	0	0.2	0.5	4.0	11.3	19.2	3.5	Tr	Tr	38.7
1980–81	0	Tr	5.4	13.5	15.0	9.7	16.9	Tr	0	60.5
1981–82	0	4	2.9	27.1	28.1	7.6	17.6	13.2	0	100.5
1982–83	0	0	2.2	6.3	6.5	8.3	11.3	3.4	0	38.0
1983–84	0	0	7.1	13.0	12.9	27.1	19.3	Tr	0	79.4
1984–85	0	0	4.0	8.9	25.5	18.2	1.2	5.9	0	63.7
1985–86	0	0	Tr	23.4	17.2	10.8	6.7	0.2	0	58.3
1986–87	0	Tr	3.1	1.1	16.4	5.0	26.2	4.0	0	55.8
1987–88	0	Tr	1.0	16.4	8.7	22.9	20.4	1.9	0	71.3
1988–89	0	Tr	1.7	17.9	6.6	13.8	9.9	4.9	Tr	54.8
1989–90	0	Tr	9.1	24.0	10.5	9.9	4.4	4.7	0	62.6
1990–91	0	0	Tr	7.4	16.6	18.9	4.2	Tr	0	47.1
1991–92	0	0	3.5	9.4	23.8	6.2	18.4	4.4	0	65.7
1992–93	0	Tr	7.1	7.1	8.7	39.1	25.4	1.1	0	88.5
1993–94	0	0.2	3.0	19.0	27.4	12.3	7.0	3.6	0	72.5
1994–95	0	0	Tr	1.0	23.4	14.7	4.3	0.2	0	43.6
1995–96	0	0	9.9	29.6	21.9	10.1	19.4	10.2	0	101.1
1996–97	0	0	23.4	5.0	13.0	8.4	5.3	0.8	0	55.9
1997–98	0	Tr	8.6	10.7	5.0	0.2	9.5	0.0	0	34.0
1998–99										
1999–2000										
2000–2001										

Cleveland's 30-Year Average: 61 inches

WINTER

❄

DEC

WINTER

DEC

WINTER STORMS

"You can tell your weather guy that I just shoveled six inches of his 'partly sunny' out of my driveway!" There isn't a veteran forecaster in Ohio who hasn't heard this unsolicited opinion, and I've found that the most passionate response from the public is that which follows a failed forecast for heavy snow. Whether you err by forecasting too much or too little, it is an event that is guaranteed to raise the public's hackles and bring down their wrath. (For that reason, there is also no greater satisfaction than knowing you've made a reasonably accurate forecast of snow accumulation.)

Predicting snowfall is about as difficult as shoveling smoke. Many things can go wrong in a snow forecast, and snowfall can vary widely over short distances.

A temperature difference of as little as one or two degrees and a variance in land elevation of 100 feet can mean the difference between heavy snow and no snow at all. A December 1962 snowstorm just east of Cleveland put down 19 inches of snow three miles inland from Lake Erie, while no snow accumulated within one-half mile of the lakeshore.

Snow forecasts can quickly go astray with the intrusion of slightly warmer air, either at the surface or a few hundred feet aloft. Then rain begins to mix with snow and a heavy-snow forecast literally turns to slush.

"TONIGHT'S HEAVY SNOW WARNING IS CANCELED DUE TO LACK OF INTEREST"

WINTER

❄

DEC

For all of the above reasons, a forecast of snowfall more than 12 hours in advance is often worthless.

The heaviest snow usually falls when the surface temperature is between 28° and 34° F (-2° and 1° C, respectively). An exception to this would be when cold air at the surface is overrun by warmer, moist air aloft. The great Thanksgiving week snowstorm of 1950 in eastern Ohio was the result of this overlapping.

Even when a forecaster is confident that a winter storm will pass nearby, that temperatures will be cold enough to produce snow, and that enough moisture will be available, the "3 Ps" must be considered:

PATH: The exact path of a snowstorm is critical, because the heaviest snow most often comes down 50 to 150 miles to the left (west through north) of an approaching storm center. Little or no snow occurs near the center of a well-developed storm. A relatively minor deviation in the path of the storm will cause a major shift in the heavy snow shield.

PACE: The rate of movement of a storm system is important, since a slow-moving storm will allow more snow to fall than a fast-paced storm. Storm systems frequently change their rate of progress.

PUNCH: The depth of a low-pressure system determines its intensity. A vigorous storm that threatens Ohio may begin to lose its energy to a deeper storm complex that develops along the eastern slopes of the Appalachian Mountains. Unimpressive low-pressure centers may suddenly deepen as they cross the Great Lakes.

A major snowstorm creates a picture of frozen motion, paralyzing and immobilizing large portions of the region. And it can kill. Forty percent of snowstorm-related fatalities are due to highway accidents; heart attacks and overexertion brought on by snow shoveling and snow removal account for 30 percent. The remaining 30 percent die from exposure, falls, contact with downed power lines, carbon monoxide poisoning (in vehicles), and building collapse.

The snowstorms that affect Ohio come from six basic situations and directions:

PANHANDLE HOOK (PH). This winter storm system brings the heaviest general snowfall into Ohio. The PH gets its name from the abrupt northeastward path the storm takes after it initially drops southeastward from the eastern slopes of the Rocky Mountains.

DEC

This low-pressure center deepens as it moves across the Oklahoma Panhandle and begins to draw moisture northward from the Gulf of Mexico. The PH that puts down heavy snow in Ohio usually travels near the Ohio River, across Kentucky, and into West Virginia. If the center of a PH passes to the west of Ohio—from Indianapolis to Detroit, for example—the heaviest snow would fall on an axis from St. Louis through Chicago. The ratio of snow to rain in a Panhandle Hook is about 8 to 1.

ALBERTA CLIPPER. In the cold-air wake of a Panhandle Hook, a fast-moving low-pressure center called the Alberta Clipper often develops. Often Clippers occur in a series. Originating in the foothills of the Rocky Mountains in the Canadian province of Alberta, these small low-pressure systems travel at speeds of 30 to 40 mph as they hurtle southeastward across the Great Lakes toward Ohio.

Since the Clipper moves quickly in its dry cold-air environment, it often brings with it one to three inches' worth of light, fluffy easy-to-shovel snow. Youngsters find it difficult to make snowmen from a Clipper, since it brings a low moisture content of about 20 to 1.

WESTERLY LOW. These poorly organized low-pressure centers carry limited amounts of moisture and usually bring light snow accumulations with a 10 to 1 moisture ratio.

GULF COAST LOW. This system, originating in the Louisiana Delta area, brings Ohio its wettest snow. If the storm center moves just west of Ohio, the mild air brought up on the east side of the storm center often changes our snow to rain. Ohio's deepest storm center, bringing with it our lowest barometric-pressure reading (28.28 inches of mercury in Cleveland on January 26, 1978), was a Gulf Coast Low. This heavy, difficult-to-shovel snow can have a snow-to-rain ratio of just 3 to 1.

EAST COAST LOW. This system can bury the big cities of the eastern United States under heavy, wind-whipped snow. Traveling northward along the eastern side of the Appalachian Mountains, the violent counterclockwise rotation of air around the storm creates the legendary "nor'easter" (winds striking from a northeasterly direction). Only the largest, most well-organized East Coast storms bring snow westward into Ohio.

LAKE EFFECT. This unusual snowfall pattern is pronounced only at four places on earth: the southeast shorelines of the Great Lakes, the southeast shoreline of Hudson Bay, the area to the east of the Great Salt Lake in Utah, and the northernmost Japanese island of Hokkaido. It results from a specific combination of topography, air temperature, and wind direction.

Lake-effect snows develop from the instability (upward motion) that is created when cold air crosses warm water. The cold air near the water surface is suddenly warmed, and it scoops up large quantities of water vapor. As the moisture-laden air reaches land, it is forced to rise rapidly over the land (orographic lifting). As a result of convective cooling and contact with the cold over running air, the water vapor quickly sublimates into ice crystals (snow).

In Northeast Ohio, the heaviest lake-effect snow sets up when frigid arctic air pours across the unfrozen expanse of Lake Erie in late autumn and early winter (November into early January).

The greatest lake-effect snow occurs when winds from the land surface up to a height of 5,000 feet are from a northwesterly direction (from 300 to 330 degrees on a compass) and the temperature difference between the Lake Erie water and the air flowing over the lake is 20 degrees or more. A wind shear (change in direction from northwest) will inhibit or destroy the potential for heavy lake-effect snow.

Because of orographic lifting, the higher the land elevation the greater the probability for heavy lake-induced snows. Moreover, the distance the incoming cold air travels across the water (fetch) is critical for heavy lake-effect snow. While the fetch across Lake Erie from Cleveland is about 55 miles, a wind trajectory that includes Lake Huron will add another 200 miles of water to the lake-effect recipe.

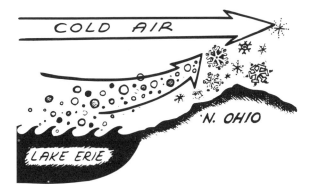

COLD AIR

N. OHIO

LAKE ERIE

WINTER

❄

DEC

Lake-effect snow can take the form of light or moderate flurries or heavy, often localized squalls. The squall is an intense burst of snow that can result in several inches of accumulation in only minutes. Usually nomadic, squalls may occasionally become stationary and drop all of their ice-crystal cargo on one location. Predicting lake-effect snowfall is extremely difficult because, unlike with other snowstorms, it develops directly over us—as a result, there is no history from which to predict its severity. Even inside the snowbelts accumulation can vary widely. A forecaster must await the arrival of the first snowflakes to get an idea of what sort of weather he will have on his hands.

Lake-effect snow affects almost exclusively the northeastern counties of Ohio, and it makes the snowbelt corridor from Ohio through northwest Pennsylvania and into western New York State one of the snowiest regions on earth.

Wind direction and wind speed play crucial roles in lake-effect snow. In Ohio, the shoreline of Lake Erie is not directly west-to-east but turns abruptly northeast as you travel from Cleveland to Ashtabula. For this reason, a wind from the west moves over dry land west of Cleveland and such a prevailing wind drops little, if any, snow west of the city. The same wind passes over water just east of Cleveland, and this water-vapor-packed wind can deposit heavy snow in Lake, northern Geauga, eastern Cuyahoga, and Ashtabula counties. This is the primary snowbelt in Northeast Ohio

A sustained west-to-northwest gale-force wind in late autumn or early winter—

Euclid Avenue after the Thanksgiving week snowstorm of November 1950.

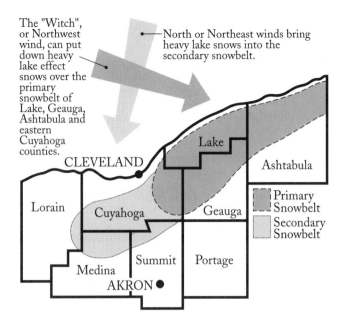

The "Witch", or Northwest wind, can put down heavy lake effect snows over the primary snowbelt of Lake, Geauga, Ashtabula and eastern Cuyahoga counties.

North or Northeast winds bring heavy lake snows into the secondary snowbelt.

WINTER

DEC

Lake

Ashtabula

CLEVELAND

Lorain

Cuyahoga

Geauga

Primary Snowbelt
Secondary Snowbelt

Medina

Summit

Portage

AKRON

called the "Witch" by Great Lakes seamen—can produce a monumental snow blitz over the primary snowbelt counties. Snow accumulations of more than two inches an hour may occur. (The equally gusty and cold northeast wind is known as the "Hawk.")

A secondary snowbelt lies over the higher ground to the southwest, south, and southeast of Cleveland. Wind from a due north direction can spread heavy bursts of lake-effect snow into Lorain, Medina, Summit, and Portage counties.

The speed of the air traveling across Lake Erie is an important factor, as air that moves too slowly does not reach land with much impetus and is not lifted rapidly enough to foment heavy snow.

Thunder and lightning may also accompany the heavier snow squalls, even though the tops of the clouds may grow to only 10 or 15 thousand feet (summertime thunderstorms can tower over 40,000 feet). During thundersnow conditions snowfall rates of four inches or more per hour are common.

Lake-effect clouds (except in thundersnow) are characteristically shallow, with tops of 4,000 to 8,000 feet. This is why during a lake-effect snow blitz you will frequently see blue sky and sunshine briefly appear between the squalls. Lake-effect snow is usually light and fluffy due to its low water content.

Winds from a southerly direction do not cause lake-effect snows on the opposite side of Lake Erie in Canada because air from the south is generally too warm to produce snow.

On weather radar, lake-effect snow appears as streaks or bands of snow oriented along the axis of the prevailing wind. In the dying stages of lake effect, the snow streaks can be seen "backing" from the lakeshore communities east of Cleveland into the city and points southwest.

Chardon, 12½ miles inland from Lake Erie at an elevation of 1,210 feet above sea level, has an average seasonal snowfall of 106 inches. At Hopkins International Airport, five miles inland from Lake Erie and at an elevation of 777 feet, an average snowfall of 53 inches occurs. (Lake Erie's shoreline elevation is 572 feet.) It is a fair assumption that the lake effect causes this difference.

In our state's greatest snow blitz, November 9–14, 1996, 68.9 inches of snow fell on Chardon. This set the Ohio record for snowfall in a single storm, eclipsing the old record of 42 inches at Canton and Gratiot during April 19–22, 1901. The snow accumulation of 48 inches on November 14 at Chardon was the deepest in Ohio's history.

Thompson, located 10 miles northeast of Chardon in Geauga County, may exceed Chardon in annual snowfall, but weather records there are not extensive.

The Lake Erie snow machine will continue to operate until a wind shift away from the lake surface shortens, or destroys entirely, the fetch over water. The seasonal increase in ice cover on Lake Erie often limits lake-effect snow potential after mid-January.

CHILLING OUT

I don't think of myself as a wimp. I've been in a tornado, flown through a hurricane, and witnessed the first full-yield H-Bomb detonation. At the movies when I'm asked to choose my popcorn container I always pick the Roger Ebert Tub of Death. (After brief research, however, I no longer eat the middle sections of Oreo cookies.) But I have come to dread the turn to bitterly cold temperatures in the Northeast Ohio winter.

Weather is very subjective, but surveys have shown that most people can handle hot weather much better than cold. I have great empathy for the outdoor critters, especially the feral dogs and cats—at least *I* have the option of going indoors. The fear of cold temperatures is called cheimaphobia, and while I haven't reached that point, I just don't tolerate the frigorific weather that well. Some say that this is a normal physical reaction as you age, but I suspect that today's clothing fabrics are vastly inferior to those of my youth.

This brings me to the bane of all businesses that rely on people to leave the warmth of their own homes: the insidious wind-chill factor. No one can argue with the fact that the wind has the power to make cold temperatures feel even colder. But the wind-chill index used to determine human discomfort was never designed for the purpose it now serves. And this is due not to a government conspiracy by the National Weather Service, but primarily to the zeal of television and radio weather reporters. How often have we been warned to stay indoors or face imminent death?

The wind-chill factor used in the United States came from the research of an Ohioan, Dr. Paul Siple, and his colleague at the base station called Little America at the South Pole in 1941. The military wanted to know the type of clothing that should be worn during winter, and Dr. Siple hung out plastic, water-filled cylinders to measure how long it took for the water to freeze under varying temperatures and wind speeds. That was the birthplace of the wind-chill factor, and the information was eventually applied to the effect of cold on human skin.

Wind chill results when air moves past your body and blows away the thin, five-millimeter layer of body-warmed air molecules that surrounds each of us. The stronger and more persistent the wind, the less chance your body has to replace the protective warm layer.

The wind-chill index, as it is used today, is flawed for many reasons. It does not take into account the age, health, and body type of each person. It does not consider the heat-robbing potential of moist air, nor the fact that sunshine can ameliorate the effect of bitterly cold temperatures as well as provide a psychosomatic benefit. The amount, type, and fabric of the clothing being worn are a major consideration. (Without head cover, more than 50 percent of body heat will be lost through your dome.) Is the person walking, jogging, or sitting? Physical activity allows our bodies to radiate more heat, and if properly layered clothing is worn, the insulation it provides can effectively negate all but the most frigid Northeast Ohio temperatures most of the time.

The dangers of wind chill should not be underestimated: it can bring on frostbite (which can lead to amputation of a body part) and hypothermia (which can lower your body's core temperature and cause death). Some parts of the human body will freeze more quickly than others, especially the extremities—fingers, hands, toes, feet, nose, and ears. Simply cover as much skin as you can.

There can be no argument that the Venturi effect (the funneling and constricting of air through narrow passages) can produce violent and explosive bursts of wind in cities. In Cleveland, the ingrown eyelash award should go to the corner of East Ninth and Lakeside, where the winter winds can blow the hair off a dog. However, a serious question arises from the manner in which the National Weather

Service records wind speed. The official anemometers are 33 feet high, not at ground level where people are. Because there is generally much less wind at ground level due to the frictional effect of rough surface terrain, it has been suggested that the wind-chill numbers should be divided by two. That means a wind chill of -20° F would more appropriately be -10°. In addition, wind speeds of over 40 mph add little additional wind chill.

The answer to the problem would be to create a new wind-chill scale that would take into account more of these variables. Even the National Weather Service's *Operations Manual* states that "no specific rules exist for determining when the wind chill becomes dangerous." A wind-chill value of -20° F is the current figure used for issuance of a wind-chill warning. Using the current wind-chill table, it can truly be said that many are cold, but few are frozen.

No, wind chill does not apply to car radiators. Although you should face your car away from the wind to slow the speed of the temperature drop, the radiator temperature cannot go below the air temperature.

WIND-CHILL TEMPERATURE

ACTUAL TEMPERATURE (FAHRENHEIT)

WIND SPEED (MPH)	50	40	30	20	10	0	-10	-20	-30	-40	-50	-60
	APPARENT WIND-CHILL TEMPERATUER (FAHRENHEIT)											
CALM	50	40	30	20	10	0	-10	-20	-30	-40	-50	-60
5	48	37	28	16	6	5	-15	-26	-36	-47	-57	-68
10	40	28	16	4	-9	-21	-33	-46	-58	-70	-83	-95
15	36	22	9	-5	-18	-36	-45	-58	-72	-85	-99	-102
20	32	18	4	-10	-25	-39	-53	-67	-82	-96	-110	-124
25	30	16	0	-15	-29	-44	-59	-74	-83	-104	-113	-133
30	28	13	-2	-18	-33	-48	-63	-79	-94	-109	-125	-140
35	27	11	-4	-20	-35	-49	-64	-82	-98	-113	-129	-145
40	26	10	-6	-21	-37	-53	-69	-85	-102	-116	-132	-148

EL NIÑO, LA NIÑA, OR EL VIEJO?

With about 71 percent of Planet Earth covered by water, it has long been suspected that our oceans and seas hold the key to our weather. In recent years the phenomenon known as El Niño (the boy child) has captured the minds and imagination of both scientists and the general public.

El Niño is still a meteorological mystery, its cause unknown. Its earliest recorded occurrence was in the year 1567, and its effect becomes pronounced about every two to seven years. El Niño occurs when a nearly 6,000-mile swath of Pacific Ocean water from Australia to the waters off the coast of Peru in South America becomes abnormally warm. (El Niño is part of what is known to scientists as the Southern Oscillation, a reverse in normal high and low air pressure across the Pacific Ocean— the combination is called ENSO.) In effect, the change in air pressure causes the Pacific Ocean to slosh back and forth like water in a bathtub. As the warmer water from the western Pacific reaches the coastline of South America, the normal northeasterly trade winds weaken and the wind may actually blow from west to east.

An NOAA-satellite view of the 1997/98 El Niño.

El Niño has consequences all around our planet, because it pushes the northern jet stream even farther northward during the winter months. This shuts off the flow of arctic air southeastward into the United States and prevents a system known as the polar vortex from forming over Hudson Bay in Canada. (This vortex brings frigid air into Ohio during a more normal winter.) The Pacific prankster brings excessive rains into Southern California and other southern areas of the United States. Along with delivering torrential rains into normally dry Peru, the warmer coastal waters deprive marine life of cold-water nutrients, and the dwindling fish population devastates the fishing industry there. Drought conditions plague Australia and parts of Brazil and Africa.

El Niño drastically curtails hurricanes and tropical storms in the Atlantic Ocean by weakening the winds that come off the coast of Africa.

Periods of both good and bad weather occur during El Niño, and the phenomenon has little effect on any location from spring through summer and early autumn. A network of weather buoys strung out across the Pacific Ocean, along with satellite sensors, is allowing weather forecasters to get some advance warning on a growing El Niño. Even so, computer forecast models can fail miserably, missing both the magnitude and timing of the event.

The El Niño of 1997/98 produced the fourth-warmest winter in Cleveland weather history (1931/32 was the warmest). Only 34 inches of snow fell at Cleveland Hopkins International Airport (normal is around 60) with an all-time record low of only 0.2 inches of snow during February. The lowest temperature was 12° F (above zero). Lake Erie stayed ice-free throughout the winter, and winter sports activity was at a minimum. Characteristically, Ohio winters during a major El Niño are unseasonably mild and dry.

El Niño winters may come back-to-back, but more often El Niño is followed by its brutally cold and snowy baby sister, La Niña. (La Niña is locally known as El Viejo, "the old one.") In Cleveland's El Niño winter of 1982/83, a meager 38 inches of snow fell. That was followed by a La Niña winter of 79 inches. During our El Niño of 1994/95 we totaled 44 inches, while an unsisterly La Niña buried us under a record 101 inches the next winter.

During El Niño, our hemispheric westerly winds increase in speed and the earth actually slows its rotation. The days grow longer by four-tenths of a millisecond. Use this extra daylight wisely.

EARTHQUAKE!
THE DAY THE COUNTRY SHOOK

Animals were the first to sound the alarm. According to a white captive of the Osage Indians in Missouri, the tribal medicine man had warned that evil spirits were on the land earlier in the autumn of 1811. Squirrels and other wildlife had abruptly fled the hunting grounds near the Mississippi River, and as the first snows of winter fell in early December the shaman knew that really bad medicine was ahead. Snakes that would normally be coiled in winter hibernation below ground suddenly began to appear at the surface. Turtles that should also have been in their early winter stupor on the river bottoms were seen climbing the banks.

What the Osage shaman had seen in 1811 was a phenomenon that has been witnessed time and again: the strange and unnatural behavior of animals just prior to a major earthquake.

On December 16, 1811, at 2:00 a.m., nearly one million square miles of North America, including Ohio, were shaken by what is considered the greatest earthquake ever experienced on the continent. All creatures from the Rocky Mountains to the Atlantic Ocean and from the Gulf of Mexico to Canada felt the convulsions. The greatest of all California quakes is puny by comparison.

Actually, the December 1811 rocker was just the first of three tremendous quakes, and hundreds of smaller tremors, that shook much of the eastern United States through March 15, 1812. A Louisville, Kentucky, man counted 1,874 separate quakes over the three-month period.

Historically, these great shakes are known as the New Madrid (pronounced MAD-rid) Earthquakes, because the epicenter was near that small southeast Missouri boot-heel town. Diaries tell something of the horrors that were encountered. New Madrid, with a population of about three thousand, was "much torn to pieces . . . all that stood was rent asunder."

It was written that "the land rose and fell like waves on the ocean" and "walking was all but impossible, many were thrown to the ground." Reports of earth movements of 12 inches, to and fro, were evidently not exaggerated. Hills disappeared and were replaced by lakes. Lakes disappeared, replaced, in some instances, by "beautiful white sand upon which lay every kind of fish."

With "great horror," people near the earthquake center gazed openmouthed at the fearful chasms in the earth, out of which issued currents of steam, hissing like snakes. One of the most frightening sounds was the rush of wind—yet there was no wind. Whole forests were said to have waved like fields of wheat. Great amounts of "a black, sulfurous-smelling liquid" shot 20 to 30 feet into the air, creating small domes like miniature volcanoes.

It was said that the mighty Mississippi River "writhed like a serpent" for a length of 75 miles upstream and downstream from New Madrid. Acres of riverbanks along the Mississippi caved in, creating tidal waves 5 to 10 feet high. The river frothed and became clogged with debris when old trees that had lain on the river bottom for half a century suddenly rose to the surface. Reports that the Mississippi River actually reversed its flow for a few minutes, however, are not considered reliable.

Reelfoot Lake, an 18-mile-long, 5-mile-wide body of water, was created by the earthquake in western Tennessee. The parade ground at Charleston, South Carolina, fell one to two inches. Clocks stopped and furniture was rearranged throughout most of the eastern United States. Wells became dry as the water table shifted. Church bells rang in Boston.

Preachers found the job of redeeming sinners was suddenly much easier. With thoughts of perdition welling in every soul, the churches were filled the following Sunday.

No estimate of deaths was ever made, since the epicenter was in a sparsely populated region. Such a quake today, especially near a major metropolitan center, would bring death and destruction beyond comprehension. Unfortunately, scientists believe that such an event is inevitable.

OHIO EARTHQUAKES

When the next major earthquake does rattle the United States, it may not be centered in California. The western part of this country does have many more quakes than the east. But in Ohio (and in all areas east of the Rocky Mountains) the composition of the earth's crust can cause seismic waves to travel ten times farther.

The reason is that the earth under Ohio is composed of stratified layers of gravel, sand, and clay rather than solid bedrock. As a result, buildings and structures undergo major ground motion when the earth suddenly turns to Jell-O. The Ohio Division of the United States Geological Survey puts the highest risk for moderately strong quakes in the western, southwestern, and northeastern counties.

The earth has moved noticeably in Northeast Ohio nearly two dozen times since 1836. Most were minor tremors (the word temblor is synonymous) that caused little or no damage. However, on January 31, 1986, an earthquake with an epicenter southeast of Painesville was felt in nine other states and parts of Canada. On September 25, 1998, a quake with an epicenter near Sharon, Pennsylvania, shook northeast Ohio as well as Western Pennsylvania and New York, but caused little damage. Ohio's most damaging quake on record—a 5.5 on the Richter scale—occurred in March 1937, at Anna in Shelby County, about 50 miles north of Dayton. There was damage to a school and homes, but as has been the case in all of Ohio's 120 recorded quakes since 1771, there were no major injuries or deaths.

It was an Ohioan, Charles Richter, who devised the widely used intensity scale (in cooperation with a seldom-credited colleague, Beno Gutenberg). Logarithmic in structure, the Richter scale measures quake force in whole numbers, with each whole number representing a tenfold increase in amplitude (wave intensity). A 5 on the Richter scale, for example, is 10 times stronger than a 4. A 7 is 1,000 times greater than a 4! (Many seismologists prefer to use a different intensity scale known as the Mercalli.)

So don't be surprised if the earth shrugs and Cleveland and Akron move a little closer one of these days. And please don't blame Charles Richter. It's not his fault.

By the way, earthquake insurance in Ohio can be inexpensively added to a homeowner's policy.

EARTHQUAKE SCALES: WHICH IS THE MOST ACCURATE? WHAT DO THEY MEAN?

The Richter Magnitude Scale
Seismic waves are the vibrations from earthquakes that travel through the earth; they are recorded on instruments called seismographs. The time, locations, and magnitude of an earthquake can be determined from the data recorded by seismograph stations.

The Richter Scale was developed in 1935 by Charles F. Richter of the California Institute of Technology to compare the size of earthquakes around Southern California. Magnitude is expressed in whole numbers and decimal fractions.

Earthquakes with a magnitude of about 2.0 or less are usually called microearthquakes; they are not commonly felt by people and are generally recorded only on local seismographs. Events with magnitudes of about 4.5 or greater are strong enough to be recorded by sensitive seismographs all over the world. Severe earthquakes, such as the 1964 Good Friday earthquake in Alaska, have magnitudes of 8.0 or higher. Although the Richter Scale has no upper limit, the largest known shocks have had magnitudes in the 8.8 to 8.9 range.

The Modified Mercalli Intensity Scale

The effect of an earthquake on the earth's surface is called the intensity.

The intensity scale consists of a series of certain key responses such as people awakening, movement of furniture, damage to chimneys, and finally—total destruction. Although numerous intensity scales have been developed over the last several hundred years to evaluate the effects of earthquakes, the one currently used in the United States is the Modified Mercalli (MM) Intensity Scale. It was developed in 1931 by the American seismologists Harry Wood and Frank Neumann. This scale, composed of 12 increasing levels of intensity that range from imperceptible shaking to catastrophic destruction, is designated by Roman numerals. It does not have a mathematical basis; instead it is an arbitrary ranking based on observed effects.

The Modified Mercalli Intensity value assigned to a specific site after an earthquake is a more meaningful measure of severity to the nonscientist than the magnitude because intensity refers to the effects actually experienced at that place. After the occurrence of widely felt earthquakes, the Geological Survey mails questionnaires to postmasters in the disturbed area requesting information so that intensity values can be assigned. Structural engineers usually contribute information for assigning intensity values of VIII or above.

The following is an abbreviated description of the 12 levels of Modified Mercalli intensity.

I.   Not felt except by a very few under especially favorable conditions.

II.   Felt only by a few persons at rest, especially on upper floors of buildings.

III. Felt quite noticeably by persons indoors, especially on upper floors of buildings. Many people do not recognize it as an earthquake. Standing motor cars may rock slightly. Vibrations similar to the passing of a truck. Duration estimated.

IV. Felt indoors by many, outdoors by few during the day. At night, some awakened. Dishes, windows, doors disturbed; walls make cracking sound. Sensation like heavy truck striking building. Standing motor cars rocked noticeably.

V. Felt by nearly everyone; many awakened. Some dishes, windows broken. Unstable objects overturned. Pendulum clocks may stop.

VI. Felt by all, many frightened. Some heavy furniture moved; a few instances of fallen plaster. Damage slight.

VII. Damage negligible in buildings of good design and construction; slight to moderate in well-built ordinary structures; considerable damage in poorly built or badly designed structures; some chimneys broken.

VIII. Damage slight in specially designed structures; considerable damage in ordinary substantial buildings with partial collapse. Damage great in poorly built structures. Fall of chimneys, factory stacks, columns, monuments, walls. Heavy furniture overturned.

IX. Damage considerable in specially designed structures; well-designed frame structures thrown out of plumb. Damage great in substantial buildings, with partial collapse. Buildings shifted off foundations.

X. Some well-built wooden structures destroyed; most masonry and frame structures with foundations destroyed. Rails bent.

XI. Few, if any (masonry) structures remain standing. Bridges destroyed. Rails bent greatly.

XII. Damage total. Lines of sight and level are distorted. Objects thrown into the air. Seismic waves visible seen on ground surface.

SOURCE: *THE SEVERITY OF AN EARTHQUAKE* (1996). REPRINTED WITH PERMISSION OF THE NATIONAL EARTHQUAKE INFORMATION CENTER, U.S. DEPARTMENT OF THE INTERIOR/U.S. GEOLOGICAL SURVEY.

MILLENNIUM MADNESS

Fasten your seatbelts as we approach the third millennium. Doomsayers and Jeremiahs will soon fill the tabloids, bookstores, and airwaves with predictions of all sorts of natural disasters.

Can we expect earthquakes, tornadoes, tsunamis, and floods, not to mention volcanic eruptions and near-earth-orbiting asteroids? Of course. That's just business as usual on our small, rocky planet. Blaming any meteorological calamity on the millennium would make as much sense as blaming the wet road for the rain.

We humans have an inflated idea of our impact on a mysterious universe whose outermost edge—according to the Hubble Space Telescope—is an ever-expanding 17 trillion light years away. (One light year is about six trillion earth miles.) The universe is oblivious to time, and it is unrealistic to believe that turning a page on a human calendar can trigger natural disasters.

How was it at the last millennium in Anno Domini 1000? (Certainly Roman stonecutters and engravers had to have been thrilled when the year DCCCCLXXXXIX suddenly became just M.) Many earthlings at that time believed that the Day of Wrath was at hand and the earth would soon turn to ashes.

Although the propheteers are now at it again, the only impending worldwide calamity—and it *could* be a big one—is the fact that many computers recognize years as only two digits and will not be able to comprehend that the new "00" is the year 2000 and not 1000. Your next bank statement may say that you owe roughly 100 years of interest. Could Social Security payments suddenly stop because a person born in 1899 would be considered to be only one year old?

If you think that could be a problem, think of the tough sell the folks will have at 20th Century-Fox. Somehow, 21st Century-Fox just doesn't make it.

By the way, I hate to spoil the party, but it can be argued that since our calendar did not start with the year zero we cannot celebrate the passage of a thousand years until January 1, 2001. On the other hand, modern research indicates that the Roman monk who calculated the time of Christ's birth—upon which the Gregorian calendar is based—missed the correct date by anywhere from three to six years. This means the world could still have legitimately celebrated the start of the next millennium on January 1 in any year from 1995 through 1998.

WINTER

SUNSHINE %: 30
DRIEST MONTH: 0.31"/1871
WARMEST MONTH: 40.2°/1932
COLDEST MONTH: 11.0°/1977
LIQUID PCPN AVG.: 2.04"
RAINIEST DAY: 2.93"/1995
RAINIEST MONTH: 7.01"/1950
THUNDERY DAYS: 0
SNOWIEST DAY: 10.8"/1996
SNOWIEST MONTH: 42.8"/1978
LEAST SNOWFALL: 0.5"/1932
DAYS ONE INCH SNOW: 5

January is named after the Roman god Janus, the two-faced Keeper of the Gates. Janus usually shows us only his cold and snowy countenance, however. Paradoxically, in early January Planet Earth is three million miles *closer* to the sun than in July. It is the angle of the incoming solar radiation—acute in winter and more direct in summer—that makes our winter cold and our summer hot. In many Januaries a welcome small reward comes in the form of the legendary January thaw, usually during the third week. The milder weather quickly leaves and Northeast Ohio plunges back into the depths of winter. Another psychological uplift comes as the seed catalogs arrive—like the one that has the guy on the cover holding up an 80-pound rutabaga and saying, "You can imagine my surprise...." On the 26th day of the month in 1978, Ohio's deepest storm, literally a white hurricane, ravaged the state from south to north. On the 19th day of 1994, Cleveland's temperature fell to an all-time record 20 degrees below zero; temperatures remained below zero for a benchmark string of 56 hours. Our coldest January was in 1977, our warmest in the El Niño year of 1932. Depending on the strength of the cold, the first flower of the year, the snowdrop, will appear by month's end. Mosquitoes are never a problem this month.

JANUARY

Day	Hi	Lo	Rec Hi	Rec Lo	Sunrise	Sunset	Lake°
1	33	20	69 / 1876	-4 / 1968	7:53	5:09	35
2	33	19	66 / 1876	-12 / 1879	7:54	5:09	34
3	33	19	65 / 1874	-16 / 1879	7:54	5:10	34
4	32	19	65 / 1874	-7 / 1679	7:54	5:11	34
5	32	19	66 / 1939	-13 / 1884	7:54	5:12	34
6	32	18	66 / 1946	-9 / 1884	7:54	5:13	34
7	32	18	63 / 1907	-9 / 1884	7:53	5:14	34
8	32	18	66 / 1937	-10 / 1968	7:53	5:15	34
9	32	18	61 / 1937	-13 / 1875	7:53	5:16	34
10	32	18	61 / 1939	-12 / 1875	7:53	5:17	34
11	32	18	67 / 1890	-9 / 1899	7:53	5:18	34
12	32	18	65 / 1916	-9 / 1886	7:52	5:19	34
13	32	17	69 / 1890	-10 / 1977	7:52	5:20	34
14	32	17	70 / 1932	-6 / 1893	7:52	5:21	33
15	32	17	68 / 1932	-7 / 1972	7:51	5:23	33
16	32	17	57 / 1889	-15 / 1977	7:51	5:24	33
17	31	17	60 / 1973	-17 / 1982	7:50	5:25	33
18	31	17	64 / 1996	-15 / 1994	7:50	5:26	33
19	31	17	67 / 1907	-20 / 1994	7:49	5:27	33
20	31	17	65 / 1906	-18 / 1985	7:49	5:28	33
21	31	17	71 / 1906	-17 / 1985	7:48	5:30	33
22	31	17	71 / 1906	-10 / 1936	7:47	5:31	33
23	31	17	68 / 1967	-17 / 1963	7:47	5:32	33
24	32	17	35 / 1909	-19 / 1963	7:46	5:33	33
25	32	17	73 / 1950	-15 / 1897	7:45	5:34	33
26	32	17	69 / 1950	-9 / 1897	7:44	5:36	33
27	32	17	69 / 1916	-6 / 1966	7:44	5:27	33
28	32	17	59 / 1914	-10 / 1977	7:43	5:38	33
29	32	17	65 / 1914	-17 / 1873	7:42	5:39	33
30	32	17	62 / 1916	-4 / 1873	7:41	5:41	33
31	32	17	62 / 1989	-5 / 1971	7:40	5:42	32

*The limits of my language
mark the limits of my world.*
– LUDWIG WITTGENSTEIN

GRAY DAYS, WINTER BLUES

Cold winds blowing across Lake Erie create lake-effect cloudiness that makes sunshine often just a rumor here in December, January, and February. It's no wonder that the gloomy skies, combined with the naturally short daylight hours, can bring on a mild meteorological malaise. But, if the long, dark days of the Northeast Ohio winter tend to make you chronically irritable and depressed, you now have a medical explanation for your mood swings. You are a victim of SAD, the acronym for seasonal affective disorder.

Some researchers believe that the lessening of sunlight during winter causes a rearrangement of chemicals within the brain that triggers the onset of SAD. This is given credence by the estimate that the frequency of SAD in the cloudier far-northern climates of the United States is more than four times that in the sunnier southern latitudes. The cure for most of those afflicted is a change to a brightly lit environment.

Studies have also shown that about one in five of us is supersensitive to a change in ions, the positive and negative electrical charges within our atmosphere. A buildup of positive ions—brought on by dry, hot air, for example—can bring on moodiness and hostility. A proliferation of negative ions (released during a rainstorm or by a cascading waterfall) produces a feeling of well-being and euphoria.

Actually, it's a wonder that any of us are ever able to climb out of bed at all. We go around each day carrying more than a ton of air on our shoulders (outward pressure within our bodies equals the external weight of the atmosphere and keeps us from turning into pancakes). At Ohio's latitude, we are spinning counterclockwise at about 700 mph, and cosmic rays are constantly piercing our bodies. Is it any wonder we often feel tuckered out? Toss in cheimaphobia—the fear of cold—and chionophobia—the fear of snow—and you've got yourself the potential for a major wintertime meteorological malady.

But it could be worse. Thank goodness for gravity. Otherwise we would slide off this small planet and sail into the utter blackness of space. So, at least we've got that goin' for us.

WINTER

JAN

WINTER WEATHER WORRIES

ICE STORMS

An ice storm develops when rain or drizzle freezes on contact with a surface whose temperature is below freezing.

When glazing is expected to create hazardous travel for pedestrians and vehicular traffic, an ice storm warning is issued.

While such ice coatings are usually thin, buildups (accretions) of up to eight inches have been recorded. Such a heavy ice buildup is devastating to trees and power lines. (A 50-foot-high, 20-foot-wide evergreen may be burdened with up to five tons of ice.)

A light snow covering atop an ice coating is especially dangerous to travelers. Eighty-five percent of ice-storm fatalities are traffic related. Black ice is also extremely hazardous. This is a thin layer of ice that is so transparent that the darker ground colors show through. Because of this transparency, black ice, unlike milky rime ice, is almost invisible.

Ohio was along the northern rim of the giant ice storm of January 28–February 4, 1951. This most damaging of all United States ice storms produced a glaze up to four inches thick as it laminated the area from Texas through Pennsylvania. Twenty-five people died from the storm, and damage totaled $100 million.

Ice buildup topples power lines in Summit County, 1951.

"OONAK IS STILL THE BEST LEAD DOG IN THE BUSINESS"

SAFETY ON ICE

Pond ice one to two inches thick is NOT considered safe for skating or winter sports. A three-inch layer of clear, firm ice is safe for one person.

Four inches will support a small group of people spaced several feet apart, in single file. This thickness will also support snowmobiles, if spaced at 33-foot intervals.

Be wary of a lake or pond with heavy snow cover, as the ice underneath could be weak. New ice is stronger than old, and ice that turns to a darker shade of gray is thinning.

Always test before you step onto ice. Toss a large rock onto the ice surface to determine support. Eskimos carry ice chisels and thump the ice frequently, remembering that "when ice cracks it will bear, when ice bends it will break."

Another potential for serious injury during very cold, wet weather is the buildup of icicles from frozen, overflowing rain gutters and other structural overhangs where ice can accumulate readily. While it might be picturesque, this icicle buildup presents two immediate hazards: first, a sharp, heavy icicle can cause serious bodily harm if it falls on you directly; second, the puddling effect caused by the melting of icicles (which often freeze again, as even bigger icicles!) can result in very slippery, dangerous footing. So watch your step when you see these beautiful yet hazardous ice formations.

FROSTBITE

When Jack Frost comes nippin' at your nose (and feet, ears, and hands), frostbite can occur.

The first stage of frostbite is a painful burning or stinging in the affected part, usually fingers or toes. Skin will be bright pink at the onset as ice crystals begin to form under the skin. Numbness sets in as skin color turns to pale white, showing gray or yellow spots.

Frostbite victims should be brought indoors or at least taken to a sheltered area. Cover the affected part with any wool or synthetic fleece material; place fingers under the armpits or in the mouth for warmth. Flexing fingers or toes can make the temperature rise. You can warm the frostbitten area by bonfire, but do not expose flesh to open flame. Immerse the skin in warm (not hot) water, at all times treating the part gently. Never rub snow on frostbite (it is believed this false "remedy" originated with Napoleon's Grand Army of the Republic when it was driven homeward by the savage Russian winter of 1812). Rubbing snow on frostbitten skin may break the skin and destroy tissue.

HYPOTHERMIA

While frostbite is seldom fatal, hypothermia can be.

Hypothermia is the cooling of the interior body core below its normal temperature of 98.6° F (37° C). Temperatures do not have to fall below freezing for this condition to set in. A relatively small drop in inner-core body temperature can be fatal. Hypothermia can be sneaky, gradually overcoming someone who has been chilled by wet clothing, low temperatures, and brisk winds. Shivering is the first step toward hypothermia and is nature's way of trying to warm the body. Speech becomes difficult as violent shivering is replaced by muscle rigidity. The victim becomes irrational and may drift into fatal sleep.

Hypothermia victims should be taken quickly indoors, if possible. Warm liquid should be given, since the body has lost the ability to reheat itself. Wet clothing should be replaced with dry. (Blue jeans are totally unsuitable for any lengthy winter pursuits, since they wet easily, retain the wetness, cling to the skin, and do not allow protective insulation between the fabric and the body.)

For lengthy outdoor trips, dress in layers of warm, loose clothing that permits warm air to be trapped next to the body. Wool or synthetic fleece is always preferable since even when wet it gives protection. Always wear a head covering, since up to 50 percent of body heat can be lost through this part of the body.

THE WHITE HURRICANE

It was Sunday, four days before the great blizzard of January 26, 1978. A number of people from the television station were at the annual dogsled races east of Cleveland. As we waited for the sleds to be hitched, an Alaskan malamute walked over to anchorman Doug Adair and pretended he was a fire plug. Amid the avalanche of laughter came the obvious conclusion, "He must have watched your show!"

As Doug good-naturedly dried off his pant leg, I kiddingly suggested that we shouldn't be too flippant, since Greenland Eskimo lore says that when a sled dog piddles on a human, a big storm is on the way. More laughter.

Eighty-four hours later the most massive, and deepest, storm in Ohio weather history passed from south to north across the state.

The first hint of what was to come appeared on Wednesday evening, January 25, when air pressure began to fall rapidly in the Louisiana delta. A storm center quickly kicked out and began to collect isobars at an alarming rate as it headed northward. By the time the storm center crossed the Ohio River early Thursday morning—headed for Canada's Ontario Province—it appeared on weather maps as a gigantic coiled snake, ready to strike. Fourteen isobars surrounded the low-pressure center as it ravaged Ohio, and it literally became a Valley of Death for 51 Ohioans.

On the late-night Wednesday weather show, for the only time in my television career, I told viewers they should not plan on highway travel for the next day. I then went home, put on a large pot of coffee, and stayed up to welcome the monster's arrival. By 3 a.m. not only was there no rain or snow, there wasn't even a hint of wind. At that point I began to think about a new line of work. Where did the storm go? There was no Weather Channel for updates in 1978.

Then, just before 4 a.m., my cats—Floozie and Blanco—went berserk, running from room to room, knocking books from shelves, and even tipping over a lamp. A few minutes later hurricane-force winds rattled the windows and raindrops sounded like small firecrackers as they hit the glass. At 4:05 a.m. the air pressure at Hopkins International Airport fell to 28.28 inches of mercury, the lowest ever recorded in the state of Ohio. (Akron-Canton registered 28.33, while I have a barograph trace from Chardon that showed 28.18 inches.)

From a reading of 44° F, the Cleveland temperature dropped 30 degrees between 4 a.m. and 6 a.m., bottoming out at 5° hours later. The 82 mph sustained wind at Hopkins Airport was the highest ever recorded in Cleveland weather annals. Gusts of 70 to 100 mph were common that morning, with a peak gust of 103mph at the Lake Erie water intake crib three miles north of Cleveland. An ore carrier stranded in ice off Sandusky registered a wind burst at 111 mph. A wind gust of this speed, coupled with an air pressure of 28.28 inches, made the storm the equivalent of a Category III hurricane.

As shards of shattered window glass and unidentified flying objects filled the air, the wind chill approached -100° F. The wind seemed to be blowing from every direction at the same time. The Ohio Turnpike closed from gate to gate for the first time in its history, and the United States mail service was halted for the first time since the great Thanksgiving week snowstorm of 1950. No highway traffic deaths occurred, simply because most roadways were made impassable by the drifting and blowing snow. Miraculously, a Cleveland trucker, James Truly, was found alive in the cab of his 40-foot flatbed five days after the storm. His truck was buried along Ohio Route 13 north of Mansfield by a snow drift 20 feet high and a half mile long.

The hurricane-force winds made snowfall measurement impossible, but the official NWS observer put down a modest 7 inches in the record book (this was atop 13 inches of old snow).

Most Ohio schools were closed from Thursday until the following Monday. President Jimmy Carter declared Ohio a federal disaster area.

The malamute was right.

Ice and whiteout conditions resulted in hazardous driving on Northeast Ohio's roadways.

One of many fallen trees from the blizzard—a victim of the storm's hurricane-force winds.

MEASURING THE WEATHER:
AIR PRESSURE, WIND, TEMPERATURE, & HUMIDITY

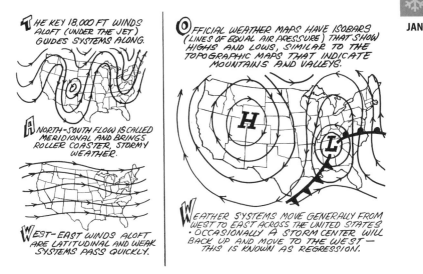

THE KEY 18,000 FT WINDS ALOFT (UNDER THE JET) GUIDES SYSTEMS ALONG.

A NORTH-SOUTH FLOW IS CALLED MERIDIONAL AND BRINGS ROLLER COASTER, STORMY WEATHER.

WEST-EAST WINDS ALOFT ARE LATITUDINAL AND WEAK SYSTEMS PASS QUICKLY.

OFFICIAL WEATHER MAPS HAVE ISOBARS (LINES OF EQUAL AIR PRESSURE) THAT SHOW HIGHS AND LOWS, SIMILAR TO THE TOPOGRAPHIC MAPS THAT INDICATE MOUNTAINS AND VALLEYS.

WEATHER SYSTEMS MOVE GENERALLY FROM WEST TO EAST ACROSS THE UNITED STATES. OCCASIONALLY A STORM CENTER WILL BACK UP AND MOVE TO THE WEST — THIS IS KNOWN AS REGRESSION.

AIR PRESSURE

Just as fish live in an ocean of water, we live at the bottom of an ocean of air.

Air, like fluids, exerts a pressure on everything within and around it. That last milkshake you enjoyed was an example of the effect of air pressure. When you drew it through the straw, the liquid was forced upward by the air pressing down on the area surrounding the straw. For this you can thank the troposphere, stratosphere, mesosphere, and thermosphere.

Pressure is a measurement of the weight of the air and is very important to meteorology. An isobar is a line that forecasters draw on a weather map to connect points of equal pressure. When plotted and analyzed on a weather map, isobars give us a good idea of wind speed and direction. Air flows from high pressure into low pressure, and the steeper the fall, the stronger the wind.

It has been determined that each square yard of the earth's surface has about 22,000 pounds of air above it. This is equal to approximately 14.7 pounds per square inch.

THE BAROMETER

In 1643, Evangelista Torricelli graphically showed the effect of air pressure. He took a straight, narrow tube closed at one end and filled with mercury, and inserted the open end of the tube in a bowl filled with mercury. While some of the mercury flowed out of the tube and into the bowl, a column of mercury about 30 inches long remained in the tube. This would only be possible, Torricelli reasoned, if the atmosphere was pressing down on the surface of the mercury in the bowl. That force supported the weight of the mercury in the tube.

The instrument that is used to tell us the weight of the air is a barometer. While no single barometer setting will guarantee any particular kind of weather, the tendency or trend of a barometer (especially when combined with wind direction) can be very helpful in determining what weather is headed our way. A fast and steadily falling barometer foretells the approach of a storm center; a fast and steadily rising barometer favors gusty winds and a change to fair weather.

Since the barometer measures the weight of the air, it also follows that air pressure will be affected by temperature changes in the atmosphere. As air is heated, it becomes less dense and begins to rise from the earth's surface, thus causing the barometer to fall. When air is cooled, it becomes denser and heavier, causing the barometer to rise.

It has been found that the standard air pressure at sea level is 29.92 inches of mercury. (Meteorologists use a unit called the millibar in map plotting and analysis: one millibar is equal to 1,000 dynes per square centimeter. Standard sea-level pressure in millibars is 1,013.)

While long, cumbersome, mercury-filled barometers are used by meteorologists to determine air pressure, the standard barometer used in the home is called an aneroid (a Greek word meaning "without fluid"). A small accordion-like cell expands and shrinks as the air pressure changes.

Use the barometer setting you hear on radio or television for your local setting. Tap the barometer lightly when you read it and reset your instrument whenever it gets about $1/10$ inch out of kilter with the official setting. Adjust the home barometer's black hand by inserting a small-machine screwdriver into the slot on the back. The large, usually gold-colored, hand on the front is just an indicator: it will never move until you turn it. When you begin setting the black and gold hands on top of each other, their eventual separation will tell you how far the pressure has risen or fallen since you last adjusted the barometer.

WIND

On one of those blustery, ingrown-eyelash-type November days, I asked my very young daughter, "What is wind?" After about a minute of profound meditation she replied, "Air that gets pushy."

While that meteorological wisdom can scarcely be improved upon, a more generally accepted definition of wind is the one offered by the Greek scientist Anaximander in the sixth century B.C. "The wind," he said, "is simply moving air."

Greek mythology demanded an explanation for the occasionally violent and uncontrollable wind, and this was the legend:

The lesser god Aeolus, king of winds, kept the north, south, east, and west winds (Boreas, Notus, Eurus, and Zephyrus) captive in a cave on Mount Haemus in Thrace. In order to help Ulysses on his epic sea voyage, Aeolus securely tied all the winds in a bag and presented them to the hero. Ulysses' mutinous crew believed that the bag contained more mundane treasures, however, and waited for the first opportunity to open the container. The ship was nearing its final port when Ulysses briefly dozed. Seizing the bag, the crew untied the knot and the hostage winds immediately rushed out, never to be constrained again. This sent Ulysses on his perilous odyssey.

The importance of the wind on our planet cannot be questioned. While it is the sun that sets the atmospheric machine in motion, it is the wind that makes the weather. Wind not only keeps our planetary thermostat in order; it also distributes heat and precipitation.

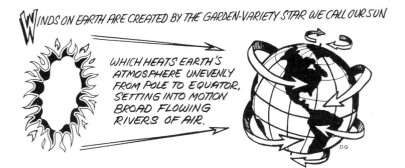

WINDS ON EARTH ARE CREATED BY THE GARDEN-VARIETY STAR WE CALL OUR SUN WHICH HEATS EARTH'S ATMOSPHERE UNEVENLY FROM POLE TO EQUATOR, SETTING INTO MOTION BROAD FLOWING RIVERS OF AIR.

WARM AIR RISES, COLD AIR SINKS

The power of the wind is stupendous. If all the winds of the world suddenly stopped blowing, we would need more energy than all the electrical plants in the United States could generate in 100 years to get them going again. Energy equivalent to seven million atomic bombs would be necessary to set the winds back in motion.

As we noted earlier, a pressure gradient force must be created in order to get the wind flowing. This happens because the sun heats the earth's surface unevenly: warm, lighter air begins to rise, and cold, heavier air moves in to replace it. Air flows from high pressure into low pressure, but not in a direct, linear path, since friction and the Coriolis force modify its movement.

In the northern hemisphere the air revolves clockwise around a high-pressure center (anticyclonic) and counterclockwise around a low-pressure center (cyclonic). In 1850, C. H. D. Buys Ballots, a professor at the University of Utrecht, Holland, gave us this rule for locating high and low pressure: with your back to the wind, low pressure is to your left, high pressure is to your right.

Wind speeds at the earth's surface will be lower than wind speeds just above the surface, because of frictional retardation. The wind is slowed by contact with the rough earth surface. The rougher the terrain, the greater the slowing of the wind.

Frictional retardation of wind across a smooth water surface is about 15 percent. Over smooth land the wind speed is slowed by about 30 percent—over rough terrain, approximately 65 percent.

The pressure force of the wind is staggering—in more ways than one. You might imagine that a wind blowing at 100 mph would be 10 times as strong as a wind of 10 mph, but not so. Wind creates a pressure proportional to the square of its velocity: a 100 mph wind is 100 times as forceful as a 10 mph wind.

Although the atmosphere is not rigidly attached to the earth's

surface, there is a frictional attachment due to gravity. For this reason the atmosphere turns with the spinning earth.

When we speak of the wind direction, we mean the direction the wind is coming from. A south wind, for example, is blowing from the south toward the north.

Of all the winds that flow around the earth, the single most important system is known as the jet stream. A jet stream is an expressway in the sky, an icy river of high-velocity air that is the wholesale distributor of weather around our globe.

The jet stream resembles a squashed tube some 300 miles wide and only about 4 miles high. It usually exists between altitudes of 20,000 to 40,000 feet. At the center of this wind tunnel the air may be traveling at speeds from 100 mph to more than 300 mph. Velocities decrease outward from the core.

Four such upper-air currents circle the globe, two in each hemisphere. The polar jet stream is found between latitudes of 30 and 70 degrees and is very irregular in its path. The subtropical jet exists between latitudes of 20 and 50 degrees and is more consistent in its location. Hustling along in a general west-to-east direction, the polar jet stream sends special-delivery weather into Ohio and North America and is actually the southern edge of the prevailing westerlies. This jet separates cold air on its northern side from warm air to

JET STREAMS ARE ICY, HIGH SPEED RIVERS OF AIR THAT TRAVEL FROM 25,000 TO 40,000 FEET ABOVE THE EARTH.

WINDS IN A JET MUST BE 50 KNOTS (58 MPH) AND MAY EXCEED 200 MPH.

THE JET STREAM RISES AND DIPS, COMES AND GOES, GUIDES STORM CENTERS AROUND THE HEMISPHERE.

AIRLINE PILOTS SEEK OUT THE JET FOR TAIL WINDS, AVOID THE JET'S HEAD WINDS.

its south. Surface low-pressure centers usually follow the path of the jet stream, just as a boat is drawn into the mainstream of a river.

In summer, the polar jet stream is usually weak and is positioned north of Ohio; in winter the polar jet strengthens and is often over, or just south of, Ohio.

Torrential rains, heavy snow, and other types of severe weather frequently accompany the jet stream's wavy course across the United States. Since the jet is constantly shifting, it is often difficult to locate.

WINTER

❄

JAN

BEAUFORT WIND-VELOCITY SCALE

Rating	Wind speed	Type	Impact
0	0–1	Calm	None; smoke rises vertically.
1	1–3	Light wind	Smoke drifts slowly.
2	4–7	Slight breeze	Leaves rustle; wind vanes move.
3	8–12	Gentle breeze	Leaves and twigs in motion.
4	13–18	Moderate breeze	Smaller branches of trees move; dust, fallen leaves, and loose paper swirl about and become airborne.
5	19–24	Fresh breeze	Small trees sway.
6	25–31	Strong breeze	Large tree branches creak and sway; telephone and electric wires whistle and sway.
7	32–38	Moderate gale	Whole trees in motion; walking becomes difficult.
8	39–46	Fresh gale	Twigs and small branches ripped from trees.
9	47–54	Strong gale	Large branches break off; shingles ripped from rooftops.
10	55–63	Whole gale	Trees snapped or entirely uprooted; moderate damage to buildings; temporary structures unstable.
11	64–74	Storm	Some damage to chimneys and television antennas.
12–22	74–201	Hurricane	Hurricane-level damage.

Meteorologists use computer models to estimate the jet's course from day to day, while weather-recording (radiosonde) balloons, satellite photographs, and high-altitude jet aircraft help in the detection. Long wisps of feathery cirrus clouds occasionally paint the jet stream in Ohio skies.

Forecasters for commercial airlines and the military seek out the jet stream to take advantage of, or avoid, its tailwinds or headwinds. It has been found that the strongest jet winds occur over Japan and New England. On April 12, 1934, the polar jet stream dropped to the 6,288-foot summit of Mount Washington, New Hampshire, and produced a wind gust of 231 mph, the highest wind speed ever recorded on the earth's surface.

With this planet's energy crisis and the steadily deteriorating quality of our air due to the burning of fossil fuels, the possibility of harnessing wind power is gaining attention. In many countries, including the United States, wind machines—multibladed windmills—have been installed in an attempt to produce a practical, environmentally "clean" source of electricity and direct mechanical power.

The wind, as we have seen, is created by sunlight splashing on the earth. While only a seemingly trivial 2 percent of sunlight is converted to wind energy, this is actually a very large amount—more energy than is consumed worldwide in any given year.

Critical to the success of a wind machine is the average speed of the moving air at each location. It is estimated that an average wind speed of 12 mph, or greater, is necessary to make an electricity-producing wind machine practical. Air movement is seldom constant, so where wind speeds are too variable such a power source would not work.

But as windmill technology grows in the decades ahead, that *whoosh!* sound we'll hear will be coming from clusters of wind turbines that have sprouted on "wind farms" across the country.

The instrument that measures wind speed is called an anemometer. A wind vane arrow, for determining wind direction, is usually attached. The most common anemometer has three or four cups that rotate horizontally on a vertical spindle or shaft. An electrical connection runs from the anemometer to an indoor recorder or meter, and as the wind catches the cups and whirls them around, the speed is registered in miles per hour or knots (one knot equals 1.15 mph, or 1.85 kilometers per hour).

The wind vane arrow points to the direction the wind is coming from, and this is also electronically recorded.

TEMPERATURE

Our air, like all other substances, is made up of molecules that travel in more or less rapid motion. Temperature measures the speed of these molecules, which determines how hot or cold a substance is. The faster the molecules move, the higher the temperature.

It is temperature that energizes the weather machine, through four effective methods of heat transfer within our atmosphere: radiation, conduction, convection, and advection.

RADIATION is the transfer of energy through space from one location to another. This happens when the sun radiates heat energy to earth.

CONDUCTION is heat transfer by contact. Air near the earth is heated and cooled by this process.

CONVECTION is heat transfer by vertical movement within the atmosphere. Warmed air near the earth's surface becomes buoyant and rises like a balloon.

ADVECTION is heat transfer by the horizontal movement of air by the wind, heating or cooling an area.

The incoming solar radiation that heats the surface of the earth is called insolation, while heat that is radiated and lost from the earth at night is called terrestrial radiation. This day-night heat exchange, and the unequal heating of the earth's surface (as well as the earth's yearly motion around the sun) are the basic causes of seasonal and geographical variations in the weather conditions around the planet.

Air loses temperature at a lapse rate that is determined by its moisture content. As long as a parcel of air rising through the atmosphere remains warmer than the surrounding air, it will continue to rise. Such air is considered to be unstable. (Thunderstorms and severe weather can be a result of such instability.) When a rising parcel of air cools below the temperature of the surrounding air, it will begin to sink. Such air is considered to be stable (and turbulent weather subsides).

While the temperature of our atmosphere normally decreases with height, occasionally a reversal occurs and the air temperature increases aloft. This is called an inversion. Intense radiational cooling of the earth's surface overnight, for example, can cause the air near the ground to be colder than a layer of air just above. This type of inversion is frequent during the long and calm nights in autumn and traps pollutants against the earth's surface.

The thermometer that measures the temperature contains either mercury or red-colored alcohol. Mercury-filled (silver-colored) thermometers are more accurate, because that fluid reacts quickly to a rise in temperature and expands at a steady rate.

The two most common temperature scales are Fahrenheit and Celsius. The melting point of ice is 32° F or 0° C; the boiling point of water is 212° F or 100° C. At -40°, the scales meet.

To convert temperatures from Fahrenheit to Celsius, subtract 32 degrees and divide by 1.8; to convert from Celsius to Fahrenheit, multiply by 1.8 and add 32 degrees.

												F°
−140	−120	−100	−80	−60	−40	−20	0	20	40	60	80	100
−100		−80		−60		−40		−20		0		20	40 C°

HUMIDITY

HUMIDITY is the amount of invisible water vapor in the air. Relative humidity is the percentage of water vapor the air is holding in relation to the amount it is capable of holding at a given temperature. When air contains all the invisible water vapor it is able to hold at its temperature, the humidity is 100 percent—the air is saturated and has reached its dew point. At 50 percent humidity, the air is holding one-half the vapor it is capable of holding at a given temperature. Generally, our air is not saturated and contains only a fraction of its possible humidity content.

THE DEW POINT is that temperature (at a given air pressure) to which air must be cooled to become saturated. It is the point at which condensation takes place. (When the dew point is within three degrees of the air temperature, fog is likely to form.) The dew point is that point at which the relative humidity is 100 percent.

You may have wondered why it can be raining when the humidity is reported to be far below 100 percent. That happens because the rain from a saturated cloud is falling through much drier air near the earth's surface.

An important characteristic of air is that as its temperature rises its capacity to produce water vapor increases. The warmer the air, the more it behaves like a sponge. At a temperature of 40° F, the air can accommodate several times the amount of moisture that it can hold at 10° F. The capacity of the air to hold moisture approximately doubles for each 20-degree temperature increase.

No matter how dry the air, or how cold the temperature, there is always a small amount of water vapor available. For that reason it can never be too cold to snow.

Humidity is measured by an instrument called a hygrometer. The hygrometer consists of two thermometers: a dry bulb and a wet bulb. The dry bulb is an ordinary thermometer and gives the current air temperature. The wet bulb is also an ordinary thermometer, but with a muslin sock at the lower end. The muslin is dipped in water, and the evaporative cooling that occurs will usually record a lower temperature than the dry bulb (unless the air is saturated). By referring to a hydrometric table you can convert the difference between the two thermometers into the percentage of relative humidity. When the dry bulb and wet bulb readings are identical, the humidity is 100 percent. The larger the temperature spread, the drier the air.

Studies have been made that suggest the ideal relative humidity for human activities is close to 50 percent, with a temperature of 65° F.

WINTER

❄

JAN

The hygrometer that is used to measure humidity in the home uses a strand of human hair (usually blond) as the activating element. The hair changes length as the moisture increases and decreases, and this causes a pointer to move on the face of a calibrated dial.

Remember that the humidity percentage you hear on radio or television is an outdoor measurement; your indoor humidity, especially in winter, will not match. Because of the drying effect of wintertime home heating, the indoor humidity—without the benefit of a humidifier—can reach desertlike levels of around 10 percent. Ideal indoor humidity during the winter season is between 35 and 40 percent.

RECOMMENDED RELATIVE HUMIDITY FOR YOUR WINTER INDOOR COMFORT

Outdoor Temp (°F)	Indoor Rec. RH
40	45%
30	40%
20	35%
10	30%
0	25%
-10	20%
-20	15%

THE FANTASTIC SYMPHONY OF THE WEATHER

There is music in our weather. The forest murmurs, mountains roar, and thunder crashes. From strings to timpani, winds and other weather phenomena create a meteorological orchestra that is there for the listening. Granted, it's often easy to ignore the music. Winter breezes sing a howling song that northern Ohioans seldom hear, as we are simply more intent on surviving the icy gales.

But the same wind, in the moderate days of summer, will strum the needles of tall pines along the Lake Erie shore like an aeolian harp.

And who doesn't enjoy listening to the syncopation of raindrops on the roof? Mark Twain loved this music so much he covered the roof above his bedroom with tin to amplify the sound.

When the forest murmurs, rain often follows. This sound is caused by prestorm winds moving through trees and rustling the myriad branches and twigs. Mountains roar for the same reason, but the sound of the wind through the trees is concentrated and intensified as it sweeps from the mountaintop to the valley below. In biblical times Elijah told Ahab to hurry down from the mountain, "for there is a sound of the abundance of rain."

Thunder is caused by the rapid expansion and compression of air along the path of a lightning discharge. On rare occasions, when the strike is nearby, a brief musical note can be heard. Scientists theorize that the sound is created when simultaneous discharges join pulses.

Who among us, traveling alone at night near the woods, hasn't felt a sudden chill and goose bumps when the Devil's Fiddle is played? This ghostly, discordant sound is made when tree limbs, agitated by the wind, rub together.

Another forest noise guaranteed to get your attention is the rifle-shot sound of tree bark splitting on a cold winter night. Houses also creak and groan on cold winter nights when joints and rafters contract.

If anyone is looking for a cannonlike sound to accompany the *1812 Overture,* I recommend the explosion of an iceberg. I thought I had bought the farm my first night in Greenland when one of those floating ice mountains blew up in the fiord.

Some earthly sounds, however, defy scientific explanation. In Wyoming, the bewitching Yellowstone Lake Whispers fit this category. The whispers occur most often on still, bright mornings not long after sunrise and may last for half a minute or more. Sounding like a vibrating harp, a swarm of bees, or the faint murmur of voices, the whispers begin at a remote distance, draw rapidly near, and then fade in the opposite direction.

In Bangladesh reside the infamous and mysterious Barisal Guns. For centuries natives have been hearing the dull and distant guns of an invisible artillery. A dozen or more individual booms may be heard at regular intervals, although travelers passing from Calcutta to the Sunderbans have often reported that the cannonades came in multiples of three.

Mysterious booms have been heard along the Atlantic coast of the United States. These ghostly detonations resemble the legendary sounds of the "mistpouffer" (fog chaser), found along the coasts of Europe from the North Sea to Ireland.

In Haiti a sound called the "gouffre," akin to a heavy wagon passing over pavement, is sometimes heard—most often between 7 and 10 at night. There may come a sound of great wind, yet there is no wind. Connecticut Indians called the puzzling, booming sounds they heard "Moodus noises," believing that one of their gods were angry.

The Echoes of Seneca can sometimes be heard in New York's Finger Lakes region. Some have theorized that gas stored in Lake Seneca's deep, sandy bottom occasionally escapes to the surface, where a gas bubble explodes. A Lake Seneca canoeist was startled, and his canoe almost overturned, by a great bubble that suddenly surfaced in the middle of the lake. Similarly loud explosions rarely heard near the southern shore of Lake Erie are very likely also caused by rising bubbles of gas.

SUNSHINE %: 37
DRIEST MONTH: 0.18"/1877
WARMEST MONTH: 37.5°/1930
COLDEST MONTH: 15.8°/1875
LIQUID PCPN AVG.: 2.19"
RAINIEST DAY: 2.33"/1959
RAINIEST MONTH: 7.73"/1887
THUNDERY DAYS: 1
SNOWIEST DAY: 14.8"/1993
SNOWIEST MONTH: 39.1"/1993
LEAST SNOWFALL: 0.2"/1998
DAYS ONE INCH SNOW: 4

The first two weeks of February are often the coldest of winter. King Winter is on his throne and Northeast Ohio is a still-life painting, a study in frozen motion. On the second day of the month, Ohio's official state groundhog, Buckeye Chuck (he lives in a heated burrow at a radio station in Marion), makes his end-of-winter forecast. No self-respecting meteorological marmot would be above ground at this time of the year; if it were, it would be an amorous boy groundhog looking for you-know-what. Ohio's lowest official temperature came on February 10, 1899, at Milligan, near Zanesville; the temperature may even have been under the observed -39°F reading, since the mercury probably froze (for temperatures that cold, alcohol thermometers are required). Naturalists tell us that spring in the eastern United States begins during early February deep in the Florida Everglades, then moves northward at a rate of about 15 miles each day. As the frostline moves by, insects emerge from their winter hibernation places and migrant birds follow the moveable feast northward. Each day the sun rides a little higher in the sky, and stays a little longer. Insects known as snow fleas (springtails) can be seen doing their circus act in the snow near the base of trees.

Day	Hi	Lo	Rec Hi	Rec Lo	Sunrise	Sunset	Lake°
1	32	17	59 / 1989	-6 / 1971	7:39	5:43	33
2	32	17	61 / 1903	-7 / 1971	7:38	5:44	33
3	32	17	57 / 1890	-8 / 1996	7:37	5:46	33
4	32	17	65 / 1874	-10 / 1996	7:36	5:47	33
5	33	17	61 / 1938	-13 / 1918	7:35	5:48	33
6	33	18	61 / 1938	-6 / 1895	7:34	5:49	33
7	33	18	60 / 1925	-5 / 1988	7:33	5:51	33
8	33	18	69 / 1937	-8 / 1977	7:31	5:52	33
9	33	18	59 / 1894	-14 / 1899	7:30	5:53	33
10	34	18	66 / 1932	-16 / 1899	7:29	5:55	33
11	34	18	73 / 1932	-15 / 1885	7:28	5:56	33
12	34	18	65 / 1984	-9 / 1917	7:27	5:57	33
13	34	19	68 / 1938	-9 / 1995	7:25	5:58	33
14	34	19	62 / 1918	-11 / 1905	7:24	5:59	33
15	35	19	67 / 1954	-4 / 1963	7:23	6:01	33
16	35	19	72 / 1883	-8 / 1904	7:21	6:02	33
17	35	20	62 / 1911	-7 / 1885	7:20	6:03	33
18	36	20	62 / 1981	-5 / 1936	7:19	6:04	33
19	36	20	68 / 1939	-4 / 1936	7:17	6:06	33
20	36	20	69 / 1930	-3 / 1968	7:16	6:07	33
21	37	21	68 / 1930	-3 / 1885	7:14	6:08	33
22	37	21	72 / 1930	-8 / 1963	7:13	6:09	33
23	37	21	66 / 1930	-4 / 1873	7:11	6:10	33
24	38	21	69 / 1961	-7 / 1889	7:10	6:12	33
25	38	22	70 / 1930	-5 / 1993	7:09	6:13	33
26	39	22	78 / 1900	-15 / 1963	7:07	6:14	33
27	39	22	66 / 1996	-10 / 1863	7:05	6:15	33
28	39	22	67 / 1939	-0 / 1884	7:04	6:16	33
29	39	22	68 / 1976	-4 / 1884	7:03	6:17	33

I respect faith,
but it is doubt that
gets you an education.
–WILSON MIXNER

DON'T CURSE THAT SNOW!

Snow is nature's protective blanket, and a frigid, snow-free winter can do much harm to many living things. Being 90 percent air (remember that when you're shoveling that six inches of air from your driveway), snow is a wonderful insulator, keeping the soil beneath from freezing to great depths. In a bare-ground, snowless winter, the soil freezes rapidly, killing many plants. Experiments have shown that where the air temperature fluctuated between 25 degrees below zero and 7 above, the temperature two feet deep in a snowbank remained constant. In another instance, with an air temperature of 24 degrees below zero, the temperature of the soil one inch deep under a heavy snow drift was 54 degrees above zero! That's a remarkable 78 degrees difference between air and ground.

For many animals who live under the snow, or burrow into it, the relative warmth of the snow blanket can mean life or death. Unfrozen ground under heavy snow cover will also allow animals to dig and grub just enough edible morsels to get them through until spring. During the thaws of midwinter you may see robins scratching through the soil for hibernating insects. (Contrary to popular notion, many robins spend all winter in Northeast Ohio.)

A heavy snowfall makes a Cleveland street nearly impassable.

Snow also turns into beneficial groundwater, providing it has enough time to gently soak into the earth.

Another one of snow's positive attributes is its soundproofing ability, as you may have noticed in the noise-deadened air that follows a heavy snowfall.

In addition, snowflakes are nature's vacuum cleaner, sweeping pollutants out of the air as they waft to earth. Snow that is loosely rubbed over rugs or clothing acts as an excellent cleaning agent.

From an aesthetic viewpoint, the lace and filigree of the snowflake turns each ice crystal into a frosty ice jewel whose beauty has few rivals in nature.

If anyone would have contempt for snow, you might think it would be the Eskimo, who live in an unrelenting world of ice crystals. Yet, while the Eskimo language has no word for hate, it does have more than two dozen words to describe snow that is falling or has fallen. To the Alaskan Eskimo falling snow is *anit,* fallen snow is *aput,* and fresh-fallen snow undisturbed by the wind is *api.* Our word snow is *schnee* in German, *sneg* in Russian, and *snu* in Swedish.

It can never be too cold to snow. Although the heaviest snows usually fall when temperatures are near freezing, there is always a tiny amount of water vapor in the atmosphere. Snow has been observed at temperatures of 50°F.

In your garden-variety snowstorm, 1,000 billion snowflakes fall (count quickly). It takes more than one million ice crystals to blanket two square feet with 10 inches of snow. An average snowflake contains 10 quintillion molecules of water (that's 10 with 18 zeros after it), and there are an astronomical number of ways that those molecules can be arranged. Although it is possible that no two snowflakes are ever identical, it is not probable (another assignment for you).

The heaviest 24-hour snowfall ever measured accurately was at Silver Lake, Colorado, on April 14, 1921, when 76 inches piled up. A total of 95 inches came down in little more than 32 hours.

In 1955, a snowstorm at Thompson Pass, Alaska, dropped 175.4 inches of fluff from December 26 through December 31. The benchmark for a single, continuous storm, however, goes to Mount Shasta, California, where 189 inches fell between February 13 and 19, 1959.

Paradise Ranger Station on the western shoulder of Mount Rainier, Washington, holds the world record for a single-season snowfall. During the winter of 1971–72, Paradise measured a staggering 1,122 inches of snow.

The greatest snow depth ever measured at one time in the United States was 451 inches at Tamarack, California, on March 11, 1911.

Ohio's single-storm snowfall depth record, 48 inches, was set in Chardon on November 11–12, 1996. The second greatest depth was the 45 inches on the ground in Ashtabula during the winter of 1962.

The official snowfall-depth record for the city of Cleveland is 21 inches; it's happened three times, during the winters of 1950, 1978, and 1993.

WINTER

FEB

MEMORABLE OHIO WINTERS

1816. Thirteen years after statehood, Ohio shared in the infamous "Year Without a Summer." Crops were killed and continually replanted due to frequent frosts well into summer. Diaries report that snow fell in Ohio on July 4, and so heavily in nearby Kentucky that a man and his lady friend riding to an Independence Day celebration in a carriage were forced to turn back due to heavy snow. Ice "as thick as a windowpane" was observed in north-central Ohio the morning of July 5.

1818. Between 18 and 26 inches of snow fell around Marietta on February 3–4. A temperature of 22 degrees below zero killed peach trees on February 10.

1855–56. An exceptionally cold, snowy, and icy winter; according to many diaries, "the hardest winter ever known." Snow fell at Marietta on 32 days this winter with a seasonal fall of 54 inches. On January 8, 1856, the temperature fell to -31° at Germantown (Montgomery County) and -25° at Waterford (Washington County). One-quarter to one-half of the fruit trees in Cuyahoga County were reported destroyed. A late-February snowmelt flood (a freshet) caused river ice to break loose all at once, with "disastrous" results for ships frozen in the ice.

1863–64. From December 31, 1863, through January 1, 1864, the temperature at Cincinnati fell 32 degrees in 4 hours and 60 degrees in 14 hours (from plus 50 to minus 10).

1899. Most severe outbreak of cold in United States weather history during February 8–14. Morning temperatures on February 10: -33° at Millersburg (Holmes County); -37° and -39° at Milligan (Perry County)—a state record.

1901. Blizzard rages in east Ohio, April 18–21. From Fairfield and Licking counties northeastward through Ashtabula County the extremely heavy, wet snow totaled 12 to 31 inches. Ten-foot drifts at Dover-New Philadelphia, where farmers reported that their sheep were buried "up to their noses." Snow shovelers were paid an unheard-of $1 per hour for their labor. The *Canton Repository* sent two reporters on horseback to locate a snowbound passenger between Cleveland and Canton.

1909. One of the state's worst ice storms on February 14–16. Ice accumulations of one to four inches reported in Erie, Hancock, Huron, Sandusky, and Seneca counties from two days of freezing rain and sleet.

1909–10. Perhaps Ohio's snowiest winter statewide. Season totals: Cincinnati—40 inches; Columbus—68 inches; Sandusky—65 inches; Cleveland—81 inches; and up to 125 inches in Geauga County.

1913. Nearly continuous rains fell on all 88 counties for five days, March 23–27. From 8 to 10 inches of rain fell over most of Ohio and all areas suffered high water. The flood of March 1913 was the greatest in Ohio history. The Dayton area was especially hard hit; 430 people perished in Ohio and damage exceeded $300 million.

1913. The legendary Freshwater Fury, considered to be the worst storm ever to strike the Great Lakes, ravaged the northern half of Ohio on November 9–11. Hour after hour, winds of gale to hurricane force piled snow into 10-to-15-foot drifts. This storm gave Cleveland its heaviest 24-hour snow accumulation—17.4 inches. Total storm snowfall: Cleveland—22 inches; Akron-Canton—20; Summerfield—23; Hiram, Columbiana—21; Cambridge—24; Cadiz—20; Wooster, Millersburg—18; Medina, Hudson—22. Thirty-two ships on the Great Lakes were either sunk or destroyed in the storm and more than 200 seamen drowned.

WINTER

❄

FEB

1917–18. A very snowy winter. January 11–12, 1918, saw blizzard and cold-wave conditions with 60 mph winds and up to 16 inches of snow in the Toledo area. Toledo's temperature fell 43 degrees in eight hours. The "greatest ice jam in Ohio River history" below Cincinnati backed high water 100 miles upstream.

1918–19. Considered Ohio's most snow-free winter (following one of our snowiest!). Only 8.8 inches of snow fell this winter in Cleveland with 1.6 inches at Cincinnati.

1937. On January 26, 1937—during the Great Ohio River Flood—the Ohio River rose to 80 feet at Cincinnati, the highest level on record (flood stage is 52 feet). The water at the Cincinnati Reds' Crosley Field was 21 feet above home plate. (Lowest Ohio River stage at Cincinnati: 1.9 inches on Sept. 17, 1881.)

1944–45. Extended snow cover began on December 11, 1944. The Akron-Canton area established a record 70-day string of days with snow cover of one inch or more. On February 2, 1945, Groundhog Day, snow depths ranged up to a foot in northern counties with up to one-half foot over the southern counties.

1950. The great Thanksgiving week snowstorm broke many snowfall records across the state for both depth and duration. From November 23 to 28 snow accumulated from 6 inches in the extreme northwest of Ohio to 40 inches in the extreme east. Youngstown set the state 24-hour snowfall record with 20.7 inches. Steubenville totaled 36 inches in three days, the state-single storm benchmark. Schools and the Post Office closed, and the Ohio State Buckeyes played the Michigan Wolverines in the legendary "Blizzard Bowl."

A car is buried under a drift during the Thanksgiving week snowstorm of Nov. 1950.

1954. Winds hit 60 to 70 mph in the March 1–4 snowstorm in northern counties. Cleveland gets 15 inches of snow as hundreds of cars, trucks, and buses are abandoned amid eight-foot drifts.

1959. Following heavy rains, the most devastating floods since 1913 struck Ohio on January 21. Just 20 days later on February 10, Greater Cleveland and Northeast Ohio were again hit by heavy rain and damaging floods. The Cleveland Zoo was inundated and all the reptiles drowned.

1962–63. This Big Bad Winter was presaged by record snows in late October (8 inches at Cleveland, 17 inches at Novelty). A storm that set in on December 6, 1962, put down snow that stayed on the ground until the following March in parts of Northeast Ohio. Cleveland set a record low temperature the morning of January 24, 1963: -19° (-22° Twinsburg, Summit County), -28° Thompson, Geauga County. A monthly record of 70 inches of snow fell on Chardon in Geauga County during December of 1962, with a maximum snow depth of 33 inches. Cleveland measured a record December total of 30 inches.

1976–77. Coldest winter in Ohio history—and for much of the eastern half of the country. A snowpack of one foot or more was common throughout Ohio from early January into early February. Cincinnati has a record January snowfall of 32 inches with 54 inches for the season. Cleveland suffers 55 consecutive hours with no temperature above zero (January 16–18) and has no temperature above freezing for 38 straight days (December 26–February 3). Greater Cleveland has 66 days in a row with one inch or more of snow cover; Akron-Canton has 59 days. Cincinnati records its coldest temperature: -25° on January 18, 1977.

A mountainous drift alongside an airport-access road, January 1977.

1977–78. The second very cold and snowy winter in succession. Cleveland received over 90 inches of snow, with 43 inches falling during January of 1978 (snowiest month ever). The severe blizzard that struck Ohio on January 26, 1978, was the deepest storm ever to move across the state. Air pressure at Cleveland fell to 28.28 inches of mercury, and the wind gusts of 70 to over 100 mph turned the snowstorm into a veritable "white hurricane." The storm center passed from south to north across Ohio and the combination of snow, wind, and a 40-below-zero wind-chill factor closed the Ohio Turnpike for the first time in its history. Snow cover on January 20, 1978: Cleveland—19 inches; Columbus—17 inches; Cincinnati—14 inches

1981–82. Two powerful January blizzards put exclamation points on this snowy, frigid winter. The Siberian Express of January 16, 1982, produced wind-chill factors of -55° F over much of Ohio. Morning temperatures on January 17: -17° at Cleveland, -16° at Columbus, -19° at Cincinnati, -18° at Youngstown, and -30° at Alger (Hardin County).

1983–84. Christmas of 1983 was Ohio's coldest. Wind chill factors were close to -60° F on December 24, 1983, and Christmas Day saw these frigid high and low temperatures around the state: Cleveland—1 above and 10 below zero; Columbus—1 above and 12 below; Akron-Canton—zero and 14 below. The cities of Ashtabula and Conneaut in the extreme northeast of Ohio were snowbound, with Interstate 90 closed by eight-foot snow drifts. Wind chills on Christmas Day of 1983 were running near 50 below zero. January 21, 1984, saw these low temperatures: Cleveland, -17°; Columbus, -16°; Mansfield -17°; Possum Run Rd. (near Mansfield), -27°; Doylestown (Wayne County), -26°; Bainbridge (Geauga County), -26°. A blizzard on February 27–29 closed schools in six northern Ohio counties and left a 26-inch snow cover on the city of Ashtabula.

1985. The intensely cold temperatures of January 19–21 were accompanied by wind-chill factors that reached -69° in Cleveland and -80° at Akron-Canton. Some of the lowest maximum and minimum temperatures since the winter of 1899 were recorded: Cleveland, -5° and -18°; Columbus, -7° and -18°; Akron-Canton, -8° and -24°; Mansfield, -7° and -22°. January of 1985 was the cloudiest month in Cleveland's 114-year weather history, with only a few fleeting sunny breaks in the continual overcast.

1987. March 30–31 saw extremely heavy, wet snowfall that totaled 16 inches at Cleveland and 18 inches at Brecksville, just south of the city. Another blast of very heavy, soggy snow came on April 4 with Akron-Canton receiving 21 inches and Columbus 12 inches.

1994. On January 20, the temperature at Cleveland fell to an all-time record low of -20° F, amid a record 56 hours with no temperature above zero. That same morning Burton, in Geauga County, registered -32°, while Possum Run Rd., in Richland County, came in at -36°. Chardon snowfall for the winter totaled 154 inches.

1995–96. The winter of 1995–96 broke the record for most snowfall in a season, 101.5 inches, with the last measurable snowfall coming in late April.

1996. Snowfall totals from November 9–14 were the greatest single storm amounts in Ohio weather history: Chardon—69 inches; Hambden—63; Thompson—61; Shaker Heights—50; Jefferson—48; Geneva—38; Mayfield Heights—37; Kirtland—28; North Royalton—25; Hopkins International Airport—19.

1998. An exceptionally strong El Niño dominates the nation's winter and produces the fourth-warmest winter on record in Cleveland weather history. An all-time record low of only 0.2 inches of snow falls in Cleveland during February, with only a trace to one-inch totals statewide.

WINTER

FEB

SNOWROLLERS

A s I remember, it was Groucho Marx who said that a mirage has to be believed to be seen.

You'll probably still not believe what you've seen if you ever witness the phenomenon known as the snowroller.

The rarely seen rollers are doughnut-like cylinders of snow that may appear in small numbers or by the hundreds, covering acres of ground. A field of snowrollers makes it appear as if schoolchildren had been interrupted halfway through making snowmen.

Snowrollers form under unique weather circumstances. The first requirement is an old, smooth, crusty layer of snow. This happens when a substantial snowfall is followed by clear, cold nights and mild, sunny days. A fresh snow then falls atop the old and temperatures begin to rise to just above freezing. This makes the new snow sticky and cohesive. A sudden gust of wind comes along, peels away a small chunk of snow, and sends it scooting a short distance. Another gust of wind picks up the snow particle, adds another coating of sticky snow, and propels the growing snow blob a little farther. If the wind continues to gust, and the snow is adhesive enough, you will eventually have an upright cylinder of snow with (usually) a hollow center: a giant and fragile snowy doughnut!

As the snowroller grows, the sides often begin to cave in, and some of the largest rollers flop over on their sides. The roller leaves a shallow trench, or path, in its wake so you can easily see the point from which it started.

Resembling rolled-up carpet, snowrollers up to seven feet in circumference and four feet long have been observed.

Snowrollers may form over level ground, but they are most often created on an incline, where gravity conspires with the whimsical wind to roll the snow-doughnuts downhill. The life of a snowroller is short, as they easily collapse with a small rise or fall in temperature.

History of Forecasting

"*WE NEVER HAD THIS KIND'A WEATHER TILL THEY STARTED SENDING THOSE ROCKS UP!*"

Mankind has been both blessed and bullied by the weather. Weather has determined which societies have thrived and which have disappeared. You may not care about isobars and the winds aloft, but weather will affect you every day of your life. Love it or curse it, every morning it is lurking just outside your door, waiting to color your day, to change your mood.

We have no way of knowing who made the very first weather forecast, but it may have been the caveman who felt the air suddenly rush out of his stony cavern and decided to call off the next day's woolly mammoth hunt. Prehistoric cave dwellers didn't know about the changing air pressure ahead of a storm, but simple experience told them they would soon be peering out through the primal mist and pelting rain.

Because primitive peoples believed that human behavior brought down the anger of the gods, or earned their favor, early societies wanted someone who could talk to the gods—a meteorological Dr. Doolittle. The tribes and clans sought out their most wise (or

WINTER

❄

FEB

cunning) member, and that person became the first weather forecaster and weather-control expert. The weather wizard was given the job of explaining the reason for a calamitous event and making sure that it didn't happen again. An example of this was the American Indian medicine man, or shaman, who was the tribe's chief meteorologist. The rain dances he recommended never failed, since the dancers just kept at it until the raindrops began to fall. Shooting arrows toward clouds was another favored rain-making ritual of many Plains tribes.

Worry about the weather is as old as the history of man. While the science of meteorology is in its infancy, the earliest records of weather lore date back more than 6,000 years. Locked in constant battle against nature, the ancient Babylonians devised a system of weather forecasting based on their interest in astrology. If, for example, cold Jupiter, windy Mercury, and watery Neptune were thought to be in alignment, that day on earth would be cold, windy and wet. Astrometeorology still has its advocates, but there is little scientific evidence to prove its validity.

Ancient Greece had a pantheon of mythological and meteorological gods. Their great god Zeus, whose symbol was the lightning bolt, lived atop Mount Olympus and this easily angered deity continually zapped mere mortals for their misdeeds. This explanation for lightning served early man's need to blame undesirable weather events on something familiar.

It wasn't until about 350 B.C. that the Greek scholar Aristotle gathered all of the previous thoughts and teachings on the weather in four books under the title *Meteorologica.* Although most of Aristotle's observations were correct, most of his explanations were not. He believed in a spherical universe, and thought that the earth gave off various "emanations" and "vapors," correctly concluding that a cloud consisted of tiny drops of water. Aristotle very likely gave us the word "meteorology," from the words *meteor*—"of the sky"—and *logy*—"discourse."

While Aristotle's work was mainly theoretical, Theophrastus, a friend and student of Aristotle, compiled a practical list of weather signs that he presented in a treatise called the *Book of Signs.* Based principally on the observation of animals and insects, Theophrastus gave 80 signs of rain, 50 of storms, 45 of wind, and 24 of fair weather. Detractors claimed that he undoubtedly overdid it, citing many examples of meteorological nonsense: "It is a sign of rain when a toad takes a bath, also when a dog rolls on the ground."

For nearly 2,000 years, Aristotle's *Meteorologica* was the major source of weather information. It wasn't until the 13th century that the English scholar Roger Bacon questioned the archaic assumptions of Aristotle with his text *In Meteora.* Bacon insisted on fresh experimentation and observation rather than accepting centuries-old perceptions. Still, it would be another 400 years before the science of meteorology progressed.

A major and understandable problem was that up until this time the only weather conditions that could be accurately measured were wind direction and rainfall. It wasn't until the 17th century that the three most important basic weather-measuring instruments were invented: the thermometer, barometer, and hygrometer.

Credit for the first thermometer (about 1603) belongs to the Italian physicist and astronomer Galileo Galilei. Galileo's thermometer was a crude, water-filled glass tube. In 1661 the German physicist and mayor of Magdeburg, Otto Von Guericke, produced an alcohol-filled version that was an incredible, and unwieldy, 20 feet long! A three-foot linseed oil thermometer by the acclaimed English scientist Isaac Newton proved to be equally unpopular.

GALILEO

A thermometer with an appropriate fluid and a reliable scale did not evolve until 1714. Gabriel Fahrenheit's mercury-filled glass tube used 32 degrees as the "commencement" of the freezing point of water. Although there was, literally, a large degree of difference in their measuring scales, Anders Celsius and Rene de Reamur also produced scientifically acceptable thermometer gradations.

The barometer, a vital instrument that measures atmospheric pressure, or the weight of the air, was invented in 1643 by Evangelista Torricelli, Galileo's fellow Italian and disciple.

Torricelli's barometer, unfortunately, was a massive 60-foot column that used water as the measuring fluid. Later, using mercury—the heaviest liquid—Torricelli reduced the length of his tube to about 34 inches.

The hygrometer is used to measure moisture in the air, and its name comes from the Greek word *hygros,* meaning "wet." The ancient Greeks believed that water could exist as "air," but they did not realize that the water simply vanishes into an invisible vapor stage.

It wasn't until the 17th century that most scientists accepted the idea that moisture could exist as vapor, yet the first hygrometer was invented by German cardinal Nicholas de Cusa much earlier, in about 1450. The cardinal used a large balancing scale with a great quantity of wool on one side and an assortment of stones on the other. When the wool absorbed moisture, the scale tipped in its favor. As the wool dried, the stone side became heavier and was lowered.

For nearly 200 years this hygrometer was used, until the Italian genius Leonardo da Vinci invented an improved mechanical moisture indicator. In the decades that followed many substances were used in hygrometers as the absorbent, from whale bone fiber and string to catgut and wild oat beard. But it was human hair, especially blond hair, that finally emerged as the most ideal moisture indicator.

Without the benefit of instruments, the Pilgrims who landed at Plymouth Rock in 1620 could not include actual measurements of temperature, wind speed, and air pressure in their weather record diaries. The first, although necessarily generalized, weather observations in this country are attributed to Reverend John Campanius Holm, the chaplain at New Sweden, a settlement near present-day Wilmington, Delaware. He began his weather record keeping 24 years after the Pilgrims landed. (It doesn't seem quite fair that National Weatherman's Day is February 5, the birth date of Dr. John Jefferies, a Loyalist from Boston who began keeping records more than 100 years later.)

John Tulley, a mariner from Saybrook, Connecticut, could rightfully be called America's first forecaster. Tulley, a good-natured fellow, printed an almanac in 1687 and began the practice of making weather predictions for each month. His "forecasts," like most in early almanacs, were based more on astrology than on meteorology and were so generalized—and so inaccurate—that they were of little practical use.

Some of our nation's most famous presidents and patriots were fascinated by the weather. The last entry in George Washington's weather diary was made the day before he died. Thomas Jefferson began to record an extensive series of observations in his diary at his Monticello home in Virginia. Benjamin Franklin, in 1743, was the first to recognize that weather traveled in a general west-to-east direction across the United States. By corresponding with his brother in Boston, Franklin, who lived in Philadelphia, deduced that storms moved in that manner. Luckily, Franklin survived his famous 1752 experiment in which he flew a kite with a metal key attached into a massive thunderstorm, attempting to prove that lightning was electricity—the hard way.

In the late 1700s, the area west of the Appalachian Mountains was still mostly virgin, unexplored land and the "Ohio Country Myth" was born. Rumors persisted that the region west of the Appalachians was blessed by a much more temperate and beneficial climate than the same latitude along the Atlantic Ocean coast.

This, of course, was not true—a "vulgar error," proclaimed one naturalist—but the promise of such a mild climate opened the door to the unsettled Ohio country.

Thomas Jefferson's weather log, showing entries recorded in Philadelphia, July 1776.

The government of the United States was aware of the importance of weather to the health and well-being of the military and in 1814 ordered hospital surgeons to keep a diary of the weather. One displeased doctor complained that most of the health problems at his outpost were caused by cheap whiskey, not anything meteorological. Rain gauges at the more remote sites sometimes went unread for days, "due to the danger of Indian attack."

By 1820, newspapers were carrying accounts of weather as far west as the Mississippi Valley, and for the first time the American people became aware of the wide range in climates over their rapidly expanding nation. At the end of the Civil War in 1865, daily weather observations were being taken by army surgeons at 143 stations.

With little understanding of the speed and complexity of weather systems, an early attempt was made to send forecasts by letter. The folly of this was immediately evident, since on the rare occasions when the forecast was reasonably accurate, the weather had arrived and departed well ahead of the mail.

It wasn't until Samuel Morse demonstrated his telegraph to Congress in 1844 that a weather-forecasting network became possible. The message Morse sent from Baltimore to Washington was "What hath God wrought?" One thing Morse had unknowingly wrought was the beginning of our national weather service.

In 1849, the Smithsonian Institution in Washington began an ambitious effort to collect and study weather reports from around the country. Within a year, 150 volunteers were sending regular reports.

In 1868, following a series of shipping disasters on the Great Lakes due to unanticipated storms, Professor Increase Lapham of Milwaukee petitioned the United States government for a national

WINTER

❄

FEB

weather forecasting agency. On February 9, 1870, President Ulysses S. Grant signed the national weather service into existence. The agency was made a part of the Signal Service, which was under the aegis of the War Department.

By 1878 there were 284 stations contributing three observations each day and telegraphing the information to Washington. Since there were then no means of getting weather information to the general public other than through the newspapers, the Signal Service used a simple flag display on buildings to indicate the weather expected for the day at hand. Searchlights, sirens, whistles, and even rockets were used by some local communities to warn of approaching storms.

In 1892, about 2,000 volunteers were taking observations in the United States, and by 1901 the weather service—now christened the Weather Bureau—was sending forecasts by telegraph to 80,000 recipients. It was estimated that by 1904 some 60,000 farmers in Ohio were receiving daily weather forecasts by telephone.

(The first forecasts were 24-hour estimates, while by 1888 the forecast period was extended to 36 hours. By 1898, 48-hour forecasts were prepared, and in 1910 weekly projections began. In 1950 the Weather Bureau started its 30-day outlooks.)

But real progress in the science of weather forecasting proceeded at a glacial pace. It was not until after the end of World War I that Norwegians Jacob and Wilhelm Bjerknes introduced the theory of fronts to weather forecasting. They reasoned that it was along these battle

A Signal Corps weather-kite release, ca. 1870.

zones that air is lifted, expands, and cools, causing the invisible water vapor to condense into rain or sublimate into snow.

This concept turned seemingly random and chaotic weather events into meteorological sense. But old weather precepts die hard and new ones are slow to prosper. It wasn't until 1936 that the familiar blue and red fronts finally appeared on official weather maps in the United States.

Another Norwegian-nurtured idea was air mass formation. This, too, was only grudgingly accepted.

In 1939, Carl Gustav Rossby, a Swedish meteorologist, advanced ideas on atmospheric middle latitude motions that led to the first application of wave action theory to the atmosphere. The movement of waves in our air mirrors that of the waves in our oceans, Rossby concluded.

The effects of weather on agriculture and military strategy gave the initial push to weather prediction, and its impact during military operations in World War II was of paramount importance. It was the use of Rossby's wave theories that allowed Allied forecasters to out-forecast the Germans for the D-Day landings on the beaches of France. Although British meteorologists disagreed, American forecasters anticipated a brief break in the terrible weather along the Normandy coastline for the June 6, 1944 invasion. The German weather service told its high command that the foul weather would continue and an invasion would not be possible at that time.

The invention of aircraft- and ship-searching radar during World War II set the stage for the development of raindrop-seeking technology in the 1950s. It is radar that has given local meteorologists their most important short-range storm-tracking tool.

On April 1, 1960, the 270-pound Tiros I, a prototype of today's sophisticated satellites, was launched. The orbiting of the first satellite gave forecasters their first overall view of the cloud patterns on earth. Until then only one-fifth of the globe was under weather observation. Huge, ocean-spawned storms, hurricanes, and typhoons often developed unnoticed until a luckless sea captain radioed that his ship was caught in the raging winds and high seas.

Today, under the guidance of the National Oceanic and Atmospheric Agency (NOAA), weather satellites hover over us, orbiting some 22,300 miles above our planet.

The theory that weather forecasts could be derived from mathematical formulas was the dream of a few imaginative scientists in the early 1900s. One of the first to foresee the possibility of numerical forecasting was a British meteorologist, Lewis Fry Richardson. His first attempt at a calculator-and-slide-rule forecast was made in 1922

WINTER

❄

FEB

for Central Europe. It was an unmitigated disaster. A lack of data and inaccurate information doomed his effort.

Richardson wrote a book in which he envisioned 64,000 humans pounding away at desk calculators in an attempt to stay one step ahead of the ever-changing weather. On a podium at the center of a gargantuan weather office would be a concertmaster—a meteorological Toscanini—who scanned the room in an effort to keep everyone in tempo and on the same weather page.

Richardson's impractical dream did not approach reality until 1945, when the first generation of electronic computers began to ingest complex meteorological equations and churn out the answers. By 1955, operational computer forecasts were being routinely prepared by John Von Neumann and his staff at Princeton University.

At the dawning of the computer age, some scientists expressed confidence that the difficult job of weather forecasting could be readily mastered by high-speed computers. All they had to do was turn the voracious computers loose to crunch the numbers. They theorized that the atmosphere could be reproduced by mathematical "models." These whirling, computer-guided models would then be put into motion to accurately project the weather for hours, days, even weeks ahead.

That optimism quickly vanished.

While the computer has been a great help in weather forecasting, the atmosphere has proven to be more inexplicably complex than anyone could have imagined. The so-called "Butterfly Effect," the slightest deviation from the model's starting point, will send the entire forecast careening down an increasingly chaotic and erroneous path. It's the second law of thermodynamics at its fleeting best: with the passage of time, all things fall apart.

In the decades ahead, computers even faster and more powerful than the Crays of today will try their luck at cracking the weather forecast barrier.

But those barriers may be too tall, too deeply entrenched: the day of the guaranteed weather forecast may never dawn. It has become increasingly apparent that randomness and chaos are the rule, not the exception, within our atmospheric ocean. Weather forecasting is simply one of the most difficult assignments science will ever face.

WINTER

❄

FEB

ALMANACS

Almanacs date almost from the invention of writing. One has been traced as far back as about 3000 B.C. in Egypt. The word "almanac" comes from an Arabic word meaning "calendar," but the first almanacs dealt primarily with astronomical calculations and seasonal changes. The heavenly happenings were combined with notations of feast days and popular legends. Christopher Columbus used an early German almanac to aid his navigation to the New World.

The second piece of literature printed in America (1639) was *An Almanac Calculated for New England.* Since then, hundreds of almanacs have come and gone. In 1687 John Tulley's almanac introduced the first weather forecasts to America. Known also for his unique humor, Tulley asked for a "charitable censure" when the forecasts went astray. Tulley, according to David Ludlum, this country's foremost weather historian, "sought to educate by entertaining."

Benjamin Franklin was responsible for the most famous of American almanacs, printing the first edition of *Poor Richard's Almanac* in 1733. For the next 25 years, that almanac presented poems and sayings recommending that life be lived on what Franklin perceived as a high moral plane. Franklin invented an author, Richard Saunders (Poor Richard), and patterned his annual publication after England's famous *Poor Robin's Almanac.*

While Franklin's almanac was full of preaching, it was written with wit and general good humor. By the fifth edition, however, Franklin decided to answer critics who derided the almanac for its inaccurate weather forecasts. In the 1737 publication, Poor Richard asked for "favourable allowance of a day or two either way" on his forecasts and, tongue-in-cheek, put a portion of the blame on the printer, saying that since he had a part in making the almanac he should at least share some of the criticism.

Perhaps the benchmark of weather hedging had been established in the 1664 edition of *Poor Robin's Almanac.* Poor Robin's forecast for February of 1664 read as follows:

We may expect some showers
or rain this month,
or the next,
or the next after that,
or else we shall have a very long, dry spring.

Robert Bailey Thomas founded the most enduring of the American almanacs, *The Old Farmer's Almanac,* in 1792. The *OFA* is supposed to have gained immortality through an incident that took place in 1805. The story goes that Thomas somehow neglected to fill in the weather for July 13, 1806, when he sent his copy to the printer. With the printing deadline at hand, and with no way of quickly contacting Thomas, the printer decided to put down the most ridiculous weather he could imagine for that summer day: "Rain, hail and snow." The rest is legend. When people received their copies of the 1806 *OFA* they chuckled at the absurd weather that was forecast for New England on July 13. You guessed it. An incredible, freak storm struck Boston and other parts of New England on July 13, 1806, dropping rain and hail—and snow!

Many almanacs have forged great reputations on just one such memorable forecast. Patrick Murphy, in his *Irish Almanac,* predicted that January 20, 1838, would be England's coldest day that winter. It was.

While most almanacs jealously guard their arcane formulas for making weather forecasts, many admit to a combination of earthly and heavenly considerations.

Astronomical weather forecasting interested the 17th-century German scientist, Johannes Kepler, and he advanced a number of theories based on the alignment of planets. Unfortunately, most of the time the planets have not cooperated.

A definitive study of almanac forecast reliability was made in the early 1980s by research meteorologists at the Laboratory for Atmospheric Research of the University of Illinois at Urbana. Using the best-selling *Old Farmer's Almanac* in a 60-month study, the research team determined that the almanac's precipitation accuracy over the period was 52 percent, while the temperature prognostications showed an accuracy of 51 percent. Considering that the rate of accuracy for outright guessing is 50 percent, the almanac's accuracy figures were not impressive.

An old Scandinavian saying seems to put things in perspective:

> *The almanac writer makes the almanac,*
> *but God makes the weather.*

Spring

IN OHIO, THE FIRST DAY OF SPRING IS
ONE THING, THE FIRST SPRING DAY ANOTHER.
BUCKEYE FOLKLORE SAYS THAT SPRING
DOESN'T REALLY ARRIVE UNTIL YOU CAN
STEP ON FIVE DANDELIONS WITH ONE FOOT
(WITHOUT USING A SNOWSHOE).

Astronomical spring—the vernal equinox—comes every March when the sun crosses the equator on its journey northward. While the word equinox means "equal night," don't be surprised that the timing of sunrise and sunset in Ohio does not produce an equal 12 hours of darkness and 12 hours of daylight on our first day of spring. The reason for this is refraction, or a bending of the rays of sunlight by earth's atmosphere. This bending causes the sun to appear higher in the sky than it actually is, especially at sunrise and sunset. The sun is seen to "rise" before it is up, and it "sets" several minutes after its rim has actually gone below the horizon.

Spring in Ohio comes in fits and starts, and true spring does not embrace most of the state until mid- to late April. A late spring is not always undesirable at our latitude, because it retards any premature burgeoning of buds and tender plants that then succumb to frosty nights in May.

If the month of March comes in like a lamb in Ohio, it's just pulling the wool over our eyes. Windy, rowdy March—named for Mars, the Roman god of war—has buried Ohio in some of our heaviest snows and greatest rains.

Torrential rain during March of 1913 brought the highest water-related loss of life in history to the state of Ohio. Heavy January rains that year soaked into the ground and then froze. February was cold but not memorable. In late March, temperatures rose into the 70s, and nearly continuous

CLEVELAND'S TOP 5 WETTEST AND DRIEST SPRINGS (RAINFALL)
Wettest
1) 16.33" / 1989
2) 14.57" / 1947
3) 14.31" / 1955
4) 13.70" / 1956
5) 13.62" / 1913
Driest
1) 4.45" / 1895
2) 4.64" / 1900
3) 4.70" / 1915
4) 4.82" / 1941
5) 5.17" / 1874

rain pelted all of our 88 counties for five days, from the 23rd to the 27th. Eight to ten inches of rain fell throughout the state, bringing the heaviest general flooding in Ohio weather records. Rivers and streams overflowed their banks, and the city of Dayton was devastated by the unprecedented flooding of the Miami River. The swollen Scioto River inundated much of the area around Columbus. An estimated 430 people perished in the great flood of 1913. This watery calamity was responsible for the creation of roller dams and reservoirs in Ohio, and their erection has minimized the possibility of such disastrous flooding recurring.

During March, the Ohio soil begins to warm under the lengthening, strengthening sunshine, and by month's end the first real signs of nature's rebirth are evident. By the 15th day, the buzzards have returned from their Florida vacation to Whipp's Ledges at Hinckley. (Ohio's turkey vultures beat the fabled swallows of Capistrano by four days.) On a mild March evening, we'll hear the first sleighbell chimes from the tiny and seldom seen tree toads, the spring peepers.

By the end of the month the first butterfly of the year, the velvety brown-and-yellow-striped mourning cloak, can be seen flitting and darting over melting clumps of snow.

In the March nighttime sky the spring constellation Leo, the lion, is now chasing the winter constellation Orion, the hunter, across the heavens.

April has been called the cruelest month, the month of fools, and we all know what Ohio's April showers bring. That's right—doubleheaders in August!

Sandusky Street in Delaware, Ohio, lies submerged by the Great Flood of 1913.

The foolhardy part comes early in April when the changeover to Daylight Saving Time, coupled with a few unseasonably warm days, gives many Buckeye gardeners the urge to get a jump on the planting season. Jack Frost prowls and paints the Ohio landscape regularly during the month of April, and even the extreme southern counties seldom escape his hoary brush.

CLEVELAND'S WARMEST AND COLDEST SPRINGS (BY MEDIAN TEMPERATURE)

Warmest: 53.4°/1991
Coldest: 41.3°/1885

Heavy snow is unusual in Ohio during April, but one of our greatest snowstorms ravaged the eastern counties in 1901. The blizzard raged from the 19th through the 21st, with the region from Canton to Dover and New Philadelphia buried under a 20-to-31-inch snowfall. Newspaper accounts of the storm lamented that the snow was so heavy "no ordinary man can shovel it," and even horse-drawn snowplows were "useless."

SPRING

If April, the coquette, denies us, the emerald month of May does not. There always comes that exhilarating morning when you're driving down a tree-lined road and you realize you are enwrapped in a dazzling green chlorophyll canyon that wasn't there the day before. (It's like the thrill that Dorothy, Toto, and the gang have as they hit Emerald City.) And there is nothing greener than the first vibrant blades of grass in Ohio's springtime.

While the month of May will have some meteorological disappointments for us—gutsy thunderstorms and some unseasonably chilly days—the fragrance of lilacs and apple blossoms assures us of the fruitful season just ahead.

Debris from the Great Flood of 1913 piles up in downtown Dayton.

On a warm late-May evening we'll be startled by a sudden thump on the window screen announcing the arrival of the first June bug of the season. Called May bugs in southern states and tumble bugs in the West, June bugs, for all their impressive-looking armor, can neither bite nor sting.

Mid-spring produces Ohio's most fitful and chaotic weather of the year. There is a continual parade of weather fronts through the state. Onrushing warm and humid air from the Gulf of Mexico often collides with cool Pacific Ocean air directly over our state, resulting in frequent severe thunderstorm and tornado watches. Nearly 70 percent of all Ohio tornadoes have occurred during the spring season.

Adding to the springtime weather forecast problems in northeastern Ohio is the fact that the Lake Erie water is slow to release its wintertime chill. After the seasonal low of 33° in February (the lake water temperature is taken at a depth of 35 feet, where freezing does not take place), the Lake Erie water temperature rises into the 40s in April and 50s during May. Even though warm air is covering the entire state, a sudden wind shift to the north will often drop nearshore temperatures 20 degrees in a few minutes. It is not uncommon in early spring to find readings in the crisp 40s along the Lake Erie shoreline with 60-degree temperatures at Cleveland Hopkins International Airport, just five miles inland.

This early-spring influence of Lake Erie not only keeps northeastern Ohio temperatures at snappy levels; it also brings frequent periods of clouds and showers. As a result, the chance for prolonged sunshine in our corner of the state is minimal. If you see anyone sporting a tanned or bronzed look in Northeast Ohio in early spring, it can mean only one thing: rust.

If you see anyone sporting a tanned or bronzed look in Northeast Ohio in early spring, it can mean only one thing: rust.

While spring may be just a rumor near the Lake Erie shore, places such as Columbus, Cincinnati, Zanesville, and Marietta often bask in 70- and 80-degree warmth. The Cincinnati Reds often enjoy comfortable weather for their April baseball opener while the Cleveland Indians are dodging snow squalls.

From the weather forecast standpoint, the seven-week period from mid-April through May can give meteorologists their most difficult time of the year. The Ohio atmosphere is a constant battleground for weather fronts.

Nature's spring starts when the daily mean temperature (the

midpoint between the daily maximum and daily minimum temperature) rises high enough to trigger plant growth: 43° F.

Many veteran gardeners in the northern counties of Ohio are unwilling to play meteorological roulette with Jack Frost until Memorial Day. The date of the last killing frost in Ohio varies widely. In autumn, areas near the slow-to-cool waters of Lake Erie have a growing season several weeks longer than that in inland areas. (Don't grumble in September when you are sent scurrying into the tomato patch to rescue the still-green fruit from frost: ten thousand years ago we were at the tip of a retreating ice-age glacier and the Ohio growing season was six weeks long!)

Since cold air is heavy and sinks, low-lying spots will have frost dates later than nearby, higher elevations.

You should be aware that "winterkill" can occur in springtime at temperatures that would not be as harmful in late autumn. That is because plants are more susceptible to cold temperatures after growth has begun. Plants die because the juices within freeze and expand. Swelling causes the fragile cells to burst.

Surprisingly, official temperatures as high as 36° F could result in frost over much of the region. This is because official thermometers are five feet above the ground, and there is a very good chance that readings at ground level are 32° or lower.

Ideal conditions for the formation of frost are a cool and relatively dry air canopy, clear skies, little or no wind, and long nights. A cloudy sky usually prevents the formation of frost, since clouds absorb terrestrial radiation and then reradiate the energy back to earth. (It is often incorrectly assumed that clouds act as a blanket, simply trapping the earth's warmth.)

For frost protection you can cover tender plants with a sheet or light blanket. This will cause temperatures under the cover to remain from three to six degrees warmer than the outside air, often just enough to prevent damage. Baskets, newspaper, or hot caps serve the same purpose. Just remember to remove the protective cover as soon as the sun comes up, otherwise you'll cook your plant.

Never use plastic as a covering, because the plant will be frostburned or injured wherever the plastic touches it.

Sprinkling your plants or trees with a fine spray of water can prevent frost or freeze, but certain rules must be followed.

The misting technique works because heat is released when the water turns to ice on the plant. This allows the surface temperature of the plant or tree to hover near 32° as long as the spray of water is continuously applied. If you stop spraying too soon, the plant could still be lost.

Sprinkling should begin when the air temperature approaches freezing and be continued until the ice that forms begins to melt and water is dripping from all surfaces. The recommended rate of fine spray is .05 to .25 inches per hour, no more. Use the heavier figure for the coldest temperatures and do not attempt the spray technique when wind speeds are more than 10 mph. Overspraying will cause heavy ice accretion, and plants and tree limbs could collapse under the weight.

The growing season is the period of days when temperatures don't fall below 32° F. The last spring frost in Ohio ranges from about April 12 to May 19, while the first frost in autumn varies from around September 23 to November 6. Ohio's longest growing season is the average 208-day frost-free period at Put-in-Bay on South Bass Island in Lake Erie. The shortest growing season is at Tom Jenkins Dam in the rugged hills of Athens County in southeast Ohio. This cold-air drainage location has an average annual growing season of 129 days.

By comparison, here are the growing seasons, in days, for some other cities around the country . . .

Atlanta: 237

Aroostook, Maine: 107

Chicago: 195

Denver: 171

Los Angeles: 359

Palm Beach: 322

New Orleans: 292

New York: 211

Butte, Montana: 110

In the Northeast Ohio Sky This Season

In spring that childhood favorite, the Big Dipper (Ursa Major, the Great Bear) is almost directly overhead in the Northeast Ohio sky.

Rising in the east is the constellation Bootes (boo-OO-tees), called the Herdsman for no obvious reason. The lowest star in Bootes is the orange-yellow Arcturus (arc-TO-russ) the second-brightest star in the Ohio sky (do not confuse stars with the bright planets Venus, Mars, Jupiter, or Saturn that masquerade as stars).

To the lower right is the blue-white royal star, Regulus (REG-you-luss), the Little King.

On a late-spring night try to find Zubenelgenubi (zoo-BEN-el-je-NEW-be) low in the southern sky. Nothing special, I just like the name.

SPRING

SUNSHINE %: 45
DRIEST MONTH: 0.41"/1910
WARMEST MONTH: 49.5°/1946
COLDEST MONTH: 24.0°/1960
LIQUID PCPN AVG.: 2.91"
RAINIEST DAY: 2.76"/1848
RAINIEST MONTH: 8.31"/1913
THUNDERY DAYS: 2
SNOWIEST DAY: 16.0"/1987
SNOWIEST MONTH: 26.3"/1954
LEAST SNOWFALL: Trace/1927
DAYS ONE INCH SNOW: 3

The winds of March that make your heart a dancer have occasionally brought record amounts of snow with them. On March 30–31, 1987, Cleveland received its second-heaviest 24-hour snowfall, 16.4 inches. Several days later the Akron-Canton area was buried under a record 20.6 inches. Curiously, many of Northeast Ohio's monumental snowfalls have come in November and March, on either side of what is officially winter. Snows in March are usually very wet and hard to shovel, but the crystals melt quickly. March is the month of reawakening, and on mild nights the tiny tree frogs known as spring peepers begin their vernal concerts. Spring, the vernal equinox, arrives on the 20th of the month; this is one of only two times each year that our sun rises due east and sets due west. We now enjoy three more hours of daylight than we did in dark December, and we'll gain another three hours by the summer solstice in June.

SPRING

MAR

Day	Hi	Lo	Rec Hi	Rec Lo	Sunrise	Sunset	Lake°
1	46	23	69 / 1912	-2 / 1984	7:02	6:18	34
2	40	24	64 / 1991	-4 / 1978	7:01	6:19	34
3	41	24	74 / 1974	2 / 1984	6:59	6:20	34
4	41	24	76 / 1983	2 / 1943	6:58	6:21	34
5	42	25	81 / 1983	-2 / 1873	6:56	6:22	34
6	42	25	74 / 1973	-2 / 1960	6:54	6:23	34
7	43	25	76 / 1983	3 / 1960	6:53	6:25	34
8	43	26	72 / 1987	-1 / 1960	6:51	6:26	34
9	43	26	73 / 1878	-5 / 1984	6:50	6:27	34
10	44	26	72 / 1973	5 / 1983	6:48	6:28	34
11	44	27	73 / 1973	-3 / 1983	6:46	6:29	34
12	45	27	75 / 1990	-5 / 1948	6:45	6:30	34
13	45	27	76 / 1990	3 / 1960	6:43	6:31	34
14	46	28	79 / 1990	6 / 1993	6:40	6:32	34
15	46	28	80 / 1990	3 / 1993	6:38	6:34	35
16	46	28	78 / 1945	7 / 1885	6:38	6:35	35
17	47	29	72 / 1945	0 / 1900	6:36	6:36	35
18	47	29	75 / 1903	0 / 1877	6:35	6:37	35
19	48	29	76 / 1903	7 / 1885	6:33	6:38	35
20	48	30	76 / 1995	0 / 1885	6:31	6:39	35
21	48	30	76 / 1938	-4 / 1885	6:30	6:40	35
22	49	30	83 / 1938	0 / 1885	6:28	6:41	36
23	49	30	77 / 1966	5 / 1885	6:26	6:42	36
24	50	31	83 / 1910	8 / 1888	6:25	6:44	36
25	50	31	83 / 1945	8 / 1888	6:23	6:45	36
26	50	31	80 / 1967	16 / 1894	6:21	6:46	36
27	51	32	80 / 1989	12 / 1982	6:20	6:47	36
28	51	32	80 / 1945	9 / 1982	6:18	6:48	36
29	52	32	81 / 1910	11 / 1887	6:16	6:49	36
30	52	32	82 / 1986	16 / 1987	6:15	6:50	37
31	52	33	77 / 1943	11 / 1923	6:13	6:51	37

Nothing is to be feared.
It is only to be understood.
– MARIE CURIE

SWEET SOUNDS OF SPRING

Unfortunately, in Northeast Ohio the promise of the first spring day is like the sign in the saloon that proclaims "Free Beer Tomorrow." That tomorrow, of course, never comes. Our first day of spring, as often as not, arrives in the guise of a miniblizzard. But if you listen hard enough, you can sometimes hear signs of the arrival of spring.

According to the famed naturalist Edwin Way Teale, springtime in the eastern United States begins in the Florida Everglades during the first week in February. Spring then moves slowly, but inexorably, northward at about 15 miles each day. The key to vernal rebirth, of course, is the steady climatological rise in the average temperature. Once the air temperature reaches 60 degrees or above, insects emerge from their winter hideaways. With the doors to the cafeteria unlocked, the birds that migrated southward in autumn follow the food supply north.

True spring reaches the Ohio River counties of our state the first week in April and the shores of Lake Erie during the third week in April. (So plan on having that lawn mower sharpened by April 20.)

Perhaps the sweetest sound that announces the advent of spring in Northeast Ohio is the bell-like chorus of the tiny tree (or cricket) frog known as the spring peeper. On the first mild evening in March take a trip to the nearest marshy woodland and treat yourself to the peeper's sleighbell symphony. You'll never see the members of the all-male orchestra, however, since the less-than-one-inch-long musicians stay hidden and temporarily stop their tintinnabulations at the slightest noise.

That whirring sound frequently heard across the region now is not caused by the flapping wings of newly arrived blackbirds, phoebes, or bluebirds. It's the sound of eager gardeners rapidly thumbing through the pages of this spring's seed catalogs. Northern Ohio gardeners need to be reminded that the average date of the last frost or freeze here ranges from late April through mid-May. Many veteran green-thumbers, stung by the fickle cold fronts of early spring, refuse to put any frost-sensitive plants into the soil until Memorial Day weekend.

SPRING

MAR

SPRING IS FOR...THE BUZZARDS?

Legend decrees that the swallows always return to the mission at San Juan de Capistrano, California, on March 19th (following their six-week, 6,000-mile return flight from the Goya region of Argentina).

Ohio's answer to the swallows are the buzzards (turkey vultures, actually) that traditionally arrive at Hinckley in Medina county on March 15th—just in time for the pancake-and-sausage breakfast on Sunday.

It is still not clear if the Ohio buzzards are the same carrion-eating critters that winter around the courthouse in Dade County, Florida. The Miami Chamber of Commerce is not fond of the birds, who sun themselves in the morning, fly off to the local dump for brunch, then return for a late

afternoon siesta. Definitely not a tourist attraction, the buzzards also have a nasty habit of regurgitating both while in flight and while at rest on the dome of the courthouse. As the courthouse superintendent and dome cleaner, Red Jones, says, "No one here gives a whoop about them, and they're a rotten-looking piece of equipment when you see them up close!"

While the buzzards may lack the aquiline grace and beauty of the eagle, remember they're one of Ohio's signs of spring!

THE ATMOSPHERE, OUR OCEAN OF AIR

The air—or atmosphere—that surrounds earth is an invisible mix of colorless, tasteless, and (mostly) odorless gases that protect us from harmful waves of incoming cosmic and solar radiation and energy. This protective umbrella causes small meteors from interplanetary space to harmlessly burn away before they collide with our planet. Without this atmospheric shield, earth would be intensely hot on the side where the sun is shining and insufferably cold on the dark, sunless side. Our atmosphere also acts as an air conditioner and distributes rainfall around the earth.

Earth's ethereal shell is several hundred miles deep, but the outer limits are difficult to measure. There is no definite boundary, no stop sign before you sail off into the blackness of space.

The stuff we call weather occurs only in a shallow layer that extends from 5 to 11 miles above the surface of the earth. In less than 1 percent of the atmosphere's depth, 100 percent of our weather is created. The relative thickness of this weather-producing layer of air, called the troposphere, can be compared to the thickness of the skin of an apple.

The pressure, or weight, of the atmosphere is heaviest against the earth's surface. The air thins out so rapidly that one-half of our atmospehere's weight lies within 18,000 feet of the surface. (More than 99 percent of the atmosphere is within 40 miles of the surface.)

Without our atmosphere there would be no weather. Just as it is on the airless moon, the sky would be black and there would be no clouds, no rain, no snow or wind. We would still not experience the things that we call weather if our atmosphere was not mixed and disturbed. But like our rolling oceans of water, our ocean of air is in constant, restless motion, intersected by rivers and streams of air.

The ladle that stirs the earth's atmosphere is the heat we receive from the medium-sized, yellow-white star we call our sun. Some 93 million miles from our planet, the sun is a gigantic, fiery ball of burning, exploding gases.

This atomic furnace heats our atmosphere unevenly from pole to equator. That heat, combined with the spinning of the earth, creates the wind that moves the weather systems along. (Earth revolves,

SPRING

MAR

counterclockwise, at speeds that range from zero at the poles to about 700 mph at Ohio's latitude, to just over 1,000 mph at the equator.)

Out atmospheric ocean is a meteorological Crock-Pot of many gases, the most important of which are nitrogen (78 percent), oxygen (21 percent), argon (about 1 percent), and carbon dioxide (less than 1 percent). Other gases occur in small amounts, but they are vital. Ozone, for example, prevents harmful ultraviolet rays from getting through. Water exists in minuscule amounts, but this moisture is the most important weather-producing ingredient. The total amount of water vapor (water in an invisible gaseous form) in our atmosphere never changes, but can vary locally—ranging from just over a trace over arid desert regions to a maximum of between 3 and 4 percent in moist tropical locations. While we sometimes hear of rain falling in biblical amounts, it is estimated that if all the moisture in our atmosphere fell at the same time, it would cover the earth with a layer of water only one inch deep. (Water on earth never goes away—it just changes form. A molecule of water in your morning coffee may have been in Cleopatra's bath!)

Water is the only readily abundant substance that exists in three forms on earth: vapor (invisible gas), liquid (rain), and solid (snowflakes, ice crystals, hail). And it changes form frequently.

The weight of the air pressing down on us from above is more than 2,000 pounds per square foot, and more than 10 tons of air surrounds us, squeezing our bodies. We are not crushed by this tremendous weight because there is enough air pushing outward in our bodies to balance the atmospheric pressure.

CIRCULATION

The spinning of the earth on its axis results in broad flowing belts of air around our globe. If you are a regular viewer of television weather programs you cannot help but notice a nearly uninterrupted parade of weather from west to east across Ohio and nearly all of the coterminous United States. This is because almost all of this land mass lies between 30° and 60° north latitude, the belt of wind circulation known as the "prevailing westerlies."

Above 60° north is the zone of the "prevailing easterlies," while between the equa-

A satellite view of earth.

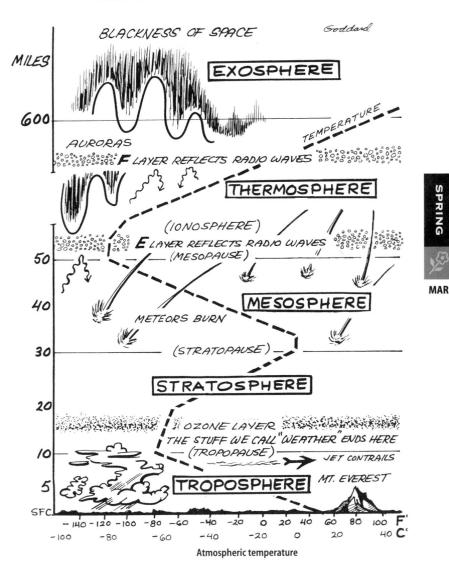

Atmospheric temperature

tor and 30° north lies the "trade winds" belt, so called because ships sailing from Europe used the reliable northeasterly air flow at these lower latitudes to bring them to the New World. (Christopher Columbus and his tiny caravels rode this route.)

Ohio forecasters know that the weather to the west will eventually head our way, so it would seem that the job of guessing tomorrow's weather would not be difficult. A woman once told me that all I needed to do was listen to Don McNeill's *Breakfast Club* radio program out of Chicago to know what the weather would be in Cleveland the next day. Well, sometimes it is the same weather. The problem is, weather systems can quickly change their character as they move along, and a snowy Monday in Chicago is no guarantee that we'll be shoveling snow in northern Ohio on Tuesday.

To understand why weather moves in an almost unfailing west-to-east course across Ohio we must consider what is known as the general circulation of the winds around our planet. This circulation is complicated and not totally consistent, but the climates of earth are determined by this primary air flow.

A key rule to remember about the workings of the weather is that expanding gases become colder (you feel this when using an aerosol spray) and compressed gases become warmer (have you felt the nozzle of a hand pump?). In warming air, the molecules become more widely separated and this less dense air becomes buoyant and rises through the surrounding cooler air. This process of lighter, warmer air rising and being replaced by heavier, cold air is called convection, and this is the most important method of heat transfer in our atmosphere. (Convection is vertically moving air; advection is horizontally moving air.) Simply put, warm air rises and cold air sinks.

Where air sinks, the atmospheric gases are compressed and the weather is most often dry and settled. These are the regions where air "piles up" and fair-weather high pressure results.

Where air rises, the weather is often unsettled and disturbed because the rising air expands and cools. This frequently results in clouds and precipitation. These are the regions of low pressure.

There are various belts around the earth that tend to produce high and low pressure, fair and foul weather. Low pressure dominates at the equator and 60° north latitude, while high pressure is the rule at 30° and 90° north latitude.

THE DOPPLER EFFECT

If you are pulled over because police radar has caught you exceeding the speed limit, don't curse Christian Doppler.

I'm sure that when the Austrian physicist discovered in 1842 that sound waves could be bounced off moving targets and would return like a boomerang, he wasn't thinking of law enforcement.

The principle of radar (transmission of radio light waves) might best be described by using sound waves as an example. When an emergency vehicle with its siren blaring moves toward you, the siren's pitch appears to be higher than when the vehicle is moving away from you.

Doppler applied this principle of sound-wave projection to electromagnetic radio-wave vibration. Traveling at the speed of light, radio waves are sent out through an antenna. The light waves bounce off a target (raindrops, hail, dust, etc.) and an echo returns to the antenna, where it is then displayed on an electronic screen. A light source moving toward the observer will show on the screen as blue. A source moving away from the observer will be red.

Using this color key (along with a number of other colors) Doppler radar can tell you not only the size, movement, and intensity of a thunderstorm, but it can also tell the speed and direction of raindrops and ice particles within the storm. It is this ability to pick up violently circulating wind patterns within the cloud that can give advance warning that a tornado is forming *before* it emerges from the cloud.

Conventional radar cannot discern rotation within a cloud. It was only with the development of modern high-speed supercomputers that the Doppler effect could be put to full use.

Can Doppler radar guarantee that we'll have warnings well in advance of a violent thunderstorm or tornado? No, since some storms can form so quickly that even Doppler radar may be briefly blinded.

OUR DEADLIEST TORNADO

The gates of hell opened in Reynolds County, Missouri, in 1925, and when they slammed shut some three and one-half hours and 219 miles later, 695 were dead.

Few who witnessed the great Tri-State Tornado of March 18, 1925, actually saw a classic tornado funnel. At the beginning, around 1 p.m., a single vortex appeared, while near its end some saw three twisting, elephant's trunk–like clouds reaching earth. For most of its life, the twister was a black-and-green boiling cloud that hugged the ground and blotted out half of the horizon.

The Tri-State Tornado set a record for having the longest continuous track and for being the longest-lived. The twister was, at times, at least one mile wide—four times the average width of a tornado. The path extended from southeastern Missouri across southern Illinois into southwestern Indiana. Using the present-day Fujita scale, the Tri-State Tornado would be at the top of the chart, an F5 with winds of over 300 mph.

Steadily traveling on a heading of northeastward, the tornado veered slightly to the left at its very end. The remarkably high forward speed of the tornado, averaging 62 mph, but at times as high as 73 mph, meant that the normally weather-wise people in rural areas had only seconds to realize their fate. Warning communities down weather from the storm was impossible, since telephone lines were quickly destroyed and no radio-type alert system was available.

Of the 695 that perished in the Tri-State Tornado, 234 were at Murphysboro, Illinois. It was the largest death toll within a single city in United States weather history.

The town of Gorham, Illinois, was 100 percent destroyed, and 34 died there. Judith Cox remembered opening the door of the Wallace Cafe in Gorham and exclaiming "My God, it's a cyclone and it's here!" At this point the "cyclone" (tornado) had already killed 13.

Judith Cox slammed the cafe door shut and then, suddenly remembering her two children in school, flung it open again and dived headlong into the ferocious wind. After she had taken two steps, the violent wind hurled Mrs. Cox back into the cafe and against a hot stove. The entire building then caved in, knocking her unconscious.

When she awakened amid the debris, Judith Cox recalled seeing a red cow lying beside her. Joe Moschenrose, who had climbed over the debris looking for his sister, Lulu, helped Mrs. Cox to her feet and together they helped the still very much alive cow to stand.

They soon found Moschenrose's sister under the wreckage, but there was a terrible gash on her head. Lulu was dead.

As her sensibilities returned, Judith Cox ran stumbling through the ruins of Gorham toward her children's schoolhouse. On the way she passed her tattered raincoat that was dangling from a plank. She reached into a pocket and quickly picked out her husband's paycheck, which she had put there earlier that day. Upon reaching the nearly demolished school she found parents frantically tearing away at the wreckage, searching for their children. There Mrs. Cox found her two daughters, Catherine, 14, and Ernestine, 12. Splinters and particles of dirt were embedded in their faces, but they had survived.

A few miles northeast of Gorham at Murphysboro, the evangelical services at the Moose Hall had just begun, with Mrs. Everett Parrott singing "More About Jesus." Sister Parrott had just rendered the first verse when what were thought to be hailstones came crashing through the ceiling. As thunder rumbled and lightning illuminated the hall, it was quickly discovered that the objects coming through the roof weren't hailstones but rocks.

Everyone panicked. The Methodist minister dived under the front of the piano and was met by Brother Parrott arriving from the opposite side. Mrs. May Williams, a visiting evangelist, proclaimed that the end of the world was at hand and announced that she was willing to die.

It is estimated that within the first 40 minutes, 540 died in the great Tri-State Tornado of 1925.

WHEN YOUR TANG GETS TOUNGLED UP

They are called "spoonerisms" and it's fair to say that anyone who has the power of speech has fallen prey to this type of linguistic transposition. Those who chronically suffer from the mixing up of words are the victims of what is known as metathesis. Fortunately, metathesis is not fatal, although its victims sometimes feel as if they are about to die of embarrassment. There is also no cure for this affliction, aside from keeping your mouth shut.

I've spent a career butchering the King's English on Cleveland television, and I enjoy verbal somersaults as much as anyone. Three times over the years, Dick Clark's television blooper show has exposed my shortcomings. (The derision of my newsroom friends turns to envy, however, when a check for eight hundred bucks shows up—at which time comes the question, "Now where do I send my tape?") A recent blunder came when I referred to a cold air mass coming our way from Canada as "a cold mare's ass." That one is awaiting national distribution.

The word "spoonerism" has come to us from the verbal misadventures of the Rev. Dr. William Archibald Spooner who, for 62 years, was an esteemed professor, theologian, and warden (president) at New College, Oxford University in England. Dr. Spooner passed from this tail of years . . . make that veil of tears . . . in 1930 at the age of 86.

All who knew Dr. Spooner agreed that he was a kindly and conscientious teacher whose only problem was that he inadvertently savaged the English language.

Perhaps the initial storm warning of Dr. Spooner's affliction came the first Sunday that he was asked to address the church congregation. Dr. Spooner mounted the pulpit and asked the elders to "please, make sure the congregation is sewn to their sheets."

Once, after introducing a church speaker, Dr. Spooner headed for his favorite spot in the pews, where he found a comely lass solidly entrenched. "Mardon me, padam," whispered Dr. Spooner, "I believe you are occupewing my pie."

As Dr. Spooner's years at Oxford multiplied, so did the spoonerisms. Students began to mimic their beleaguered professor, and eventually there arose a list of verbal blunders falsely attributed to Dr. Spooner. By 1955 the word "spoonerisms" had been firmly established. Apocryphal or not, here is a sampling of Dr. Spooner's most precious tongue twisters:

Admonishing a student whom he believed had wasted two terms and repeatedly missed his history lectures, Dr. Spooner chided, "Not only have you tasted two worms, but you have hissed my mystery lectures."

In a speech welcoming Queen Victoria to Oxford, Dr. Spooner wanted to confide to Her Majesty that "In my bosom I have a half-formed wish" which, unfortunately, came out "In my bosom I have a half-warmed fish."

In everyday conversation a spoonerism is usually met with a smile or chuckle, but when a spoonerism is committed by a public figure before a large audience, the verbal gaffe will live on in perpetuity.

Anyone who has done radio or television for any length of time will pile up a steadily growing list of speaking blunders.

The late Cleveland sportscaster, Jim Graner, who had Johnson's Jay Wax for a sponsor, told his listeners one evening to be sure to pickup a can of "Jackson's John Wax."

A radio station in Northern Ohio directed its disc jockeys always to follow the reading of the local weather forecast with the words, "Now, let's take a look out the window." You can imagine the embarrassment of the morning jock—and the glee of his listeners—when he substituted the word "leak" for "look."

Stage performers often come acropper at critical moments. The famous actor Rex Harrison recalled his first role. He played the part of a new father and, at the moment of delivery, shouted, "It's a doctor ... fetch a baby!"

A fine example of a spoonerism at its best came when an aspiring Hollywood actor was introduced to the famous British film star, Walter Pidgeon. "Mr. Privilege," gushed the young man, "this is indeed a pigeon."

Spoonerisms have claimed victims from all professions, including presidents of the United States. During the 1976 presidential campaign, President Gerald Ford concluded a speech by declaring "Jimmy Carter speaks loudly and carries a fly spotter ... a flyswasher ... It's been a long day." And consider these remarks by Vice President George Bush: "For seven and a half years I've worked alongside President Reagan. We've had triumphs, made some mistakes. We've had sex ... uh ... setbacks!"

In all my years of kicking around the English language on televi-

SPRING

MAR

sion there is one indelible moment that I will never top. It was at the 21st annual Jerry Lewis MDA telethon, which was headquartered at the just-renamed Stouffer's Tower City Plaza. To make matters even worse, I was standing next to a nun, Sister Angela. As Ed McMahon cued the return to local stations, the little red light on the camera went on, the floor director pointed at me, and in my best announcing voice I greeted everyone with "Welcome back to Cleveland. I'm here with Sister Angela at the beautiful Stouffer's Sour Tity Plaza!"

I remember Sister Angela's beatific smile.

SUNSHINE %: 51
DRIEST MONTH: 0.65"/1915
WARMEST MONTH: 55.9°/1955
COLDEST MONTH: 39.6°/1874
LIQUID PCPN AVG.: 3.14"
RAINIEST DAY: 2.24"/1961
RAINIEST MONTH: 6.61"/1961
THUNDERY DAYS: 4
SNOWIEST DAY: 11.6"/1982
SNOWIEST MONTH: 14.3"/1943
LEAST SNOWFALL: Trace (most recently in 1991)
DAYS ONE INCH SNOW: 1

April is also known as the month of fools. It's foolish, indeed, to set out any tender plants during this fourth month of the year. April marks the beginning of the tornado season in Northeast Ohio, and April tornadoes are often strong, accounting for the highest monthly death toll from twisters in the United States. The April 11, 1965, Palm Sunday tornado killed 19 at Pittsfield in Lorain County. The massive F5 twister that struck Xenia, Ohio, on the 3rd of April in 1974 killed 35. (That tornado was part of the greatest "family outbreak" of tornadoes in American weather history.) Thanks to Ben Franklin, who came up with the idea, we revert to Daylight Saving Time on the first Sunday of April. At 2 a.m. we'll loose an hour's sleep by setting our clocks ahead to 3 a.m. Raucous and cunning crows are returning from the depths of the winter woods. Juncos (snow birds) have returned and bluebirds often arrive by the third week in April. Woollybear caterpillars, who spent all winter in their larval stage, will be munching on dandelion and plantain weed before spinning cocoons out of their body hair. In a few weeks a beige, purple-spotted tiger moth will emerge and flit away in the spring sunshine. Each moth lays thousands of eggs, which will become the woollybears of autumn. If snow should cover your flowers, don't bother to brush it away; snow acts as a protective, insulating blanket.

SPRING

APR

Day	Hi	Lo	Rec Hi	Rec Lo	Sunrise*	Sunset*	Lake°
1	53	33	80 / 1986	10 / 1964	7:11	7:52	37
2	53	33	81 / 1963	19 / 1883	7:10	7:53	37
3	53	34	77 / 1981	19 / 1954	7:08	7:54	38
4	54	34	77 / 1882	19 / 1971	7:06	7:55	38
5	54	34	81 / 1988	17 / 1881	7:05	7:57	38
6	55	34	84 / 1929	21 / 1982	7:03	7:58	38
7	55	35	83 / 1929	17 / 1982	7:01	7:59	39
8	55	35	79 / 1871	11 / 1982	7:00	8:00	39
9	56	35	81 / 1931	17 / 1972	6:58	8:01	39
10	56	36	83 / 1978	20 / 1997	6:56	8:01	39
11	56	36	82 / 1945	22 / 1982	6:55	8:02	40
12	57	36	82 / 1977	21 / 1874	6:53	8:03	40
13	57	36	85 / 1941	20 / 1950	6:52	8:04	40
14	57	37	85 / 1883	20 / 1950	6:50	8:05	41
15	58	37	81 / 1976	22 / 1935	6:48	8:06	41
16	58	37	84 / 1896	18 / 1875	6:47	8:07	41
17	58	38	84 / 1896	15 / 1875	6:45	8:08	41
18	59	38	85 / 1896	17 / 1875	6:44	8:09	42
19	59	38	84 / 1941	22 / 1887	6:42	8:11	42
20	60	39	83 / 1985	23 / 1904	6:41	8:12	42
21	60	39	86 / 1942	24 / 1875	6:39	8:13	42
22	60	39	84 / 1985	23 / 1875	6:38	8:14	43
23	61	40	86 / 1985	27 / 1994	6:36	8:15	43
24	61	40	88 / 1925	28 / 1930	6:35	8:16	44
25	61	40	87 / 1990	27 / 1888	6:33	8:17	44
26	62	41	87 / 1948	26 / 1972	6:32	8:18	44
27	62	41	86 / 1990	27 / 1971	6:31	8:19	45
28	62	41	88 / 1986	25 / 1947	6:29	8:20	45
29	63	41	84 / 1899	25 / 1977	6:28	8:21	45
30	63	42	88 / 1942	28 / 1969	6:27	8:22	46

* DAYLIGHT SAVING TIME BEGINS ON THE FIRST SUNDAY IN APRIL

*Be nice to people on your way up,
because you'll meet them again
on the way down.*
– WILSON MIXNER

CLOUDS

Henry David Thoreau observed, "A sky without clouds is like a meadow without flowers." Satellite photographs over the years have revealed that about 59 percent of earth's meadow is flowered at any one time.

Clouds range in height from earth-hugging fog to the towering and majestic cumulonimbus, the thunderstorm cloud. The distinctive anvil-shaped top of the cumulonimbus may tower to over 60,000 feet, piercing the stratosphere.

Clouds are messengers, the press agents for the next weather show coming to town. They also serve as wind vanes, indicating the prevailing air currents. It is the cloud that carries water around the earth and sustains life on our planet.

When you see your breath on a cold day, you have a good example of how a cloud forms. A tiny cloud plume is created when we expel warm, moist air that suddenly cools to its saturation (or dew) point—the point at which the air can no longer hold water vapor in its invisible state. The vapor condenses on invisible particles of dust in the air. The dust motes are hydroscopic, meaning that they attract water. Without these minute magnets, or aerosols (billions of which could fit inside a thimble), clouds could never develop; rain or snow would never fall. Ironically, pollution—at least a certain amount of it—benefits mankind.

A cloud is made up of billions of tiny water droplets or ice particles. Each droplet or particle is too minuscule to be seen individually, but crammed together they become visible as a cloud.

Almost all of our clouds, and the precipitation that falls from them, are caused by unstable, rising air.

While clouds can form when warm and cold air masses mingle and mix, almost all of our clouds, and the precipitation that falls from them, are caused by unstable, rising air. This uplifting process—convection—involves a phenomena called adiabatic cooling. The heated air near the earth's surface becomes lighter than the surrounding cool air and rises like a balloon. As the rising warm air expands, it gradually begins to cool. The average temperature fall, or lapse rate, is 3.5° F for each 1,000 feet, but that depends on how much water vapor is in the rising air. The drier the air, the greater the temperature declines.

SPRING

APR

SPRING

APR

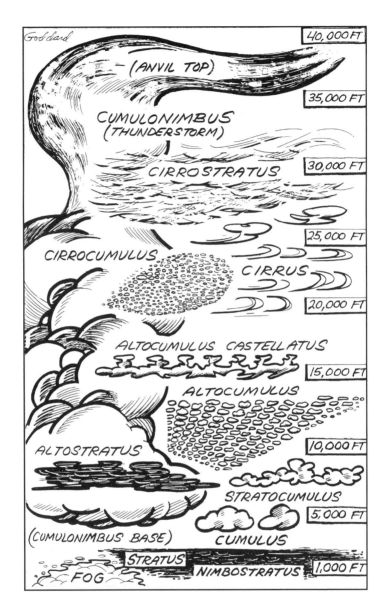

A cloud will form when the air has cooled so much that the invisible water vapor condenses onto microscopic water droplets, ice crystals, or particles of ice.

The bottom of a cloud will tell us at what level the humidity has reached 100 percent: the air is so saturated with moisture it can no longer keep it concealed in vapor form. The top of the cloud shows the point at which the air has stopped rising and become stable.

Aside from convective currents, clouds can also develop when a warm air mass simply climbs over a cold air mass (as happens with a warm front), or when the wind forces the air to flow over mountains or high terrain (orographic lifting). Another process, known as convergence, takes place when similar air masses collide, but that is restricted to areas near the equator (the Intertropical Convergence Zone—ITCZ).

Condensation creates a cloud; evaporation will make it disappear.

In low-pressure areas, the air rises and the adiabatic cooling process produces clouds. In areas of high pressure, the air sinks and this subsidence warms the air and clouds evaporate. In the satellite cloud photographs you see on television, the clear sky regions tell us where the air is sinking, while the white cloud swirls and curlicues reveal rising air.

An equally important process in understanding how clouds form and precipitation falls is sublimation. While condensation occurs when invisible water vapor changes into liquid water droplets, sublimation occurs when the vapor freezes directly into ice particles (or the opposite, ice into water) without first turning to liquid water.

When water vapor continues to condense and sublimate, the thickening and expanding cloud makes it increasingly difficult for sunlight to penetrate, and the cloud base darkens. As a result, a dark, threatening cloud is still no guarantee of precipitation—it may only be an "empty" coming in from Indianapolis.

There are two basic cloud types, the cottony, vertically rising variety and the sheet-like, horizontal clouds that spread out with little upward movement.

In 1803, Luke Howard, an English chemist who admitted he had no idea how clouds formed, devised the cloud classification system that is still used today. Using Latin names, Howard called the clouds formed by rising air currents "cumulus," meaning "heaped." Clouds without vertical movement were named "stratus," meaning "layered."

Clouds are categorized depending on their height (low, middle, and high), form, and composition.

SPRING

APR

High Clouds

Called cirrus (Latin for "curl"), high clouds exist from 20,000 feet to the top of the troposphere. Composed mainly of ice particles/crystals, cirrus clouds appear to move slowly, yet are often traveling over 100 mph.

CIRRUS: Thin and feathery, standard cirrus clouds forecast continued fair weather when remaining solitary and surrounded by blue sky. When cirrus thickens into cirrostratus, it often portends rain or snow.

CIRROSTRATUS: A milky veil that covers the sky from horizon to horizon. A pale halo, or circle, may develop around the sun or moon. The brighter and larger the ring, the higher the probability that rain or snow will fall in 12 to 18 hours. Precedes a warm front.

CIRROCUMULUS: A cloud infrequently seen, it appears as small puffs, rippled like sand on a beach. Resembling fish scales, this "mackerel sky" cloud is usually a companion to other cirrus clouds.

Middle Clouds

Called alto, or "middle" clouds, there are two types, with bases ranging between 6,500 feet and 20,000 feet.

ALTOCUMULUS: These clouds are composed of water droplets and appear as masses of puffy cotton balls (larger than cirrocumulus) surrounded by bright patches of sunlight or blue skies. Considered the most beautiful by many, this cloud permits shafts of sunlight—crepuscular rays—to penetrate and produces dramatic sunsets. A faintly colored ring (blue inside, red outside) called a corona may encircle the sun. Altocumulus castellatus, with parapets resembling those on a turreted castle, indicates an unstable atmosphere and is a reliable precursor of thunderstorms.

ALTOSTRATUS: Mainly a water-droplet cloud, although the upper portion may be ice particle/crystal. This cloud draws across the sky as a gray-blue blanket and causes the sun or moon to become diffused, as if appearing behind ground glass. When lowering and darkening, this cloud will obliterate the sun or moon and foretell the arrival of rain or snow.

Top Left: Cirrus clouds.
Top Right: Cirrostratus clouds.
Middle Left: Cirrocumulus clouds.
Middle Right: Altocumulus clouds.
Bottom Left: Altostratus clouds.
Bottom Right: An exceptional cloud formation over Lenox, Ohio.

us

Cirrostratus

SPRING

APR

cumulus

Altocumulus

ostratus

SPRING

APR

Cumulus

Cumulonimbus

Cumulonimbus mammatus

Stratocumulus

Stratus

Nimbostratus

LOW CLOUDS

Bases of low clouds range from the earth's surface (fog) to 6,500 feet. These clouds are almost entirely composed of water droplets, but where the temperature within the cloud is below freezing, ice particles/crystals exist.

CUMULUS: This cloud forms convectively and is most common over land areas during the warmth of a summer day. It has a relatively flat bottom, but the upper portion takes on ever-changing shapes. (What child hasn't seen a cumulus cloud dragon turn into a lion or bear?) These clouds remain small cotton balls if there is little vertical movement. If there is enough instability, the cumulus will continue to grow and build until it becomes the giant thunderstorm cloud, the cumulonimbus. Looking buoyant, fluffy, and light, even a medium-sized cauliflower cumulus cloud may weigh over 500 tons.

CUMULONIMBUS: The King of the Sky, this exceptional cloud is in a category all by itself. With its base at low cloud level, a dramatic upward development allows this cloud to extend through middle and high cloud levels. Some of these monstrous clouds grow to 70,000 feet, where the strong winds at the top of the troposphere shear the cirrus cloud top into a flattened, anvil shape. The cumulonimbus is composed of water droplets at its lower levels with a mix of water droplets and ice particles/crystals in its midsection and all ice above. The impressive-looking and glowering cloud called cumulonimbus mammatus is a thunderstorm cloud with rounded, balloon-like shapes at its base. Mammatus indicates extreme instability and often accompanies severe weather.

STRATOCUMULUS: Undulating and dark-to-light in color, this cloud shows rounded forms that appear to be lighted by sunlight from behind. Patches of blue may also appear. A familiar cloud during Northeast Ohio's lake-effect weather, it can produce light showers of rain or snow as it moves along.

STRATUS: A dull, sheet-like cloud in varying shades of gray. The drizzle, light rain, and snow that attend this cloud may linger for days. Fog is simply a stratus cloud resting on earth.

NIMBOSTRATUS: This ominous, threatening cloud is dark gray to black and often shows a ragged or torn bottom. Its name comes from the Latin word *nimbus,* meaning "dark." With water drops at its base and ice particles/crystals above, this somber, gloomy-looking cloud can bring heavy and long-lasting rain. Lower scud clouds often form amid the steady precipitation.

VIRGA: An entrained veil of raindrops suspended in the air. The droplets usually evaporate before reaching the ground.

SPRING

APR

Top Left:	*A large, towering cumulus cloud.*
Top Right:	*Cumulonimbus clouds (aerial view).*
Middle Left:	*Cumulonimbus mammatus.*
Middle Right:	*Stratocumulus clouds.*
Bottom Left:	*A stratus cloud deck.*
Bottom Right:	*Nimbostratus clouds.*

PRECIPITATION

The rain it raineth every day,
On both the just and unjust fella.
But more upon the just because
The unjust has the just's umbrella.

—ANONYMOUS

SPRING

APR

You may have wondered why some clouds give us abundant rain while others of the same apparent size and shape give us none at all. Actually, there is no important difference between these clouds except in respect to the movement of air within the clouds and the size of the cloud droplets. Just because a cloud has formed is no guarantee that it will eventually rain or snow on us. Something has to happen before a crowded cloud begins to cry.

Before minuscule water droplets or ice crystals (snow) can fall on our heads they must become large enough, and heavy enough, for gravity to pull them down. There are two ways this happens.

The simplest process is called coalescence. Larger rain droplets collide with smaller droplets and become even larger. Cloud droplets average $1/1200$ inch in diameter. If the jostling and colliding continue, the cloud droplet will grow to a diameter of $1/100$ inch, at which point it will be heavy enough to overcome gravity and fall from the cloud as a raindrop.

This coalescence growth process causes the "warm rain" in the tropics and is thought to be the main cause of rain from all very low clouds.

The second precipitation process is responsible for most of the rain and snow in Ohio and in all other temperate regions. This involves water droplets, ice particles/crystals, and supercooled water droplets in the upper part of clouds. (Supercooled droplets are liquid droplets that remain liquid at temperatures well below freezing). The water droplets evaporate and condense on the ice particles/crystals. Snowflakes or ice pellets result from this process, and they then fall to earth. If the air temperature near the surface of the earth is below freezing, the precipitation will remain as snowflakes or ice pellets. If the air near the earth's surface is warm enough, the frozen precipitation turns into raindrops. That is why rain in Ohio feels so chilly even on a sweltering summer day: it starts out as snow.

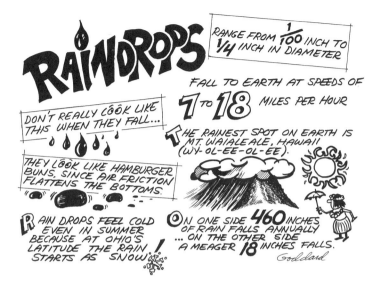

RAINDROPS RANGE FROM 1/100 INCH TO 1/4 INCH IN DIAMETER

FALL TO EARTH AT SPEEDS OF 7 TO 18 MILES PER HOUR

DON'T REALLY LOOK LIKE THIS WHEN THEY FALL...

THE RAINEST SPOT ON EARTH IS MT. WAIALEALE, HAWAII (WY-OL-EE-OL-EE).

THEY LOOK LIKE HAMBURGER BUNS, SINCE AIR FRICTION FLATTENS THE BOTTOMS.

RAIN DROPS FEEL COLD EVEN IN SUMMER BECAUSE AT OHIO'S LATITUDE THE RAIN STARTS AS SNOW!

ON ONE SIDE 460 INCHES OF RAIN FALLS ANNUALLY ... ON THE OTHER SIDE A MEAGER 18 INCHES FALLS.

Goddard

SPRING

APR

The precipitation process is not fully understood and in fact is so complex it seems a wonder that it ever rains or snows at all. We do know that it takes a lot of cloud to produce heavy rain or snow. Such clouds must be several thousand feet thick, and there must be an active upward motion within the cloud.

The ancients puzzled over how so much water could exist on earth though so very little of it seemed to fall. It wasn't until the 17th century that the hydrologic cycle was discovered.

Powered by energy from the sun, water from the earth's surface evaporates into the atmosphere, where it condenses into clouds and eventually falls as precipitation. Only a small fraction of earth's water is involved in this unending hydrologic cycle, though that is still a lot of water. An estimated 16 million tons of water are picked up by the air every second from oceans, rivers, lakes, soil, and vegetation. This evaporated moisture, now in its invisible gaseous form, is carried through the atmosphere and around our planet by the wind.

CLEVELAND'S TOP 5 WETTEST AND DRIEST YEARS (RAINFALL)
Wettest
1) 53.83" / 1990
2) 53.51" / 1878
3) 50.38" / 1950
4) 48.53" / 1992
5) 48.34" / 1972
Driest
1) 18.63" / 1963
2) 21.81" / 1934
3) 24.17" / 1933
4) 24.53" / 1899
5) 24.54" / 1897

The evaporation from the earth's surface is continuous. Once precipitation has fallen on earth it drains into the oceans or percolates into the ground, where it moves horizontally. Some of the water that infiltrates the soil is absorbed by plants and vegetation; it then returns to the atmosphere through their leaves in a process that is called transpiration.

Even though the snow that falls in cold polar regions may become part of a glacier, it will eventually melt and continue its part in the hydrologic cycle. Ice covers 7 percent of the earth's surface, and 95 percent of earth's fresh water is frozen in glaciers.

In Ohio, the hydrologic process brings an average annual precipitation of 30 to 45 inches across the state. It is estimated that if precipitation were evenly distributed over the earth, the average annual total would be 35 inches. In reality, precipitation varies to wide extremes. For example, atop Mount Waialeale, on the Hawaiian island of Kauai, an average of 460 inches of rain falls each year. At Arica, Chile, in the Desierto de Atacama, no measurable rain has ever been recorded.

Precipitation is considered to be water that is falling from the sky in either liquid or solid form. Here are those forms:

RAIN: This is precipitation that appears as sizable drops of liquid water. Raindrops range in diameter from about one-hundreth to one-quarterof an inch. Any drop larger than that will be broken into smaller drops by friction as it falls. Contrary to the idealized pear-shaped raindrops seen on the Saturday-morning cartoons, high-speed photography has revealed that raindrops have flattened bottoms and mushroom-shaped tops. Raindrops fall at speeds between 7 and 18 mph. The single word "rain" in a forecast indicates that a fairly steady fall of precipitation is expected. The word "shower" suggests a come-and-go, here-and-not-there character. Showers may be light or heavy, but they are transient.

DRIZZLE: Placid rain. Tiny raindrops that fall with uniform intensity. Intensity of drizzle is determined by its effect on visibility, not its accumulation. The term Scotch Mist is locally used to describe the drizzle that seems to float in the air during periods of low visibility.

FREEZING RAIN: Rain or drizzle that immediately freezes on contact with surfaces whose temperature is below freezing. Such ice storms can cause monumental damage to trees and power lines due to the weight of the ice accretion. A thin, nearly invisible layer of black ice (so-called because the dark earth colors show through) can cause severe highway and pedestrian travel problems. Rapidly changing temperatures near the earth's surface can cause freezing rain to change to rain, sleet, or snow, and then back again. It's about that time that forecasters start thinking about a new line of work.

ICE PELLETS: Also called sleet, these are small beads of clear, or transparent, ice. Ice pellets result when rain falls through cold air near the earth's surface. The pellets resemble tapioca and bounce when they hit a hard surface.

SNOW PELLETS: A first cousin of the snowflake, these small, white granules are too soft to bounce. Snow pellets often precede snowflakes in the Northeast Ohio autumn.

SPRING

APR

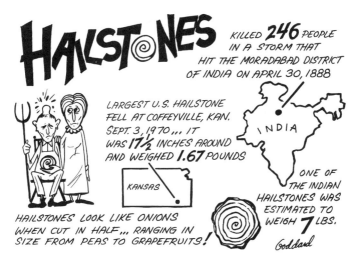

HAILSTONES KILLED **246** PEOPLE IN A STORM THAT HIT THE MORADABAD DISTRICT OF INDIA ON APRIL 30, 1888

LARGEST U.S. HAILSTONE FELL AT COFFEYVILLE, KAN. SEPT. 3, 1970 ... IT WAS **17½** INCHES AROUND AND WEIGHED **1.67** POUNDS

INDIA

KANSAS

ONE OF THE INDIAN HAILSTONES WAS ESTIMATED TO WEIGH **7** LBS.

HAILSTONES LOOK LIKE ONIONS WHEN CUT IN HALF ... RANGING IN SIZE FROM PEAS TO GRAPEFRUITS!

Goddard

SPRING

APR

SNOW: Taking the form of a hexagonal (six-sided) crystal, the snowflake is actually a piece of ice. Beginning its life as a microscopic seed of ice, no larger than the speck of dust on which it forms, the ice crystal grows by sublimation, passing directly from vapor to solid form without turning to liquid. The lace and filigree of the snowflake turn each ice crystal into a frosty jewel whose beauty has few rivals in nature. Snow, unlike rain, acts as an atmospheric vacuum cleaner, collecting pollutants as it wafts to earth. The most pure- and pristine-looking snow cover is loaded with impurities because of this, so forget about any snow ice-cream recipes.

HAIL: In parts of the Midwest, hail is known as the "white plague." More crop and property damage is caused by hail in the United States than by all our tornadoes. Hail forms when a raindrop is suddenly carried by a wind updraft into a layer of freezing temperatures. The now-frozen ice drop starts to fall and melt. The wind takes it up again and the surface refreezes. This process continues until the weight of the ice ball exceeds the force of the uplift and it falls to the ground. A hailstone, when cut in two, resembles an onion, with nearly concentric circles inside. The number of rings will tell you how many times the ice ball was taken on its roller-coaster ride. Buckeye hailstones usually run from pea-sized to marble-sized. Hail the size of golf balls—and even baseballs—has infrequently fallen on Ohio.

DEW: Technically, dew does not fall. It forms where you find it, on grass, flowers, cobwebs. The moisture on the outside of a cold glass of iced tea is dew. Dew forms on clear, windless nights because of the radiational cooling of the ground and surface objects. When the temperature of the air in contact with an object cools below its saturation point (the dew point), moisture condenses on the object.

HOW ARE HAIL SIZES CATEGORIZED IN THE UNITED STATES?

Hailstone diameters (in inches) as defined by the National Weather Service are given in the following equivalents:

0.25	Pea
0.50	Marble
0.75	Dime
1.00	Quarter
1.25	Half dollar
1.50	Walnut
1.75	Golf ball
2.00	Egg (hen)
2.50	Tennis ball
2.75	Baseball
4.00	Grapefruit
4.50	Softball

If temperatures overnight are below freezing, frost, not dew, forms through sublimation (so frost is not frozen dew). A heavy dew in the early morning is an excellent sign of a dry day ahead: "Heavy dew upon the grass, rain will not soon come to pass."

FOG: Composed of microscopic water droplets suspended in the air, fog is also not considered to be precipitation. Fog is a grounded cloud whose invisible water vapor has condensed into visible moisture. (Ice fog forms in arctic regions when vapor sublimates into ice crystals or ice needles.) There are three primary fog-forming processes:

RADIATION FOG occurs on clear, calm nights when the earth throws off its heat and the air near the ground cools by contact to below its saturation point. This ground fog is usually shallow in depth and gradually burns away under the morning sun.

ADVECTION FOG develops when warm air moves over a cold surface (a wintertime warm front passing over heavy snow fields, for example). This slow-to-clear fog can be several thousand feet in depth and cover several states.

EVAPORATION FOG is the morning fog common to Ohio River communities. In this case the warm surface water evaporates moisture into the colder air above. The vapor condenses into, literally, a river of fog. The greater the temperature spread between air and water, the better the chance for this type of fog.

SPRING

APR

BEWARE: IT'S TWISTER TIME

It is estimated that 75 percent of all tornadoes on this planet occur in the conterminous United States, and nearly all of the F5 super twisters strike within our borders. Most tornadoes develop during the months of April, May, and June, but when meteorological conditions are right, they can drop from the sky in any month, at any time.

In the U.S., an average of 1,000 tornadoes are reported each year. Ohio averages about a dozen annually. (Many twisters in rural and thinly populated areas go unseen and thus unreported.)

The rise in the number of tornadoes over the last several decades can be partially explained by an increasingly sophisticated reporting network. There has been a corresponding drop in the number of annual fatalities, and it is suspected (and hoped) that the public has become more aware and educated about this most violent storm on earth. (It is a sad statistic that an estimated seven out of ten people who are killed by tornadic winds were aware of either a severe storm watch or warning.)

A tornado's most damaging effect on a building is the savage blast of wind along the leading portion of the rotating funnel. It is there that the violent winds are augmented by the tornado's forward speed. For example, the wind velocity of a powerful, fast-moving tornado may be 100 mph stronger along the leading portion than on the trailing side.

The principal effects of tornadic winds on buildings are, in order of importance: (1) disintegration from wind pressure against the walls; (2) devastating damage from objects propelled by the wind; (3) collapse of higher portions of the building (chimneys, towers, etc.); (4) explosive pressure difference between the tornado (a partial vacuum) and the higher pressure within the building.

SPRING

APR

Because the majority of tornadoes approach from the southwest, their most violent winds often come from that direction. Rooms facing south and west, especially on the upper floors, will be the hardest hit and are the most dangerous to occupy. The basement of any building will normally be the safest place of all. If there is no basement, simply go to the lowest floor. Large rooms with free-span roofs (auditoriums and cafeterias, for example) should be avoided.

A wind-tunnel effect occurs in corridors and hallways in line with the tornado's path. Glass, stones, and pieces of metal and wood literally become bullets and spears as they speed horizontally through open spaces. Interior hallways facing north are usually the safest to occupy, followed by those facing east. Hallways that face south or west should be avoided, if possible. You should sit or crouch against a wall, with your arms over your head. Stay away from windows; flying glass can be lethal.

In summary, the safest place in any building would be on the lowest level, away from the windows, under a short-span ceiling (the smaller the roof the better) at the interior of the building.

FUJITA TORNADO SCALE			
Rating	Wind speed	Type	Impact
F0	40–72 mph	Minimal	Twigs and branches broken off trees; signs and temporary structures damaged; window panes broken.
F1	73–112	Weak	Automobiles unstable, pushed off roadway; light trailers pushed off road or overturned.
F2	113–157	Strong	Trailer homes destroyed, roofs torn from frame houses; cars and trucks blown from roadways.
F3	158–206	Severe	Trains derailed; cars lifted off the ground; walls of frame structures torn down or destroyed.
F4	207–260	Devastating	Frame structures completely destroyed; bark stripped from trees; cars, trucks, and trains blown or rolled long distances.
F5	261–318	Incredible	Entire structures torn from foundations; cars become airborne; asphalt stripped from roads.

KNOW THE ENEMY AN AVERAGE OF 100,000 THUNDERSTORMS DEVELOP IN THE UNITED STATES EACH YEAR — 10,000 BECOME SEVERE AND ABOUT 1,000 PRODUCE TORNADOES

AVOID THE "BEAR CAGE." WALL CLOUDS THAT PERSIST, AND SPIN, SPAWN TORNADOES

LOOKING LIKE BALLOONS, CUMULONIMBUS MAMMATUS CLOUDS WARN OF A STORM

DRAMATIC ARCUS CLOUDS — SMOOTH ON TOP — FORETELL A VIOLENT SQUALL LINE

TORNADOES COME IN MANY SHAPES: LOOP, HOURGLASS, CONE, NEEDLE, CYLINDER, etc.

USUAL TORNADO COLORS: BLACK, WHITE, YELLOW, GREEN (ONCE, PINK — AFTER A GERANIUM FARM HIT)

MULTI-VORTEX TWISTERS — SUCH AS AT XENIA, OH IN 1974 — ARE ESPECIALLY DESTRUCTIVE

OUR DEADLIEST TORNADO — THE GREAT TRISTATE OF 1925 — WAS HIDDEN BY DEBRIS ON ITS 219-MILE RAMPAGE

ALTHOUGH STILL DANGEROUS, DYING TORNADOES GROW THIN AND "ROPE OUT"

Over the years, some timeworn safety rules about tornadoes have proven to be erroneous. Take, for example, the following . . .

OPEN WINDOWS IN YOUR HOME EQUALIZE AIR PRESSURE. The theory is that low air pressure outside the house and high pressure within will cause the structure to explode. It has been determined that raising the windows only guarantees you will have wet carpet from incoming rain. The effect of opening windows is minimal.

SEEK SAFETY FROM A TORNADO IN THE SOUTHWEST CORNER OF A BUILDING.
As described above, this is actually a dangerous place to be. Years of study have found that the safest place is at the lowest level of a building, preferably in a closet or bathroom, especially near the center of the room. Stay away from outside walls or windows.

YOU CAN OUTRUN A TORNADO IN YOUR CAR. Perhaps, but don't bet your life on it. Although 70 percent of all tornadoes move from the southwest to the northeast, they have been known to make U-turns and remain stationary for short periods.

A classroom at the Halle School in Cleveland, damaged by the tornado of June 8, 1953.

Scissors planted into the side of a house during the Pittsfield tornado of April 1965.

TORNADOES SEEK OUT MOBILE-HOME PARKS.

Believe it or not, I've been asked this question many times over the years. Tornadoes do not, of course, target specific objects. The problem with mobile homes (even if tied down) is that they are aerodynamically designed, and without solid foundations underneath (like a permanent structure), they simply tend to "take off" in high winds. Those who live in mobile homes should abandon the unit in favor of a nearby building. In lieu of a building, seek refuge at any point below ground level. A ditch or low area would provide protection against dangerous airborne projectiles, which may travel horizontally at 100 mph or more.

Flying the Unfriendly Skies

What do Dorothy, Toto, Miss Gulch, and Roy Bennett have in common? They all traveled inside a roaring tornado—and lived to tell about it.

The three fictional characters, of course, survived a fantastical flight to Oz in a fictional Kansas tornado provided by Metro-Goldwyn-Mayer. Roy Bennett, however, survived a real trip in a real tornado provided by a severe Texas thunderstorm on April 3, 1964.

Those who have flown united with a tornado in unfriendly skies have seldom remained conscious long enough to recall what it was like. For most of Roy Bennett's trip, however, he was all too wide awake.

Roy Bennett was a master sergeant with the U.S. Air Force at Sheppard AFB, Wichita Falls, Texas. On this early April day in 1964 he was at home with his wife, Dorothy, and they were being visited by his sister and brother-in-law, the Ed Carswells.

As they chatted, a deep and throaty rumbling could be heard and they could see that the sky to the west was rapidly darkening. To get a better view, they went outside.

In a few minutes, it became apparent that they had more than a thunderstorm at hand. A black tornado funnel was snaking down from the sky and bearing down on them.

As large hail began to pelt the yard, Roy told his wife to run next door and warn her parents. Roy and the Carswells rushed back into the Bennett home to ride out the storm.

Roy dived under a piece of heavy furniture, a combination radio-TV set. The Carswells ducked under the kitchen table. Soon, what sounded like bricks began to hit the house, and a deafening roar "like a thousand freight trains" began to build.

When a garbage can came through the front window, Roy got a firm grip on the furniture he was under. Looking through the broken window, he stared in disbelief as a house trailer, traveling about five feet off the ground, came hurtling towards the house. Roy distinctly recalls seeing an elderly woman and her dog staring in equal disbelief out of a window in the mobile home.

The trailer sliced through Roy's house, cutting across the bedrooms. A flying door put a gash on his forehead. Then, for a few sec-

SPRING

APR

onds, came a deathly stillness. Roy had difficulty breathing and his ears began to pop. He was in the center of the tornado vortex.

Suddenly, the roaring began again and the vicious winds returned. He saw his sister swept from under the kitchen table and dashed against a wall. The wall then fell and both Carswells were killed.

Roy felt his grip on the furniture loosening, so he grabbed exposed water pipes with such force that he broke several bones in his left hand. At that point a terrific gust of wind broke his grip and he went spiraling up into the maw of the tornado. Completely conscious, he remembers that the inside of the tornado funnel was several yards across and he could see a tractor, automobile tires, fenders, even a bed with a mattress and covers intact, all circling near him in orbit. He thought that if he could only get over to the bed he would climb in and maybe go to sleep.

SPRING

APR

> **Roy had difficulty breathing and his ears began to pop. He was in the center of the tornado vortex.**

Roy looked down through the funnel and figured that he was at least 200 feet above the ground. The winds alternately lowered and lifted him, but finally he recalls being taken upwards in one final violent gust before he blacked out.

When Roy Bennett was found by medics, he was wrapped in a roll of barbed wire, approximately 150 feet from where he had taken off. His nearly nude body was a mass of swollen red flesh and broken bones. At the hospital a priest gave him the last rites.

But it wasn't necessary.

Twenty months later, Roy Bennett walked out of the hospital with an honorable discharge and a 90-percent disability pension, one of the few to survive the deadliest ride on earth.

CHASING RAINBOWS

Sunlight is white, but hidden inside each sunbeam is a bouquet of colors we call the spectrum.

As sunlight passes through earth's atmosphere, it strikes atoms of gas, dust particles, and water drops. It is sunlight traveling through minuscule raindrops that causes the beautiful and fleeting rainbow. The beam of light bends (refracts) within the water droplet, and the white light separates into its component colors: red, orange, yellow, green, blue, indigo, and violet.

The Muppets have explained to us that in order to make the rainbow connection you need both sunlight and water drops, and you must be in between—with your back to the sun. The best time for rainbow hunting in Ohio is in summer, following rain showers and when the sun is low in the sky, a couple of hours before sunset or after sunrise.

In reality, the rainbow is a perfect circle, as it duplicates the shape of the sun. However, because of the earth's horizon, we can see only the top half. (In an airplane you can sometimes see a less colorful perfect circle reflected off the clouds—a "glory.")

The classic mnemonic (memory aid) for recalling the proper rainbow color order is ROY G BIV. Remember that red is always on the outside of the arc, with violet inside. Many paintings by renowned artists have the colors reversed. Occasionally a secondary, fainter rainbow will appear above the primary bow with the colors backwards.

If you decide to chase a rainbow for that legendary pot of gold at the end, be sure to pack a large lunch. Better yet, forget it. The bow will always appear the same distance away. You can create your own backyard rainbow by using the garden hose with a fine spray on a sunny day. Put your hand through the iridescent mist and search for loose change.

In many cultures the rainbow is a good luck sign. To many American Indian tribes the arc was a highway to the sky for fallen warriors and animals. The fierce Iroquois, who wiped out our local Erie Indians around 1650, warned that it was bad luck to point at a rainbow; doing so would cause both the rainbow and you to disappear.

If you're a rainbow fanatic, try the Hawaiian Islands. Honolulu is the Rainbow City: I once saw five of the dazzling arches suspended over the city at once.

Other amazing and naturally occurring visual phenomena include the following:

FOGBOW. Rare and almost totally white, due to the extremely small size of the suspended droplets.

CORONA: A colorful ring that occasionally forms around the sun or moon. This is caused by light being diffracted (slightly bent) as it passes through a thin cloud that is made up of water droplets. Blue and red are the most common corona colors.

HALO: The white, or lightly colored, ring that frequently appears around the moon or sun. While the corona requires water droplets, the halo is the result of light shining through ice crystals. The halo often forms when cirrostratus clouds overspread Ohio skies ahead of a precipitation-bearing warm front. Rain or snow frequently begins some 12 to 18 hours after the halo appears. The brighter the ring, the higher the probability for precipitation. It is for that reason the old folk saying has scientific validity: "Ring around the sun or moon, expect the earth to puddle soon."

SUN DOGS: Small mock suns—usually colorless—that appear as bright spots on either side of the sun. Occasionally only one sun dog is visible. The solar canine companions result from sunlight passing through a thin layer of ice crystals.

SUN PILLARS: Tall streaks of light that appear to rise from the sun, especially at sunrise or sunset.

CREPUSCULAR RAYS: Brilliant shafts of sunlight that pierce the clouds and resemble bright stairways into the sky. This is stock artwork for church pamphlets.

AURORA BOREALIS: The northern lights that infrequently dance in our nighttime skies. Awesome and ghostly, this curtain of lights is named after Aurora, the Roman goddess of the dawn, and is the result of solar radiation energizing and electrifying atom and gas molecules near the magnetic poles some 70 miles above earth. The most common aurora color is a soft green, caused by oxygen atoms being electrified. A red aurora tells us that nitrogen gas is being bombarded. Just like those neon signs.

Auroras may take the form of wavy or stationary curtains, a flowing waterfall, undulating ribbons, or shooting shafts of light.

A stunning auroral display filled the Northeast Ohio sky in September of 1943, but such dramatic shows usually are limited to the higher latitudes in Canada. The aurora cannot be accurately forecast, but the lights often accompany peaks of sunspot activity.

On extremely rare occasions—in very clear and clean air—a momentary flash of green will be seen atop the rising or setting sun. The green flash is caused by nature's little trick called refraction, plus the ability of the atmosphere to briefly magnify the short green wavelengths. According to Scottish folklore, if you ever are fortunate enough to see the green flash, you will never be deceived in love ... probably.

MIRAGES: This false image is caused by sunlight over a superheated surface being refracted upward. We've all seen a mirage while walking or driving along a paved road on a hot summer day. A shimmering, thin lake will appear along the horizon. This near-horizon image is known as an inferior mirage.

A superior mirage results from air near the surface being colder than the air immediately above. In this case the image is inverted, or upside down.

Although we normally cannot see Canada from Cleveland, occasionally strong temperature differences in the air directly over the Lake Erie water surface will allow the city of Rondeau and the Canadian shoreline to become briefly visible.

BLUE MOON: There is no such thing ... the moon shines only by reflected sunlight and is silvery white above earth's polluted atmosphere. However, volcanic ash or debris from forest fires suspended in our atmosphere can make the moon appear to be blue—or red—or orange. The phrase "once in a blue moon" refers to the second full moon in any one month. This occurs, on the average, about every 32 months.

SPRING

APR

WHY IS OUR SKY BLUE?

The answer must involve sunlight, because our sky loses its blue color after sunset. Our atmosphere of invisible gases is equally important, as without our air canopy the sky would always be black—as is the sky on the airless moon.

Our sky is blue because the red, orange, yellow, green, and indigo parts of the color spectrum pass through our atmosphere undisturbed. Air molecules are just the right size to intercept and scatter the blue and violet rays, however. The human eye is not especially sensitive to violet, but blue is highly visible and that becomes the color of our sky.

SUNSHINE %: 58
DRIEST MONTH: 0.58"/1934
WARMEST MONTH: 66.9°/1991
COLDEST MONTH: 51.1°/1907
LIQUID PCPN AVG.: 3.49"
RAINIEST DAY: 3.37"/1995
RAINIEST MONTH: 9.14"/1989
THUNDERY DAYS: 5
SNOWIEST DAY: 2.1"/1974
SNOWIEST MONTH: 2.1"/1974
LEAST SNOWFALL: Trace (most recently in 1986)
DAYS ONE INCH SNOW: 0

The emerald month can be a cool and some-times cruel jewel. This month is notorious for claiming prematurely planted flowers and vegetables. May 20 is a safe date for most plantings, but some veteran Northeast Ohio gardeners wait until the Memorial Day week-end before digging in. A tip: when you slip on the gardening gloves that have spent all win-ter in the dark recesses of your garage be sure to squeeze each finger, vigorously. That's because spiders (the brown recluse and black widow are especially venomous) often use the fingers of gloves for cozy winter headquarters. Colorful woodland wildflowers dominate the month of May in Northeast Ohio before the spreading canopy of leaves shuts off the springtime sunlight. Ohio's only hummingbird—the ruby-throated—usually makes its first darting appearance about midmonth. Towards the end of the May and into early June, those pesky non-sting-ing insects called muckleheads (also known as midges) move inland from Lake Erie, joined by mayflies (a.k.a Canadian soldiers). On Memo-rial Day Northeast Ohioans are often reminded that the reason three-day weekends were created is because it's impossible to cram all the bad weather into only two days. Beware during those early-season picnics—strong thunderstorms that can spawn deadly tornadoes can happen at any time during May.

Day	Hi	Lo	Rec Hi	Rec Lo	Sunrise	Sunset	Lake°
1	63	42	88 / 1942	28 / 1876	6:25	8:24	46
2	64	42	86 / 1951	26 / 1963	6:24	8:25	47
3	64	43	85 / 1949	27 / 1986	6:23	8:26	47
4	64	43	89 / 1949	23 / 1971	6:21	8:27	47
5	65	44	89 / 1949	30 / 1968	6:20	8:28	48
6	65	44	92 / 1959	26 / 1968	6:19	8:29	48
7	65	44	87 / 1936	28 / 1970	6:18	8:30	48
8	66	45	88 / 1889	30 / 1976	6:17	8:31	49
9	66	45	88 / 1979	29 / 1983	6:15	8:32	49
10	67	45	90 / 1953	25 / 1966	6:14	8:33	49
11	67	46	87 / 1881	33 / 1977	6:13	8:34	50
12	67	46	89 / 1881	32 / 1976	6:12	8:35	50
13	68	46	86 / 1991	32 / 1895	6:11	8:36	50
14	68	47	91 / 1962	33 / 1994	6:10	8:37	51
15	68	47	89 / 1962	35 / 1977	6:09	8:38	51
16	69	47	89 / 1991	29 / 1984	6:08	8:39	52
17	69	48	90 / 1962	33 / 1979	6:07	8:40	52
18	69	48	91 / 1962	36 / 1985	6:06	8:41	52
19	70	48	89 / 1911	33 / 1976	6:05	8:42	53
20	70	48	91 / 1962	34 / 1981	6:05	8:43	53
21	70	49	90 / 1941	32 / 1895	6:04	8:44	53
22	71	49	90 / 1941	36 / 1978	6:03	8:45	53
23	71	50	90 / 1991	34 / 1961	6:02	8:46	54
24	71	50	89 / 1950	32 / 1963	6:01	8:47	54
25	72	50	89 / 1914	35 / 1956	6:01	8:48	54
26	72	51	89 / 1914	34 / 1969	6:00	8:49	54
27	72	51	90 / 1967	35 / 1969	5:59	8:49	54
28	73	51	91 / 1941	37 / 1971	5:59	8:50	54
29	73	52	91 / 1991	38 / 1949	5:58	8:51	55
30	74	52	92 / 1879	32 / 1961	5:58	8:52	55
31	74	52	92 / 1944	39 / 1984	5:57	8:53	56

The exact contrary
of what is generally believed
is often the truth.
– JEAN DE LA BRUYERE

THUNDERSTORM: KING OF THE SKY

Bellowing and snorting daggers of fire like some mythological dragon, the highly electrified thunderstorm is Ohio weather's Greatest Show on Earth.

Anywhere from 1,800 to 3,600 thunderstorms are roaming the earth at any moment, and while the individual thunderstorm usually lives for only an hour, a few of these lonely giants may rampage for six hours or more.

All thunderstorms result from the rapid lifting of moist air through the atmosphere. This process, called convection, is basically the same thing you see when bubbles rise in a pan of boiling water.

Convection and the resulting thunderstorms can occur in a number of ways. Frontal thunderstorms form when cold air undercuts and forcefully lifts warm air. Air mass thunderstorms are spawned by intense heating of air near the earth's surface. Orographic thunderstorms are the result of the forceful lifting of air up a mountainside by the wind. Radiatorial cooling of cloud tops and low-pressure disturbances in the upper air can also foment thunderstorms. In each case, water vapor condenses as the air is lifted, and the resulting release of latent heat adds to the buoyancy and instability of the rising air. Thunderstorms are most frequent in the warmer months during the late afternoon due to the heating of the air near the surface of the earth.

SPRING

MAY

THE KING OF THE SKY—THE MAJESTIC THUNDERSTORM CLOUD CUMULONIMBUS—CAN TOWER OVER 60,000 FT., WITH OVERSHOOTING TOPS THAT SOMETIMES ENTER THE STRATOSPHERE

I'VE DRAWN A VARIETY OF EVENTS THAT ACCOMPANY THUNDERSTORMS

TORNADOES MOST OFTEN FORM ON THE SOUTHWEST EDGE OF THUNDERCELLS

ANVIL TOP IS CAUSED BY STRONG, SHEARING WINDS ALOFT

MAMMATUS

STORM MOVEMENT

REAR FLANK DOWNDRAFT

FLANKING LINE CLOUDS

UPDRAFTS CAN EXCEED 150 MPH

VAULT

HAIL

THUNDERSTORM IS SEVERE IF IT SPAWNS TORNADOES, HAIL 3/4 INCH, OR MORE, IN DIAMETER OR WINDS OF 58 MPH, OR HIGHER

MOST THUNDERSTORMS LAST AN HOUR, OR SO, BUT THOSE KNOWN AS SUPERCELLS MAY LIVE FOR MORE THAN SIX HOURS

FORWARD FLANK DOWNDRAFT

SHELF CLOUD WITH INTENSE LIGHTNING

ARCUS CLOUD

WALL CLOUD
TORNADO

BEAR CAGE

Goddard

Even the most massive and destructive thunderstorm begins as a tiny, snow-white puff of cloud called a cumulus. If the rising air current within the cloud—the updraft—is not substantial, the cumulus will not grow vertically and may soon evaporate and disappear. The cumulus cloud will grow as long as air continues to meet and be drawn in at its bottom. The air then rises, as if in a chimney, and escapes at the top of the cloud.

It takes about 10 to 15 minutes for the thunderstorm engine to rev up. During this first stage, as the cloud builds above 15,000 feet, updrafts begin to stack layers of rain, snow, and ice particles within the cloud. A 3/4-mile-diameter thunderstorm cloud may contain some 500,000 tons of water.

During the second, or mature, stage of the thunderstorm the updrafts within the cloud may reach velocities of 30 to 60 mph or higher. Before long, the rain, snow, and ice particles will become large enough and heavy enough to overcome the updrafts and begin to fall to earth. As the updrafts and downdrafts fight it out during the mature stage of a thunderstorm, raindrops, snowflakes, ice particles, and hail are moving both up and down.

It is the falling precipitation that creates the cold downdrafts which eventually cause the thunderstorm to spread out and die.

Dazzlingly white from its billowing midsection to its top, the thunderstorm cloud—called cumulonimbus—often towers above 30,000 feet. The tallest thunderstorm can climb to 70,000 feet, scraping the stratosphere. Strong winds aloft sculpt the cumulonimbus into the familiar anvil-shaped thunderhead. The cumulonimbus may

A rotor builds atop the thunderhead that spawned the Newton Falls tornado on May 31, 1985.

literally blow its top and send overshooting clouds into the stratosphere. Such overshooting is often the clue to a tornado-bearing thunderstorm.

The dying stage of a thunderstorm comes when the cold-air downdrafts dominate the cloud. When winds no longer converge into the cloud base and rise but separate as they flow out from the bottom, the heat and moisture that drive the storm are cut off. The thunderstorm dies of thirst.

A thunderstorm may exist as a single well-organized and long-lived entity known as a supercell, or thunderstorms may gather into lines ahead of a rapidly moving cold front. Called a thunderstorm squall line, these storms often form on a southwest-to-northeast axis. Squall lines can produce strong winds, heavy rain, large hail, and tornadoes.

Miles ahead of a line of thunderstorms, the outflowing cold air may produce an explosive burst of wind called a gust front.

Thunderstorms may also collect into the phenomenon known as a Mesoscale Convective System (MCS). The word mesoscale, in this case, describes an event that can cover thousands of square miles, or several states. The MCS begins as a cluster of thunderstorms that gradually evolves into a highly organized, marauding complex of dozens of storms. Occurring mainly in the middle latitudes of our continent during the summer months, anywhere from 30 to 100 MCSs form each year. The MCS is slow-moving (10 to 20 mph), frequently develops at night, and may last for 12 to 24 hours, then regenerate. The MCS often foments intense, severe weather and appears as a huge, circular cloud mass on satellite photographs—larger than a hurricane.

The derecho (da-RAY-ko) is a unique thunderstorm complex that forms in the warm summer months when atmospheric moisture becomes extremely high (with dew points between 78 and 82 degrees). These storms can form over any heavily forested region, particularly those in Wisconsin and Minnesota, due to a natural process called evapotranspiration. On a sun-filled day, every tree can release from 50 to 100 gallons of water vapor into the lower layers of the atmosphere. This injection of moisture fuels developing thunderstorms, which can become severe as they move from northwest to southeast across the Midwest and lower Great Lakes.

The destructive phenomenon known as a downburst, or microburst, was first recognized by Dr. Ted Fujita ("Mr. Tornado") of the University of Chicago after he made an aerial survey of the damage from the great tornado outbreak across the eastern United States on April 3, 1974. He was surprised to find that much of the damage

SPRING

MAY

took on a curious "starburst" pattern, unlike the circular damage that tornadoes create. (See the "Fujita Scale" on page 126.) Turns out, this was caused by wind shear.

Wind shear is an abrupt change of wind speed and/or direction over a short distance, and the downburst—or microburst—is the most violent form of wind shear. A downburst is actually a large-scale downdraft: a veritable avalanche of cold air that descends rapidly from a cloud and then spreads out in an explosive starburst pattern along the ground (the same effect you see when the spray from a garden hose hits a flat rock).

While a downburst can cover a distance several miles in diameter, the smaller, more intense microburst may cover an area only one-half to two miles across. The microburst, with winds of 40 mph to over 100 mph, may or may not be accompanied by rain. And it may come from a relatively innocent-looking cloud.

Being invisible, the microburst is extremely hazardous to aircraft. The wind shear can cause an abrupt loss of air speed and altitude in planes that are taking off and landing. The airplane's lift is destroyed as the wind shifts quickly from a strong headwind to a strong tailwind. Most intense at 100 to 300 feet above ground, the microburst may only last for one to four minutes. A pilot may have only a few seconds to recognize and react to the problem.

Fortunately, aircraft encounters with microbursts are infrequent; it is believed that only about one in every 200 thunderstorms produces such an event.

It is estimated that an average-sized thunderstorm packs ten times the energy of a World War II atomic bomb.

It is estimated that an average-sized thunderstorm packs ten times the energy of a World War II atomic bomb, or the equivalent of a two-megaton hydrogen bomb. To be considered severe, a thunderstorm must cause one or more of the following: wind gusts of 58 mph (50 knots); three-quarter-inch hail; or a tornado. Although a thunderstorm generates perhaps 100 times the energy of the relatively small tornado it can spawn, the tornado's greater destructiveness results from its violent rotation, or torque, over a limited area.

OUR GREAT LAKE, ERIE

Sunsets over Lake Erie are often spectacular, and on summer evenings when the golden globe slides behind altocumulus clouds, the piercing shafts of sunlight known as crepuscular rays add exhilarating exclamation points.

It's difficult to believe that not long ago (geologically speaking) there was no Lake Erie. Only ice. It was twenty thousand years ago that a southward-moving ice sheet known as the Wisconsin glacier carved out the basin that became Lake Erie. Water filled the cavity when global warming set in and the ice melted.

Erie was the first of the Great Lakes to form, and its 241-mile length and 57-mile width make it the fourth-largest of the Great Lakes and the 12th-largest freshwater lake on earth. (To the Indians who lived on its shores it was the "sweetwater sea.")

Lake Erie is by far the shallowest of the Great Lakes, with an average depth of 62 feet. Depths range from around 20 feet in the far west around Toledo to 210 feet near Buffalo, New York. (Lake Superior, by

SPRING

MAY

Boats run aground at Edgewater Park by high seas after the deadly storms of July 4, 1969.

contrast, has a maximum depth of 1,333 feet.) Nearly all of Lake Erie's water—about 97 percent—flows in from Lake Huron via the Detroit River. The other 3 percent arrives from adjacent rivers and streams. It takes a drop of water 2.6 years to travel the length of Lake

Erie before it dives over Niagara Falls headed for the Saint Lawrence Seaway and the Atlantic Ocean. (A drop of water takes 191 years to traverse gigantic Lake Superior.)

The name Erie was given to the Indians who lived along the south shore of the lake by the fierce Iroquois tribes who lived farther to the east. Erie, in the Iroquois language, meant "people of the long tails" and came from the fact that the Ohio territory was rife with the animal known as the cougar. For that reason the Erie Indians became known as the "cat people." (In 1650, despite their bravery and expertise with bow and arrow, the cat people were overwhelmed and massacred by the more numerous Iroquois.)

BOATING

Because of its shallowness, Lake Erie is easily angered; the lake is famous for its choppy waters. The wind provides the energy to start the waves, but the waves will continue even after the wind subsides.

How difficult can Lake Erie become? I've talked with ship captains who have battled storms on the high seas, and to a man they say they would rather face mounting waves on the open ocean than those on the Great Lakes. Ocean waves have a dependable regularity; waves on the Great Lakes—particularly on Lake Erie—are irregular and confused. It is the fetch, or distance traveled across the water, that determines the size of the waves. Wave height is the distance from the highest point (crest) to the lowest point (trough). Wave length is the distance from crest to crest. Wave lengths in the Great Lakes are much shorter than those on the oceans.

Ship captains I've talked to say they would rather face mounting waves on the open ocean than those on the Great Lakes.

As a rule of thumb, in a body of water as large as Lake Erie, and under a long fetch, the maximum wave height will be three-quarters of the water's depth. For example, in water 10 feet deep the highest wave would be 7.5 feet. The short fetch on inland lakes prevents waves from building to their mathematical potential.

Marine wind velocities are given in knots (one knot equals about 1.15 mph). A rough but quick way to convert from knots to miles per hour is to divide the knot number by eight, then add the difference. Example: a 16-knot wind divided by 8 is 2, thus an 18 mph wind.

What is considered a small craft on Lake Erie? For years I asked mariners the question and I received a hurricane of answers. Finally, I cornered a Coast Guard captain and, without hesitation, he replied, "any vessel under 65 feet." That's a lot of craft.

Northeast Ohio boaters should attend the weather seminars conducted by the marine forecasters at the Cleveland National Weather Service. You should also take advantage of the NWS Web site on the Internet (www.csuohio.edu/nws).

Everyone who travels Lake Erie should be equipped not only with the necessary safety flotation devices, but also with the NWS 24-hour continuous broadcast radio. Wave action can change rapidly and water conditions west of Avon Point often have nothing in common with the water to the east.

Be aware that if you fall overboard the possibility of hypothermia (cooling of the inner body core) is a threat not just in the spring or autumn but in summer as well. To borrow the old aviator's mantra: "There are old sailors and bold sailors, but there are no old, bold sailors."

SPRING

MAY

WAVE HEIGHT IS MEASURED FROM CREST TO TROUGH; WAVELENGTH IS CREST TO CREST.

CREST — LENGTH — CREST

HEIGHT

TROUGH

UNLIKE OCEAN WAVES, WAVES ON SHALLOW AND EASILY ANGERED LAKE ERIE MOUNT QUICKLY AND TRAVEL IN SHORT WAVELENGTHS.

Fry Now, Pay Later

For most people, spring and its warm temperatures are an open invitation to go out and enjoy the outdoors and bask in the sunshine. Unfortunately, our zeal for great, wide open spaces should be tempered by a major weather-related environmental problem that concerns us all: ozone depletion. There now is conclusive proof of the rapid disappearance of earth's protective ozone layer, and its direct correlation to incidences of skin cancer.

Ozone is a rare gas that we often smell after a summer rain or a lightning strike. While this gas is found throughout our atmosphere, it is concentrated primarily at about 19 miles above the surface of the earth. Incredibly, for something so important, there is very little of it. It is estimated that if all the ozone in our atmosphere could be compressed into a compact layer, it would be less than one-quarter-inch thick.

Ozone is also a lifesaver, since it acts as a protective umbrella, intercepting harmful ultraviolet radiation from the sun. Medical experts warn us that continued diminution of the ozone layer will result in a dramatic upsurge in life-threatening skin cancers (melanomas). Damage to the human immune system and to terrestrial and aquatic ecosystems also will occur.

Conversely, ozone at the earth's surface can be lethal to humans and plants. Ozone can retard plant growth and reduce crop yields. Aside from irritating our eyes and making breathing difficult (health agencies issue ozone alerts in summer), ozone frequently gives the air near industrial areas its murky, hazy color (smog).

It was the British, in 1985, who first detected an atmospheric hole in the ozone over Antarctica (the South Pole), and the most recent soundings have revealed the lowest levels ever. In recent years, an alarming decrease in the ozone shield has been discovered over the northern reaches of the North American continent as well.

The main culprits in the vanishing ozone problem are chlorofluorocarbons (CFCs). CFCs are used in hair and deodorant sprays (as propellants), in refrigerants and coolants, as cleaning agents, and in styrofoam products.

The insidious feature of CFCs is their long life. The CFCs in our atmosphere today will still be there 50 years from now. Just one CFC molecule may destroy as many as 100,000 ozone molecules.

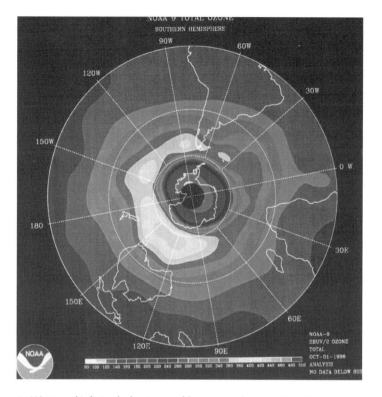

An NOAA graphic depicts the deterioration of the ozone over the South Pole in 1996.

Each May the Cleveland Dermatological Society promotes free skin-cancer screenings at local hospitals, and each year a number of pernicious melanomas are detected. When I first became aware that tiny lesions on my face refused to go away, I imagined it may have been the result of the atomic bomb tests I witnessed while with the U.S. Air Force in the 1950s. We had been told that if any "problems" developed it would take perhaps 20 to 25 years. My dermatologists, however, have decided that it was the love of sunshine in my youth that brought on the lesions. (Thankfully, none have been malignant).

Now I slather on the sunscreen—SP15 or higher—and I recommend that all fellow sun worshippers (heliophiles) do the same.

LAKE ERIE MONSTER

The monster came in the wee hours of the morning on May 31, 1942. Under a brilliant full moon, the terrifying wall of water suddenly rose from Lake Erie and slammed into 60 miles of shoreline from Bay Village through Cleveland to Geneva-on-the-Lake.

Those who saw the wave coming reported that it first appeared in the distance as a ghostly dark highway that stretched along the moonlit lake horizon.

The wind, which had been blowing out of the south, mysteriously grew calm. A few seconds later came an onrushing, chilling wind out of the north.

And then came the wave.

The wall of water, whose height was estimated at between 4 and 25 feet, struck at approximately 2:10 a.m. and resulted in seven drownings.

All who perished had been fishing in the lake—four from small boats off Geneva, two from a pier at Huntington Beach in Bay Village, and one from a jetty at Cleveland's Perkins Beach.

The death wave has been attributed to the phenomenon known as a lake seiche (pronounced saysh), a sudden, unannounced, and cataclysmic rise in water level.

A seiche can result from unequal air pressure over the surface of the water, or because of an unusual and abrupt shift in wind direction around thunderstorms.

Unusually high wind speeds are not necessary to produce large waves, and walls of water are not predictable as they move independently of the storms themselves.

Witnesses reported that lightning had been lacing the Lake Erie skies that fateful night of the Memorial Day weekend in 1942, and the lake was running choppy under a freshening south wind.

The highest part of the wave hit North Perry in Lake County. Two men putting a boat in the water there suddenly looked up just as the wave reached shore. They were picked up and carried into bushes some 150 feet inland, one man suffering a broken leg.

Another fortunate survivor at North Perry testified the wave was about 25 feet high, traveled at perhaps 80 mph, and gave off a siren-like shriek as it broke onshore.

At the Cleveland Yachting Club in Rocky River, the wooden piers were damaged but no major damage was reported to the moored boats.

Other monstrous walls of water ravaged the northern Ohio Lake Erie shoreline in 1882, 1929, 1933, and 1947.

THE DANGEROUS **Seiche** (SAYSH) IS CAUSED BY UNEQUAL AIR PRESSURE ON THE WATER SURFACE.

IN A SEICHE THE WATER LEVEL CAN RISE SEVERAL FEET IN A FEW SECONDS.

Goddard

SPRING

MAY

Summer

AH, SUMMER IN NORTHEAST OHIO.
WE CAN'T WAIT UNTIL IT ARRIVES,
WE COMPLAIN WHEN IT'S HERE,
AND WE ARE SORRY TO SEE IT END...

By June the struggle between the warm inroads of spring and the cold remnants of winter has been decided. While June supplies Ohio with its share of thunderstorm squall lines and tornado activity, the approach of the lazy, hazy days of summer brings on a more stable weather regime.

The way many Ohioans react to summer is a study in human nature: we can't wait until it arrives, we complain about it when it's here, and we are sorry to see it go when it's over.

Ohio is no stranger to periods of withering heat in summertime, especially during the traditional 40-day Dog Day sizzle from July 3 through August 11. While the northeastern counties of Ohio often find the summertime heat and humidity temporarily broken by the passage of weak cool fronts, these wind shift lines frequently fizzle out by the time they've reached the central counties of the state. Post-frontal winds across the waters of Lake Erie can provide several days of welcome air-conditioned relief for the northeast corner of the state, while the remainder of Ohio is still in the sauna

Ohio's record high temperature is 113° F at Thurman (Gallipolis) in Gallia County on July 21, 1934. Cleveland's highest is 104°, set on June 25, 1988.

Ohio heat waves (a heat wave is considered a minimum three-day run with temperatures in the 90s) are caused by the pressure system known as the Bermuda high. This dome of air is usually centered near the island of Bermuda, off the mid-Atlantic

SUMMER

CLEVELAND'S WARMEST AND COLDEST SUMMERS (BY MEDIAN TEMPERATURE)

Warmest: 75.0°/1949
Coldest: 66.7°/1927

LONGEST CONSECUTIVE NUMBER OF DAYS WHEN CLEVELAND'S TEMPERATURE TOPPED 90° (6 OR MORE)

11 days	August 25 – September 4, 1953
8 days	June 13–20, 1994
8 days	August 9–16, 1944
7 days	August 11–17, 1995
7 days	July 30 – August 5, 1955
6 days	July 5–10, 1988
6 days	August 16–21, 1955
6 days	June 11–16, 1954
6 days	July 17–22, 1991

THE HEAT INDEX

The Heat Index serves as a diagnostic measure of the combination of temperature and relative humidity. The resulting "apparent" temperature (when the meteorologist says "it feels like …") gives an estimation of what the hot, humid air feels like to the average person.

Exceptional heat indices (which can endanger your life) occur mostly during the muggy summer months. The abundance of moisture and increased heat keeps you perspiring, which is your body's involuntary attempt to cool itself. Those with health concerns should keep a close eye on the heat index during prolonged spells of hot weather, as dehydration and heat exhaustion are very serious matters.

DATES WHEN CLEVELAND'S TEMPERATURE REACHED 100°

June 25, 1988 (104°)
July 27, 1941 (103°)
August 27, 1948 (102°)
September 1–3, 1953 (101°)
June 28, 1944 (101°)
July 16, 1988 (100°)
August 19, 1955 (100°)
June 28, 1934 (100°)
August 6, 1918 (100°)

APPARENT TEMPERATURE READINGS

CAUTION: 85° to 94° F—physical activity can cause fatigue.

EXTREME CAUTION: 95° to 105° F—possible heat cramps and/or heat exhaustion with lengthy exposure to the heat.

DANGER: Above 105° F—Conditions for heat stroke if exposure to heat is prolonged; heat exhaustion and heat cramps likely.

HEAT INDEX CHART

Temp (F)	Relative Humidity (%)								
	90.0	80.0	70.0	60.0	50.0	40.0	30.0	20.0	10.0
65:	65.6	64.7	63.8	62.8	61.9	60.9	60.0	59.1	58.1
70:	71.6	70.7	69.8	68.8	67.9	66.9	66.0	65.1	64.1
75:	79.7	76.7	75.8	74.8	73.9	72.9	72.0	71.1	70.1
80:	88.2	85.9	84.2	82.8	81.6	80.4	79.0	77.4	76.1
85:	101.4	97.0	93.3	90.3	87.7	85.5	83.5	81.6	79.6
90:	119.3	112.0	105.8	100.5	96.1	92.3	89.2	86.5	84.2
95:	141.8	131.1	121.7	113.6	106.7	100.9	96.1	92.2	89.2
100:	168.7	154.0	140.9	129.5	119.6	111.2	104.2	98.7	94.4
105:	200.0	180.7	163.4	148.1	134.7	123.2	113.6	105.8	100.0

– SOURCE: NOAA

SUMMER

coastline of the United States. The invisible air mountain blocks the advance of cool fronts from the western Great Lakes and, when it expands far enough to the west, can create heat-wave conditions over the entire eastern half of the country. The Bermuda high will eventually shrink, allowing a timid cool front to penetrate Ohio, before expanding once again.

The approach of the summer cool front is often announced by the towering thunderstorm cloud, cumulonimbus. Torrential rains from such storms are possible anywhere in the state, but the area of maximum frequency is over the southwestern counties of Ohio.

The area of heaviest annual precipitation (the combination of rain and the liquid content of snow) is centered near Wilmington in Clinton County. The 45-inch average there contrasts with the 30-inch annual fall that makes Put-in-Bay on South Bass Island the dri-

SUMMER

A thunderhead builds into a major storm.

SUMMER

CLEVELAND'S TOP 5 WETTEST AND DRIEST SUMMERS (RAINFALL)

Wettest
1) 19.88" / 1972
2) 16.84" / 1885
3) 16.81" / 1987
4) 16.51" / 1902
5) 16.36" / 1992

Driest
1) 3.63" / 1933
2) 4.03" / 1910
3) 4.42" / 1930
4) 4.45" / 1895
5) 4.64" / 1900

est place in Ohio. Annual precipitation across the state averages 37 inches, with the heaviest occurring in May, June, and July and the lightest in October and February. However, severe weather accompanying downpours is always a possibility anywhere in the state; it is wise to heed storm watches and warnings.

Ohio's heaviest officially recognized short-term rainfall inundated Sandusky in Erie County on July 12, 1966. From 2 a.m. until 9:30 p.m., a total of 10.51 inches came down. Six inches fell on Sandusky between 2 a.m. and 7:30 a.m. Cleveland's 24-hour rainfall record is 4.97 inches, set on September 1, 1901.

An undocumented diary account of monumental Ohio rainfall tells of a 12-inch frog strangler "near Canton" in Stark County on June 24, 1888.

On July 16, 1914, at a point 2.5 miles northwest of Cambridge in Guernsey County, Samuel Mehaffey "carefully measured" 7.09 inches of rain in an hour and one-half. A diary recorded that those riding in a horse-drawn carriage "found it difficult to breathe" during the deluge.

The worst summertime flooding in state history, with a loss of 42 lives, came amid the 3-to-14-inch rains during nonstop thunderstorms from July 4th into the morning of the 5th in 1969. Wooster, in Wayne County, was particularly hard hit.

From 4 to 7 inches of rain soaked much of eastern Ohio during the gale-force winds from the remnants of Hurricane Agnes on June 20–25, 1972. Some shoreline homes in Eastlake were destroyed by the rough seas on Lake Erie stirred up by the storm.

On the first day of summer we receive an average of 15 hours and 11 minutes of daylight. Sunshine is a steady companion in the Ohio sky during June, July, and August. Even the northeast counties, so heavily clouded from November into March, are bathed in more sunshine during this three-month period than are such fabled Sunbelt cities as Tampa-St. Petersburg, New Orleans, and San Diego.

A melancholy paradox is that the moment summer begins the sun also begins it gradual journey southward. The days shorten, and by the end of August we notice lengthening shadows, shadows that were not there as recently as June and July.

The annual Perseid meteor shower, centered around the nights of August 11 and 12, often gives Ohio its finest display of shooting stars. Best viewing time is from midnight until sunrise, in the north-eastern sky.

By mid-August the bald-faced hornets have abandoned their papier-mâché homes, and the first brood of woollybear caterpillars are munching on plantain weed. By now the cicada symphony (we wrongly call them locusts) has reached a cacophonous crescendo. At month's end the katydids can be heard fiddling in the fields, and folklore says that when the katydids sing, the first frosts of autumn are little more than six weeks away.

On hot, sultry days in late summer and early autumn, some Ohio cities suffer when temperature inversions trap pollutants near the earth's surface. The industrialized areas in the Ohio Valley near Steubenville experience inversions more frequently than other parts of the state, and the lack of an active wind will allow moderate to heavy pollution levels to linger for days. The arrival of a cool front from the west or northwest will clear the air.

The waters of Lake Erie warm into the mid-60s during July, reach the 70-degree level in August, and hold nearly steady well into September. (The lake water temperature is taken at a 35-foot depth off Cleveland Harbor.) The warmest temperature ever recorded was 79° F in September of 1958, August of 1988, and July of 1998.

By late July or early August, local backyard gardens are ready for daily pre-dinner harvests.

SUMMER

Heavy surf from Hurricane Agnes churns up Lake Erie, demolishing an Eastlake home in June 1972.

IN THE NORTHEAST OHIO SKY THIS SEASON

The featured stars of the summer are Deneb, Vega (VEE-gah), and Altair and together they form the Summer Triangle. Nearly overhead, Vega is the brightest star in our summer sky.

Near the southern horizon you can find the Mars-red star called Antares (an-TAIR-ese). Indeed, the name means "rival of Mars."

Two prominent constellations are Ophiuchous (OFF-ih-YOU-kus) (which means "snake-holder"), and Hercules (in Greek mythology, the strongest man on earth).

Under the darkest of skies (clear, moonless nights), the Milky Way paints a ghostly river across the heavens.

SUNSHINE %: 65
DRIEST MONTH: 0.39"/1933
WARMEST MONTH: 73.9°/1949
COLDEST MONTH: 62.2°/1903
LIQUID PCPN AVG.: 3.70"
RAINIEST DAY: 4.00"/1972
RAINIEST MONTH: 9.77"/1902
THUNDERY DAYS: 7
SNOWIEST DAY: Trace/1966
DAYS ONE INCH SNOW: 0

As the old song from Oklahoma! says, "June is bustin' out all over." The first consistently warm—even hot—weather often delays until this month. Mid- to late June can sometimes be a blazer here. At 4:37 p.m. on June 25, 1988, Cleveland's temperature rocketed to an all-time high of 104° F. (Bone-dry and very windy thunderstorms added a meteorological exclamation point that evening.) Thunderstorms are common here in June and tornadoes are not strangers. The great Sandusky-Lorain tornado hit on June 28, 1924. The tornado that killed 9 in Cuyahoga County (20 in Ohio) on June 8, 1953, passed very close to Cleveland's Public Square before exiting over Lake Erie around East 40th Street. In 1959, heavy rains caused severe flooding on Cleveland's East Side, submerging many vehicles; passengers on a transit bus in University Circle were rescued by motorboats. The latest Cleveland snow—only a trace—fell on June 5, 1907. Summer arrives with the solstice occurring around the 21st (leap year can make it vary). Sun worshipers should be aware of the strengthening sunshine, especially powerful between the hours of 10 a.m. to 2 p.m. On warm, moist evenings fireflies (glowworms) will jet across the grass, eternally followed by small children carrying glass mason-jar prisons.

Day	Hi	Lo	Rec Hi	Rec Lo	Sunrise	Sunset	Lake°
1	74	53	95 / 1934	40 / 1981	5:57	8:53	57
2	75	53	94 / 1934	39 / 1966	5:56	8:54	57
3	75	53	91 / 1925	35 / 1977	5:56	8:55	58
4	75	54	93 / 1925	40 / 1947	5:55	8:56	58
5	76	54	93 / 1925	38 / 1990	5:55	8:56	59
6	76	54	92 / 1988	38 / 1945	5:55	8:57	59
7	76	55	91 / 1933	39 / 1977	5:54	8:58	59
8	77	55	98 / 1933	39 / 1977	5 54	8:58	60
9	77	55	92 / 1914	41 / 1949	5:54	8:59	60
10	77	56	91 / 1947	31 / 1972	5:54	9:00	60
11	77	56	93 / 1933	31 / 1972	5:54	9:00	61
12	78	56	92 / 1954	42 / 1980	5:54	9:01	61
13	78	56	93 / 1954	43 / 1979	5:54	9:01	62
14	78	57	95 / 1988	43 / 1978	5:53	9:02	62
15	78	57	97 / 1954	43 / 1997	5:53	9:02	62
16	79	57	96 / 1952	39 / 1961	5:54	9:02	62
17	79	57	93 / 1994	38 / 1980	5:54	9:03	63
18	79	58	96 / 1944	41 / 1950	5:54	9:03	63
19	79	58	92 / 1994	46 / 1965	5:54	9:04	63
20	79	58	96 / 1988	46 / 1962	5:54	9:04	64
21	80	58	95 / 1941	45 / 1897	5:54	9:04	64
22	80	59	98 / 1988	39 / 1992	5:54	9:04	64
23	80	59	94 / 1948	41 / 1963	5:55	9:04	65
24	80	59	96 / 1952	44 / 1915	5:55	9:05	65
25	81	59	104 / 1988	41 / 1979	5:55	9:05	65
26	81	59	99 / 1952	47 / 1984	5:56	9:05	65
27	81	59	98 / 1944	44 / 1981	5:56	9:05	65
28	81	60	101 / 1944	49 / 1988	5:56	9:05	66
29	81	60	94 / 1952	51 / 1985	5:57	9:05	66
30	81	60	95 / 1941	41 / 1988	5:57	9:05	66

SUMMER

JUN

*You can judge the character of a person
by how he treats those
who can do nothing for him.*
– ANONYMOUS

THE LORAIN TORNADO

On June 28, 1924, the deadliest tornado in Ohio weather history tore through the sultry air over Lake Erie and struck Lorain.

The storm lasted one minute and 44 seconds, killed 78 persons, injured 1,000, left 7,000 homeless, and caused property damage of $35 million. Parts of the downtown business district and nearby neighborhoods were completely demolished.

The most interesting eyewitness storm account I have heard is the one by Commodore J. A. Williams, then a member of the Cleveland Yachting Club.

Williams, commanding the 59-foot yacht *Oswichee* on her maiden voyage, left the Rocky River harbor for Put-in-Bay at 1:30 that afternoon. Two hours out of port, Williams observed the ship's barometer was falling steadily and rapidly as the wind mounted to 35 mph amid a rising sea.

Debating the prospect of finding safe harbor inside the breakwater at Lorain, he instead chose to continue battling the storm toward the Erie islands. Ten miles past Lorain he saw a pitch-black sky over Marblehead and set a southwest course for safe harbor at Huron.

SUMMER

JUN

BRETZ
MUSIC
STORE
BROADWAY
LORAIN
—o—
as left by the
TORNADO
6-28-24

Here is Williams's account of the moment he came eye to eye with the Lorain tornado:

Rain was falling so heavily that the bow of the boat could not be seen from the pilothouse. Then came a lightning flash dead ahead, the largest I'd ever seen. It had the volume of a 12-inch gun and shook the very lake.

In a few minutes we ran out of the rain and just ahead we saw an open circle, perhaps two miles in diameter, completely surrounded by black clouds and rain. There, in the center of the circle, about a mile ahead, was the most terrible monster I have ever seen. Had the tornado been made of lamp black, it couldn't have been any darker.

The funnel was round, just like a barrel, about 300 yards wide at the bottom and three-quarters of a mile wide at the top. Clouds around the tornado were as level and flat as a piece of slate and about the same color. Off to the left of the monster was a child of the tornado, a thin waterspout, resembling a twisted manila rope, about 100 feet in diameter. Left with the choice of being sucked into the tornado or the waterspout, I chose the latter.

As the waterspout hit, I immediately looked at the barometer and saw it fall an incredible three inches. Tons of water fell on us and the waterspout seemed to beat the boat down into the water about one foot. For a few seconds it was hard to get one's breath.

We were in the spout for only a few seconds and after its passage the lake all around us looked white as snow from the falling water. The waterspout had sucked out all of the ship's stovepipes.

As we rode out the rough sea following the waterspout, we could see the tornado heading for Lorain. It was only after we made safe landing at Vermilion that we learned of the destruction and death that followed. The most impressive and frightening thing about the tornado to us was the intense darkness, like midnight. It was a gruesome feeling.

Upon reaching shore the ship's cook, who had spent the entire ordeal praying in the crew's quarters, announced that his career as a Great Lakes seaman was at an end.

SUMMER

JUN

GETTING OUT THE WEATHER WORD

Visitors to this country are usually amazed at the time and attention given to weather on television. There are two reasons for this fixation: (1) ever since God allowed pictures to fly through the air, television executives have found that weather programs are an easy sell; (2) this country has a greater variety of weather than any other, and it is frequently violent.

The popularity of TV weather shouldn't be underestimated. I'm a certified sports nut, and my fellow jock enthusiasts are always surprised when I tell them that surveys continually indicate that the television weather audience is regularly four times as large as the sports audience.

Getting the weather message out to the public hasn't always been easy. Today radio and television broadcasts allow massive and immediate distribution of highly perishable weather forecasts and warnings. There was a time, and not so long ago, when weather information was just as much a rumor as the forecast itself. While the government weather service was signed into existence by President Ulysses S. Grant in 1870, the first official forecast was not made until February 19, 1871, by Professor Cleveland Abbe of the Cincinnati Astronomical Observatory. The invention of the telegraph in the 1840s made a national weather service possible, but from the 1870s into the early 1920s the government forecasters were like a puppy chasing its tail when it came to getting the weather word out to the public.

Professor Cleveland Abbe

Until the beginning of commercial radio, government weather forecasts were disseminated to the public using the U.S. mail, whistles, cannons, rockets, and bombs and by hoisting flags of different colors. In Ohio, the forecast flags bore these symbols: full sun, crescent sun, and star, in either red or blue. In red, the full sun was a forecast of rising temperatures, the crescent sun foretold lower temperatures, and the star indicated steady temperatures. A blue sun warned of general rain or snow, a blue crescent sun presaged fair weather, and a blue star forecast localized rain or snow.

An oncoming cold wave was depicted by an ominous black square in the middle of a 6-by-8-foot white flag. When winds of over 25 mph were expected, a red flag was unfurled. The forecast flags were hung from post offices and other buildings, while some trains were also adorned with the banners on their baggage cars.

> **By 1923, 140 radio stations across the country were broadcasting weather reports.**

By 1901, weather service forecasts were being distributed by telegraph, telephone, and mail to about 80,000 customers. In 1904 some 60,000 farmers in Ohio were getting the daily weather forecast from Washington, D.C. by telephone within one hour of its issue. In 1939, New York City began its automatic telephone answering system and within four days about 58,000 calls were being made daily.

Radio telegraphy started in 1914, and the commercial radio industry that followed revolutionized the business of dispensing weather information. While radio station KDKA in Pittsburgh, Pennsylvania, claims it was the first to broadcast a weather report (on April 26, 1921), it appears that E. B. Rideout of WEEI in Boston hit the airwaves with the first forecast in August of 1920. For more than 40 years Rideout's Yankee twang filled the New England air. By 1923, 140 radio stations across the country were broadcasting weather reports.

An interesting sidelight to the beginning of private weather forecasting was the professional jealousy of the government service. All weather forecasters in this country must rely on the same raw weather data provided by the National Weather Service headquartered in Washington, D.C. The animosity became so intense that in the 1930s and 1940s the government put up a vigorous fight to keep all the weather information for itself. The late Dr. Irving Krick, the iconoclastic proponent of long-range forecasting (whom I met a few years ago while doing a story on his involvement in forecasting for the Allies' D-Day invasion in 1944), told me that the United States Weather Bureau shut off all of his teletypes at CALTECH in 1938. This curious battle ended by the late 1940s when the government was forced to recognize the entitlement of the private sector to the information that is the result of taxpayer funding.

Cooperation is now the rule, but I'm sure that many government meteorologists look upon their blow-dried TV counterparts the way a golfer who shoots 105 looks down on someone who shoots 115.

Much credit for the surge in nationwide weather interest must go to the television enterprise known as The Weather Channel. TWC

SUMMER

JUN

first glowed on cable screens at 8 p.m., May 2, 1982. On that first show were two weather personalities very familiar to Northeast Ohioans: André Bernier, the ace morning forecaster on FOX 8, and the silky-smooth Bruce Edwards, from Garfield Heights. TWC, which was the idea of Chicago meteorologist John Coleman, struggled mightily for its first five years and was close to bankruptcy (average annual losses of about $800,000 were sustained each of the first three years). Many television executives called the Weather Channel a laughingstock, but they underestimated the audience for

The first television weather presenter was "Wooly Lamb," a puppet who made his debut on NBC.

weather. By 1988 TWC had turned the corner, and in the 1990s it became a solid, profitable business. Initially seen in 3.2 million homes on cable service, by 1995 TWC was available in 52 million of the 61 million homes that subscribed to cable.

The first television weather presenter was "Wooly Lamb," a meteorologist in sheep's clothing. Wooly Lamb, a puppet, made his debut in limited-area viewing on NBC in New York City in October of 1941. Wooly, who had a seven-year career and was sponsored by Botany Wrinkle-Proof Ties, would begin the report by looking into a telescope, then turn to the camera and sing the forecast. To cement the forecast in viewers' minds, Wooly would fade to black and a slide would appear with the prophecy spelled out.

In the early days of TV weather, the airwaves were populated by puppets, magicians, and comedians (my first nasty letter was from a viewer whose main complaint was "you're not funny!"). There were also well-endowed young ladies with names such as Sunny Day, and Stormy Gale (who "simply love the weather"). The turn toward weatherpeople with meteorological training began in the late 1940s. The first credentialed weatherperson to gain national attention was Chicago's rotund Clint Youle, who was a regular on John Cameron Swayze's *Camel News Caravan* on NBC beginning in 1949. (I propose that there is a public preference for weathercasters who are pleasingly plump, with large and lovable Willard Scott as the paradigm. Many of the panjandrums of prognostication are both personable and portly. The government should fund a study on this.)

By the 1960s many major-market television stations began to hire forecasters who had been trained in meteorology, often with a background in the United States Air Force or Navy. The on-air time for weather broadcasts increased to two and three minutes. By the late-1970s computer-graphics systems were generating colorful, often glitzy, and sometimes animated, maps and illustrations.

SUMMER

JUN

In Ohio, Jimmie Fidler became Ohio's first television forecaster at WLW Cincinnati in 1947. (Fidler had begun his broadcast career on WLBC-AM radio in Muncie, Indiana, in 1934. The station billed him as "Radio's First Weatherman," which of course he was not.)

WLW TV weatherman Jim Fidler.

CLEVELAND WEATHERCASTING

Those who have watched Cleveland weather programs over the years will fondly recall a number of favorites. After returning to Akron from the Air Force in 1955, I remember watching the good-humored and ebullient Joe Finan, dressed as a gas-station attendant in cap and bow tie, doing the weather as the Atlantic Weatherman on KYW. Jim Doney, the talented and affable host of *Adventure Road* on WJW, doubled as the weekend weatherman. I recall the night that Jim sent viewers into hysterics by taking nearly all of his allotted weather time trying to locate the state of Wyoming.

Some may remember the first weatherperson to offer scientific reasoning for why the forecast went wrong: Paul Annear, from Baldwin-Wallace College, was a mathematics professor who made a brief TV appearance around 1950.

Houlihan the Weatherman (Bob Wells) was a popular weather presenter at WJW in the 1960s and 1970s, while the versatile Don Webster began his weather career at WEWS in the early 1960s. Amiable Al Roker entertained viewers on WKYC from the late 1970s into the early 1980s before joining (and then replacing) his buddy, Willard Scott, on the NBC *Today* show in New York.

As the 1990s drew to a close, the FOX 8 weather team of André Bernier, Mark Koontz and Dick Goddard could claim the record for unit longevity.

Buoyed by the confidence that a 13-week contract can bring, I began my TV career on KYW, May 1, 1961. My cross-town competitors were Carolyn Johnson on WEWS and the venerable Howard Hoffmann (the station's first announcer) on WJW.

Some of my fondest memories are from the early 1970s, when I was locked in television weather combat with two other ex–Air Force meteorologists: Bob Zames, an excellent forecaster, was at WEWS (ABC), while Herbert W. Kinnan was at WKYC (NBC).

SUMMER

JUN

The early days at KYW TV-3 in Cleveland.

Wally Kinnan was arguably the best weather forecaster ever to hit town. In World War II, Wally was in a P-38 Lightning that was shot down over Germany, and he spent time in a Nazi prisoner of war stalag. After his military career, Wally became a TV legend in Philadelphia.

I admired Wally for many reasons and one of them was that he didn't suffer weather fools gladly. A major cross-country bus company sponsored his evening weathercast in Philadelphia, and a viewer had sent Wally an especially venomous letter criticizing his forecasting skills. Wally read the letter on the air and responded by telling his new pen pal that he would like to see him under the next bus leaving Philadelphia. And Wally was put into high dudgeon when a nonmeteorologist competitor, who couldn't qualify for the AMS Seal of Approval, decided to create and display his own fancy Shield of Approval.

One day when Wally and I were laughin', scratchin', and tellin' lies around the golf course, I accused him of being a meteorological Typhoid Mary for bringing the five-day forecast with him from Philadelphia. Wally shot back that since his evening weather show was about two minutes ahead of mine, I should assign an intern to copy his forecast for me.

At least Wally and I are proof that being telegenic is not a requirement for some measure of television longevity.

"YA WANNA KNOW WHAT THE WEATHER IS?
LOOK OUT THE DAMN WINDOW."

WEATHERLINE FROM HELL

I am not a profane person, limiting my swearing to when it is absolutely necessary. But I must apologize to any child who had his mouth washed out with soap by Mom in early April 1992.

On April 6, 1992, FOX 8 initiated the Weatherline, an automatic telephone weather, time, and temperature message available by calling (216) 881-0880. Since the beginning, Weatherline has averaged over 800,000 calls per month. Many children enjoy calling, and a few eagerly dial the FOX 8 Weather Center when the forecast and the weather outside have nothing in common.

It doesn't take an astrophysicist to figure how to record the forecast, but the first few days of anything new can lead to some surprises. On the third day of the Weatherline's availability, severe storms developed quickly. At that point any meteorologist becomes as busy as a fox in a henhouse, trying to update information on the changing weather conditions. As I was concluding a weather warning, the National Weather Service buzzer sounded, requiring a new statement for the Weatherline. In my haste, I pushed the wrong button, and this is the message that was recorded: "A severe thunderstorm warning is now in effect . . . Son-of-a-bitch! . . . click."

As I was scanning the latest official bulletin I saw our news director, Grant Zalba, approaching at warp speed with eyes as big as manhole covers. I felt numb, since I knew what the problem was. "Hey Goddard, Virgil (Dominic, the station manager) just called and said that you . . ."

"I know, I know! I'm changing it," I quickly informed him.

Once I had time to consider the consequences of my blunder, I could visualize children all over Northeast Ohio running to their mothers and shouting, "Dick Goddard said there's a thunderstorm coming, and it's a son-of-a-bitch!"

Again, kids, I apologize for the soap.

SUMMER

JUN

YEAR WITHOUT A SUMMER

There is one statement about summer that cannot be disputed: the coldest summer that has ever come to the United States was in 1816. In weather books it has been called "the year without a summer" and "eighteen hundred and froze to death."

There is little doubt that the reason for it was the cataclysmic eruption of the volcano Mount Tambora, on the island of Sumbawa in Indonesia in 1815. Fly ash and debris from the explosion circled the earth and spread a thick veil that diminished radiation from the sun for the next year.

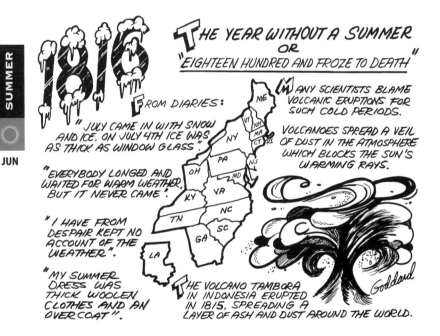

THE YEAR WITHOUT A SUMMER
OR
"*EIGHTEEN HUNDRED AND FROZE TO DEATH*"

FROM DIARIES:

"JULY CAME IN WITH SNOW AND ICE. ON JULY 4TH ICE WAS AS THICK AS WINDOW GLASS"

"EVERYBODY LONGED AND WAITED FOR WARM WEATHER, BUT IT NEVER CAME".

"I HAVE FROM DESPAIR KEPT NO ACCOUNT OF THE WEATHER".

"MY SUMMER DRESS WAS THICK WOOLEN CLOTHES AND AN OVERCOAT".

MANY SCIENTISTS BLAME VOLCANIC ERUPTIONS FOR SUCH COLD PERIODS.

VOLCANOES SPREAD A VEIL OF DUST IN THE ATMOSPHERE WHICH BLOCKS THE SUN'S WARMING RAYS.

THE VOLCANO TAMBORA IN INDONESIA ERUPTED IN 1815, SPREADING A LAYER OF ASH AND DUST AROUND THE WORLD.

Goddard

There were 18 states in the Union as the year 1816 began, Ohio having joined in 1803.

As the year started, January was very mild and February not much colder. March came in like a "small lion and went out like an innocent sheep."

April began warm, but as the days lengthened the air grew cold. In early May, young buds were frozen dead, and ice an inch thick formed on ponds and rivers. A hard frost in late May destroyed the corn crop, and snow fell in Ohio on May 22.

The first few days of June were warm and a feeling of optimism returned. The frosts of May were forgotten and corn and other crops replanted.

On June 6, the next arctic cold front arrived. From June 6 to 9, severe frost occurred every night from Canada to Virginia, "killing every green herb and vegetables of all descriptions."

The people shivered and built roaring fires, while gardens blackened and newly shorn sheep froze to death. Thousands of birds perished.

On June 11, frost killed nearly all of New England's corn crop, a major food staple.

Snow fell in June to depths of 10 inches in Vermont and 7 inches in New York and Massachusetts.

All summer long the north wind blew fresh arctic cold fronts southward. July came in with local snows and ice.

In Ohio, an Urbana newspaper told of a young gentleman and his lady who had set out for a July Fourth celebration but were forced to turn back because of heavy snow.

The few green things that survived July's ice were cut down by hard frosts on August 20 and a final devastating freeze September 27.

For the few who could afford it, hay—at $45 a ton—was shipped in from Ireland to save the starving cattle. Flour sold at $17 a barrel and potatoes at a penny a pound—unheard-of prices.

A note in the weather diary of Adino Brackett in 1816 tells the story succinctly: "This past summer and fall have been so cold and miserable that I have from despair kept no account of the weather."

The "year without a summer" triggered a great western migration the following spring and summer.

SUMMER

JUN

LIGHTNING: NATURE'S TERRIBLE SWIFT SWORD

In Ohio and across the United States, more people are killed by lightning in July than in any other month.

It has been estimated that a hundred lightning flashes lace earth's atmosphere every second, some eight million every day.

A lightning discharge travels at about 60,000 miles per second, nearly one-third the speed of light. It is believed that the temperature along the lightning bolt channel momentarily (for one millionth of a second) rises to 50,000° F (30,000° C), some five times the temperature of the sun's surface. It is because of this intense heat that objects struck by lightning may immediately burst into flame.

The garden-variety lightning bolt generates a million volts of electricity with tens of thousands of amperes. Unfortunately, we have no way of putting this force to work for us, as we have no way of harnessing the fleeting, massive burst of energy

As terrifying as it can be, lightning actually serves as earth's protective atmospheric fuse, relieving a powerful electrical buildup and preventing a more devastating and cataclysmic explosion. It is also

SUMMER

JUN

extremely important to life on our planet. The electrical discharge causes nitrogen fixation, a fertilization process that puts nitrogen compounds and nutrients into a usable form for both plants and animals.

In Norse mythology, lightning and thunder were attributed to the red-bearded and frightful Thor the Hammerer, the god of thunder, weather, and crops. Lightning bolts, it was reasoned, were sparks forged by Thor on his mighty anvil.

Lightning also plays some grim pranks:

A cow was electrocuted by lightning in New Hampshire while she was being milked, but the farmer was unharmed.

In Vermont lightning struck a large flock of sheep, killing only the black sheep in the pack.

Lightning struck a church belfry in Maryland, surged through the automatic chime system, short-circuited the wires, and touched off a long program of church hymns.

A lightning bolt in Minneapolis set fire to a house and then jumped across the street, hitting a fire-alarm box, which summoned firefighters who put out the flames.

Edwin Robinson of Falmouth, Maine, regained his sight and hearing after being struck by lightning. Hair began to grow on his previously bald head.

There is no place that is completely safe from lightning, but many situations are to be avoided: open spaces, tall solitary trees and objects, metallic objects, and water. Superstitions about lightning abound. For example, lightning cannot only strike twice in the same place, but many times. New York's Empire State Building averages 23 strikes a year (and was hit eight times in a single thunderstorm). As late as the 18th century there was a belief in Europe that the ringing of church bells would divert the bolts from the blue. Many church bells bore the Latin inscription *fulgara frango,* which translates into "I break up the lightning." During one 30-year period, some 100 bell ringers were electrocuted.

> **There is no place completely safe from lightning, but many situations are to be avoided.**

Ben Franklin invented the only practical lightning "protector": the lightning rod you still often see on barns and farmhouses. The rod actually attracts a lightning strike, but the electrical discharge is then taken down an attached wire (copper is best) to another metal rod that is driven into the ground, where the grounded energy dissipates harmlessly.

Interestingly, Franklin never patented the device, saying it was "a gift to my fellow man." (Somehow, I don't believe such altruism would happen today).

When Lightning Strikes, Be Sure You're Protected

When lightning zigs and zags across the northern Ohio skies, folks ask me about lightning protection for their homes and property. About 18,000 homes are destroyed or heavily damaged by lightning in the United States each year.

Even though a home is considered a safe place during electrical storms, statistics show that 27 percent of all persons injured by lightning were in their homes at the time.

Lightning bolts enter most homes through the roof after making contact with the highest projection, often a TV antenna or a chimney. Lightning rarely strikes the side of a building.

Lightning may also enter the home through an overhead power line (that's why you should never use any electrical appliance during thunderstorms) or by leaping into the home from an adjacent tall tree (lightning bolts seek out the better conductor).

For buildings, trees, or boats, the lightning rod that Ben Franklin invented still offers the only real solution to the problem. The three-to-five-foot rods, however, have been fancied up and are now much shorter, and referred to as "air terminals."

Air-terminal installation should be handled by experts, since an improper arrangement could invite a disastrous lightning strike.

The basic lightning arrestor plan involves building a "cone of protection" around whatever you want to shield. The protected area forms a cone whose radius is equal to the height of the air terminal conductor. A series of terminals, no more than 20 feet apart, will be needed to construct an umbrella of safety around a home.

27 percent of all persons injured by lightning were in their homes at the time.

Hardware for constructing the cone consists of copper (preferably) or aluminum air terminals connected by cables that lead into the ground several feet from the foundation of the house. The cable is attached to a copper rod that is buried at least 10 feet deep. Those tall and priceless trees in your yard can be protected in a similar manner, with a series of buried cables that extend like spokes from the base of the tree.

SUNSHINE %: 67
DRIEST MONTH: 0.74" / 1930
WARMEST MONTH: 79.1° / 1955
COLDEST MONTH: 67.6° / 1960
LIQUID PCPN AVG.: 3.52"
RAINIEST DAY: 2.87" / 1969
RAINIEST MONTH: 9.12" / 1992
THUNDERY DAYS: 6
SNOWIEST DAY: None
DAYS ONE INCH SNOW: 0

July can be a meteorological firecracker in Northeast Ohio. Lightning laces the sky more in this month than any other. The legendary Dog Days begin on July 3 and continue for 40 days. The ancient Egyptians came up with the canine idea because they believed that the dog star, Sirius (the brightest star in our skies), lent its heat to that of the sun. Sirius is unseen in our summer sky because of the brightness of our sun; indeed, Sirius comes over the eastern horizon each summer morning just ahead of the star we call our sun. Our July atmosphere is often humid, and torrential rains can fall. On July 12, 1966, a state record 10.51 inches of rain fell in 24 hours at Sandusky. Even on a blistering July day, the raindrops will feel cold. That's because nearly all rainfall at Ohio's latitude begins as ice crystals and snow high above. On July 4, 1969, 12 hours of nearly continuous thunderstorms resulted in 42 deaths, most by drowning. Just northwest of Wooster, 14 inches of rain fell from the storms. On warm and sultry July nights heat lightning can be seen. The lightning is unaccompanied by thunder, since it is coming from a thunderstorm that may be a thousand miles away, in Oklahoma or southern Canada. In this lush and verdant estival month the ubiquitous Queen Anne's lace will proliferate in unmowed fields. Katydids are fiddling away the nights.

Day	Hi	Lo	Rec Hi	Rec Lo	Sunrise	Sunset	Lake°
1	81	60	95 / 1941	45 / 1988	5:58	9:05	67
2	82	60	97 / 1954	47 / 1943	5:58	9:05	67
3	82	60	98 / 1949	46 / 1907	5:59	9:04	67
4	82	60	98 / 1990	41 / 1968	5:59	9:04	67
5	82	61	96 / 1911	48 / 1979	6:00	9:04	67
6	82	61	97 / 1988	45 / 1979	6:00	9:04	67
7	82	61	99 / 1988	45 / 1968	6:01	9:04	67
8	82	61	99 / 1988	45 / 1984	6:02	9:03	68
9	82	61	97 / 1936	43 / 1961	6:02	9:03	68
10	82	61	97 / 1936	46 / 1963	6:03	9:02	69
11	82	61	99 / 1936	48 / 1996	6:04	9:02	69
12	82	61	95 / 1936	48 / 1978	6:04	9:02	70
13	82	61	95 / 1952	51 / 1976	6:05	9:01	70
14	82	61	99 / 1954	51 / 1888	6:06	9:01	70
15	82	61	97 / 1980	48 / 1960	6:07	9:00	71
16	82	62	100 / 1988	50 / 1954	6:08	8:59	71
17	83	62	96 / 1942	49 / 1946	6:08	8:59	71
18	83	62	96 / 1878	51 / 1971	6:09	8:58	71
19	83	62	95 / 1930	50 / 1979	6:10	8:57	72
20	83	62	98 / 1930	46 / 1965	6:11	8:57	72
21	83	62	97 / 1952	46 / 1966	6:12	8:56	72
22	83	62	99 / 1952	47 / 1966	6:13	8:55	72
23	83	62	96 / 1933	49 / 1981	6:14	8:54	72
24	83	62	99 / 1934	51 / 1985	6:14	8:54	72
25	83	62	99 / 1941	47 / 1953	6:15	8:53	72
26	83	62	99 / 1941	46 / 1946	6:16	8:52	73
27	83	62	103 / 1941	47 / 1946	6:17	8:51	73
28	82	62	96 / 1993	52 / 1977	6:18	8:50	73
29	82	62	95 / 1941	50 / 1948	6:19	8:49	73
30	82	62	96 / 1941	50 / 1981	6:20	8:48	73
31	82	62	97 / 1955	52 / 1960	6:21	8:47	73

What do we live for
if it is not to make life
less difficult for others?

– GEORGE ELIOT (MARY ANN EVANS)

JULY FOURTH FIREWORKS

On July 4, 1969, at 7:40 p.m., the first wave of violent thunderstorms, with winds near 100 mph, came crashing in from Lake Erie.

For the next 12 hours, severe thunderstorms continually developed over Lake Erie and quickly swept inland, filling the nighttime sky with vivid lightning and dropping rain in biblical proportions.

In the worst summer flooding in Ohio weather history, rainfall totals for the 12-hour period ranged generally between 3 and 11 inches across northern Ohio, with one report of 14 inches near Wooster in Wayne County.

Forty-two Ohioans died in the 1969 thunderstorm blitz, most by drowning. Damage in the state exceeded $65 million.

Contrary to what many still believe, tornadoes played no part in the extensive damage to trees and buildings in Greater Cleveland. In Lakewood, for example, the hundreds of trees that were felled pointed in the same general direction, indicating a typical straight-line thunderstorm wind (tornado damage is in a circular pattern).

Flood damage in downtown Vermilion from the July 4, 1969 storms.

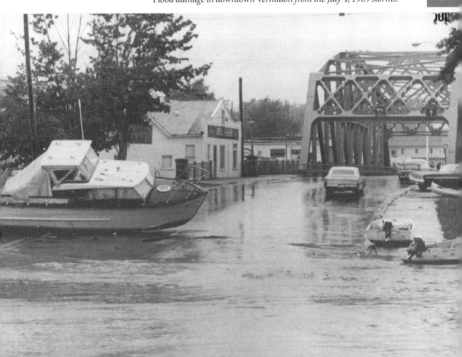

Two Greater Cleveland residents lost their lives during the July Fourth storms, but the potential for an even greater disaster was in place. Hundreds of small craft were just off the Lake Erie shoreline in anticipation of the annual Festival of Freedom fireworks display later that evening.

While weather forecasters were aware that towering 60,000-foot thunderstorms were over the lake that afternoon, the storm movement all day long had been west to east. Just after 7 p.m. the storms suddenly veered southward. The first inkling that Ohio forecasters had of the onrushing fury came when a ship 10 miles north of Lorain reported a wind gust of 110 mph.

A severe thunderstorm warning was issued just seven minutes before the first wave of storms hit land.

One of many trees struck by lightning during the storms.

SUMMER

JUL

CALCULATING A CAREER

The National Weather Service in the 1950s and 1960s was staffed primarily by ex–Air Force and Navy meteorologists (in the Navy you are an aerologist), but today a college degree is almost mandatory in the atmospheric sciences. The United States government (through the armed forces and the National Oceanic and Atmospheric Agency, or NOAA) provides most of the weather employment available on the job market, but private industry has become an increasingly important employer. (Most major airlines, for example, have their own forecasters.)

If you plan to go forth into the field of meteorology today you will be required not only to be fruitful and multiply, you'll also have to add, subtract, and divide—all the way through integral calculus. Many colleges and universities (including Ohio State University) now offer B.A. and B.S. degrees in meteorology, while others have courses in conjunction with related science and engineering fields. Those interested in research and development should plan on obtaining a master's degree (a doctorate is usually overkill).

"I'LL HANDLE THE ANALYSIS, FARNSWORTH!"

In the course of your education, you should take as many classes in math, physics, chemistry, and earth science as possible. English and foreign languages are very beneficial, as writing and other communication skills are imperative to success. Those interested in meteorology should write to the American Meteorological Society (45 Beacon St., Boston, MA 02108) and ask about becoming a student member of the AMS. The AMS, in conjunction with the University Corporation for Atmospheric Sciences, publishes *Curricula in the Atmospheric, Oceanic and Related Sciences* biannually. The book, which sells for twenty dollars, plus three dollars postage and handling, will give you information on courses and faculties at about 100 universities and colleges in the United States, Canada, and Puerto Rico.

The Department of Geography at Kent State University offers courses in meteorology, climatology, and polar environments. You may contact either Dr. Thomas Schmidlin or Dr. Robert Rohill at (330) 672-2045.

Salaries of meteorologists and atmospheric scientists range widely, from $15,000 to $35,000 at entry and basic levels, to between $50,000 and $100,000 for higher management, including research scientists, professors, and consultants. Perhaps regrettably, television meteorologists in major markets can attain salaries of $150,000 to

Preparing for a telecast in 1969.

over $350,000 (the trade-off for the large pay is the relative lack of job security).

Currently the National Weather Service employs about 4,800 meteorologists, with some 6,000 in the private sector and 1,000 in media. With the advent of the computer age the NWS has been downsizing. This followed a burst of hiring in the 1980s. Many local NWS offices (Akron-Canton is an example) have, unfortunately, been closed and replaced by the automatic surface observation system, ASOS. Another unfortunate part of the NWS "modernization" has been the institution of a confusing set of hieroglyphics known as METAR (mee-tar), which replaced the easily understood airways code. The meteorological mavens who come up with such stuff have too much time on their hands and should not be allowed to reproduce. Or, they should at least be required to listen to Dr. Laura.

LANDING A JOB AS A WEATHERPERSON

Do not assume that every weatherperson who points and pontificates on television is a fully degreed and accredited meteorologist. Many successful weather presenters get their daily weather knowledge by tearing off hard copy from teleprinters. Glibness and personality count, along with a modicum of weather knowledge. There is a lot of dark humor among television newspeople. A sense of humor and the ability to laugh at yourself are very important.

If you are lucky enough—as I have been—you'll have a job you truly love. There is great satisfaction in knowing that your weather forecast has been beneficial and that you have helped people navigate our often unpredictable climate. Conversely, you'll occasionally get some caustic criticism. That goes with the territory. As the old adage goes: If you don't want to be criticized, say nothing, do nothing, be nothing.

The look of television weather programs has changed drastically, and for the better, over the past decades. Those who presented weather in the 1950s and 1960s usually created weather maps using magnets or wide-tipped, leaky ink pens (Wally Kinnan's ties often looked like they were painted by Salvador Dali). For over four years at KYW I spent about five hours every day chalking my maps (I'm sure I was on the verge of white lung disease). Today the ink pens, magnets, and chalk have been replaced by colorful and glitzy computer-generated maps and icons.

Computers have also dramatically improved the severe weather alert system at television stations. Prior to the high-speed computers, weather warnings from the National Weather Service took many minutes before they appeared on the TV screen. At FOX 8 today our First Warning system automatically puts a warning on the screen only one second after its issuance.

Those who give the weather on television need to be acutely aware of the adverse impact a forecast can have on the general public, both from a mental and economic standpoint. I cringe when I hear a weather announcer warn viewers to stay home because of predicted weather conditions. It's one thing if a blizzard is raging or tornadoes have been sighted and large objects are flying through the air. But we must remember that forecasts are seldom a "lock" and weather

SUMMER

JUL

TOP 10 REASONS TO BE A TELEVISION METEOROLOGIST

10. You can never get lost—people are always telling you where to go.

9. It's a good feeling to belong to a non-prophet organization.

8. It's one of the few jobs where you can climb the ladder of success wrong by wrong.

7. To anyone who annoys you with a trite "Looks like a nice day," you can counter with a nifty "Not if that trough at 500 millibars continues to amplify!"

6. In only three minutes you can irritate nearly everyone in a 25-county region.

5. Weather people traditionally get to referee newsroom food fights.

4. You can blame bad forecasts on caterpillar larvae and large marmots.

3. Hanging out with Slider and Mark Koontz.

2. On your 80th birthday you'll only be 27 Celsius.

1. Management has no idea what you do.

---

conditions can vary widely over short distances. Unless a meteorological monster is rising from Lake Erie, I feel the viewer should be left to determine whether or not to venture out based on that individual's ability to navigate in foul weather.

SEAL OF APPROVAL

The meteorological Seal of Approval for television is bestowed by the American Meteorological Society. To qualify, you must submit a videotape of an on-air presentation. A  board of professional meteorologists will critique your performance based on technical competence, informational value, explanatory value, and communication skills. The candidate must be given a "satisfactory" in each category before the seal will be granted. Those who fail will be allowed to reapply in three months. A second failure will require a one-year waiting period.

This program, aimed at upgrading television weather presentations, began with the awarding of the first seals in January of 1960. Rules for application have loosened and tightened over the years. Today a minimum of 12 semester hours of study in atmospheric, oceanic, or related hydrologic sciences is required.

The Seal of Approval must be renewed annually and may be revoked for a variety of professional offenses. Possibly by writing a weather book such as this.

SUMMER

JUL

GLOBAL WARMING

In October of 1997 many whose job it was to forecast the weather on television were summoned to the White House in an attempt to win over meteorologists to the proposition that climate change resulting from global warming was a reality, not just a theory.

The event got off to a shaky start.

As about 100 of us—including high-ranking officials from NOAA, the National Weather Service, and the American Meteorological Society—were waiting in a long security-check line outside the White House, it began to rain. And not one of us had an umbrella! (If a major tabloid had had their weatherazzi on hand, we would have been a drop-dead cinch to make the next day's front page under a banner headline exclaiming, "Weather Fools Meet the President.")

In the East Room, President Clinton made a brief, cordial welcoming speech. We all knew the president was setting the table for Vice President Al Gore, who has made global warming a personal crusade. For nearly an hour the vice president made what I thought was an impressive and compelling presentation, complete with graphs and pie charts.

The problem was that the majority of meteorologists who came to the conference were unconvinced that global warming is real, and they went away with the same opinion.

In reality we are passengers on a spaceship called earth that circles a life-giving star we call our sun. However we view our earthly home, there is little scientific doubt that because of neglect and poor housekeeping we have befouled our own nest. Fortunately, planet earth has a remarkable ability to heal itself. The question is, just how much can it handle?

While core samples of glacial ice tell a story of dramatic changes in the earth's climate over millions of years, these changes have very likely come from such disparate things as collisions with comets and asteroids or the eccentric wobbling of our planet on its axis. It wasn't until the beginning of the Industrial Revolution that human beings acquired the ability to change the climate and damage our finely tuned ecosystem. Our power to alter the atmosphere cannot be minimized.

Pollution can be environmental (natural) or anthropogenic (manmade) and it can occur in our air, land, and water. An example of natural pollution is a volcanic eruption; the burning of fossil fuels (coal, petroleum, and natural gas) in factories, automobile engines, and home furnaces is an example of manmade contamination.

It is estimated that as the 20th century draws to a close the concentration of carbon dioxide (CO_2)—caused primarily by the burning of fossil fuels—is 25 percent higher than at the start of the century. Those who deny that there is any current global warming point to the fact that, with the earth 71 percent water covered, the oceans act as colossal "sinks," absorbing excessive CO_2 and thus keeping the climate in balance.

The warming of earth's climate has been labeled the greenhouse effect, although hothouse effect or heat trap effect would be equally appropriate. Short-wavelength sunlight easily passes through a greenhouse's glass, while the absorbed sunlight within is then reradiated as long-wavelength radiation, which the greenhouse glass blocks from escaping. Correspondingly, earth's atmosphere is almost transparent to incoming sunlight, but carbon dioxide gas traps much of the infrared heat energy that is reradiated from our planet.

SUMMER

JUL

Scientists recognize carbon dioxide as the largest single contributor to the greenhouse effect over the past century, but the cumulative effect of nitrogen oxides, methane, ozone, chlorofluorocarbons, and other trace gases could equal that of carbon dioxide over the next century.

Scientists recognize carbon dioxide as the largest single contributor to the greenhouse effect over the past century.

Aside from fossil fuel burning, which produces more carbon dioxide than any other activity, deforestation of the earth's surface has been the largest single source of this gas. Trees absorb carbon dioxide, and when they die and rot they unlock and release the gas back into the atmosphere. (Planting new trees is one method of reducing carbon dioxide accumulation).

Methane, a gas that emanates from landfills, the digestive tracts of cattle, termite mounds, and rice patties, also contributes to the greenhouse effect. Improved landfill procedures and new methods of managing cattle and growing rice are being examined by environmentalists.

Computer estimates suggest that with a dramatic greenhouse effect, the layer of air from the earth's surface to 12 miles aloft would warm, while the stratospheric layer above would cool. Earth's higher latitudes (including Ohio's) would warm, while the tropics would show little change. There would be catastrophic drought in grain-producing latitudes (including ours) while some now drought-plagued areas would get abundant rainfall. Glaciers and ice caps would melt and the rise in ocean water levels would inundate present-day coastal regions.

To this scenario the global-warming skeptics say, "No!" They claim that the supercomputer projections are flawed, and they reject the idea that surface temperature observations over the last decades are accurate. Satellite observations have actually shown no change, or even a lowering of temperatures. Many respected climatologists believe that any global warming (or cooling) is a natural phenomenon and that variations in global temperatures have come in cycles, over extremely long periods of time. A 1997 survey of climatologists in the United States revealed that 58 percent did not believe there is overwhelming evidence that global warming is for real. Thirty-six percent agreed with the global warming theory. Curiously, about 36 percent of climatologists believe that earth is headed for another glacial period.

I believe such skepticism is healthy, if it is maintained in an altruistic spirit with the search for truth as its goal. I have a file from the 1960s packed with magazine and newspaper articles warning that the next ice age was closing in, rapidly. With just as much zeal as today's advocates of global warming theory, the ice-age people were issuing a clarion call for immediate action if the coming deep freeze was to be somehow ameliorated (one suggestion was to spread lamp black over polar regions to absorb solar radiation and melt the ice sheets).

By the late 1970s, the frigorific forecasts suddenly disappeared and, following a brief climatological interregnum, the hothouse people emerged with their own reading of the global thermostat. During the 1997 White House conference on global warming I found a great opportunity to quiz two respected meteorologists on the subject. I told them about my three-inch-thick file from the 1960s and asked, "Where did the ice age people go?" The National Weather Service official smiled broadly and poked his finger at the American Meteorological Society member next to him. The pokee, who was obviously very sensitive to the question, returned a less-than-broad smile and a shrug.

Actually, life on earth can be adversely affected by many unpredictable events:

EARTH'S ORBIT around the sun ranges from elliptical to nearly circular, and it recycles about every 100,000 years. Earth's current 23$\frac{1}{2}$-degree tilt on its axis will range between 22 and 24 degrees, a considerable variance.

SOLAR VARIABILITY changes with incoming radiation rising and falling with sunspot activity (storms on the sun). This effect is ancient and extremely changeable, affecting not only the temperature on earth, but the amount of ozone and rainfall.

COMETS AND ASTEROIDS (miniplanets) have bombarded earth over the eons, creating enormous tsunamis (incorrectly called tidal waves) and life-threatening, sunlight-blocking ash and dust clouds. Earth's orbit and the tilt of its axis could be affected.

VOLCANOES can spread ash around the planet, shutting off sunlight and causing the earth's temperature to drop dramatically. The Year Without a Summer (1816) was caused by the eruption of Mount Tambora in Indonesia in 1815. (See page 166.)

SHIFTING OF EARTH'S TECTONIC PLATES can rearrange its geography, which would change weather patterns.

NUCLEAR WAR, with its resultant clouds and radiation, could theoretically create a life-destroying "nuclear winter."

We have no right, of course, to be in high (or even low) dudgeon when nature, which created this planet, decides to do some rearranging. In truth, beautiful planet earth, hanging like a bright blue sapphire in the blackness of space, and embellished with majestic mountains and seas, is hostile. Created in the unimaginable violence of an exploding and (perhaps) ever-expanding universe some 4.6 billion years ago, tilted and wobbling as it circles the sun, the earth is wracked by an earthquake every ten minutes. Dust from volcanoes is constantly in our atmosphere, while ice ages have advanced and retreated.

But those of us alive today should be most thankful. In the lottery of life, 20th-century Americans drew some very good numbers. Through modern science and the industrial revolution, we have been given a prosperous artificial way of life, shielded from much of nature's violence. Through no effort of our own, and in spite of highly publicized heat waves, blizzards, tsunamis, hurricanes, and tornadoes, the climate of the last 50 years has smiled benignly on the United States. Some climatologists have concluded that since the Dust Bowl days of the 1930s ended, we have been blessed with the mildest and most agriculturally productive weather in the last 10,000 years. What we have perceived as "normal" weather has instead been at the most favorable extreme possible.

JUNK SCIENCE

The American public has a large appetite for disasters, and the business of writing books based on junk science has been highly profitable. Doomsday publications on such topics as the millennium, the ice age, the greenhouse effect, and celestial calamities are continually cranked out, in hopes that the gullible public will buy enough to warrant a script for a follow-up movie or television special.

One of the most egregious examples of this came in the late 1970s when a book called *The Jupiter Effect* began to ring up sales. The idea was that a straight lineup (conjunction) of several planets in our solar system—featuring the giant gas ball Jupiter—would cause gravity to tug on the earth's surface with such force that it would trigger massive earthquakes, seaquakes, and tsunamis. In 1982, several months before the date of the planetary conjunction, the authors called a press conference to repent and say, in essence, "By Jove, there won't be a Jupiter Effect: we miscalculated." No money was refunded.

Even the media can be victimized by a scientific hoax. A few years ago a major wire service in this country distributed a story from a "respected British scientific organization" that had determined that the reason there were so many tornadoes in the United States was that Americans drove on the right side of the highways. It was the swift passing of automobiles on warm days that created a massive counterclockwise vortex of wind. The British study also revealed that most of the tornadoes occurred in rural areas on weekends when city dwellers were making a mad dash for the countryside.

As the authorities on education in this country tell us, science illiteracy and mathematical innumeracy are the norm. While worry over the pollution of our environment is unquestionably a legitimate concern, we must be on the alert for alarmists. Consider the concern over the proliferation of the chemical "dihydrogen monoxide." A petition to ban further use of this substance was signed by 43 of the 50 people who were approached with the following list of dihydrogen monoxide's effects:

- It is found in tumors of fatally ill cancer patients.
- In its gaseous state it can cause severe burns.
- Excessive inhalation can kill.
- It can cause baseball-sized objects to critically impact on the unwary.
- It is a major component of acid rain.
- It can devastate entire communities.

What is dihydrogen monoxide? Water.

SUNSHINE %: 63
DRIEST MONTH: 0.17"/1881
WARMEST MONTH: 77.8°/1995
COLDEST MONTH: 65.4°/1927
LIQUID PCPN AVG.: 3.40"
RAINIEST DAY: 3.65"/1994
RAINIEST MONTH: 8.96"/1975
THUNDERY DAYS: 5"
SNOWIEST DAY: None
DAYS ONE INCH SNOW: 0

The Perseids are coming! One of the most reliable of the meteor showers, the Perseids are most frequent around the 11th night. These night lights of August may be no larger than a bean, or grain of sand, as they become super-heated after entering our atmosphere at about 65 miles up, traveling at 150,000 mph. Shooting stars that make it through the atmosphere and strike earth are called meteorites. An especially bright meteor, called a bolide, was seen blazing across the Northeast Ohio sky in October of 1992; the bolide eventually struck the trunk of a car in New York State. While May is the month of woodland flowers, August is the month of field flowers. New England asters, with bright yellow centers and purple petals, adorn the untended countryside. The 17-year locusts—which are actually cicadas, distant relatives of locusts that have no mouths—will emerge from their sleep chambers in 1999 and again in 2016. The shrill cicadas last sang their discordant symphony in 1982. Those who live near wooded areas may resort to earmuffs before the month is through. Adding to the summertime symphony will be the stridulation of crickets and red-legged grasshoppers. Personally, I'll take the noise of summer over the silence of winter. On extremely hot August afternoons the refraction of light over Lake Erie has created a mirage, allowing the Canadian shoreline to appear—upside down.

Day	Hi	Lo	Rec Hi	Rec Lo	Sunrise	Sunset	Lake°
1	82	62	95 / 1917	47 / 1960	6:22	8:46	73
2	82	62	97 / 1988	50 / 1962	6:23	8:45	73
3	82	62	97 / 1944	58 / 1976	6:24	8:44	73
4	82	62	97 / 1930	46 / 1966	6:25	8:42	74
5	82	61	94 / 1947	46 / 1972	6:26	8:41	74
6	82	61	100 / 1918	45 / 1997	6:27	8:40	74
7	82	61	95 / 1918	48 / 1997	6:28	8:39	74
8	82	61	96 / 1941	47 / 1975	6:29	8:38	74
9	82	61	96 / 1949	50 / 1972	6:30	8:36	74
10	82	61	97 / 1944	47 / 1972	6:31	8:35	74
11	81	61	96 / 1944	48 / 1965	6:32	8:34	74
12	81	61	99 / 1881	44 / 1967	6:33	8:32	74
13	81	61	95 / 1995	47 / 1982	6:34	8:31	74
14	81	61	97 / 1944	46 / 1964	6:35	8:30	74
15	81	61	96 / 1944	44 / 1962	6:36	8:28	74
16	81	60	96 / 1944	45 / 1979	6:37	8:27	74
17	81	60	99 / 1988	48 / 1971	6:38	8:26	74
18	81	60	96 / 1947	46 / 1981	6:39	8:24	74
19	80	60	100 / 1955	47 / 1964	6:40	8:23	74
20	80	60	95 / 1947	46 / 1998	6:41	8:21	74
21	79	60	96 / 1947	45 / 1950	6:42	8:20	74
22	79	60	94 / 1936	45 / 1982	6:43	8:18	74
23	79	60	93 / 1914	48 / 1969	6:44	8:17	74
24	79	59	94 / 1947	44 / 1952	6:45	8:15	74
25	79	59	97 / 1948	45 / 1951	6:46	8:14	73
26	79	59	97 / 1948	47 / 1958	6:47	8:12	73
27	79	59	102 / 1948	49 / 1963	6:48	8:10	73
28	79	59	98 / 1953	42 / 1968	6:49	8:09	73
29	79	59	98 / 1953	38 / 1982	6:50	8:07	73
30	76	58	96 / 1953	45 / 1976	6:51	8:06	73
31	78	58	99 / 1953	46 / 1890	6:52	8:04	73

*A man's worst enemies
can't wish on him what he
can think up for himself.*

– FOLK SAYING

HURRICANES

The hurricane is a storm that forms in tropical seas where the water temperature exceeds 80 degrees. The storm grows and is sustained by the energy from water vapor that is drawn upward into the system. June to October is considered to be the hurricane "season," with the peak period culminating September 10.

Hurricanes are the largest storms on earth, with diameters that can reach 500 miles. In the Pacific Ocean west of Hawaii the hurricane is known as a typhoon (from the Mandarin Chinese words *tai,* meaning "great," and *feng,* meaning "wind"). The same storm in the Indian Ocean is called a cyclone, while off the northern coast of Australia it's a willy-willy.

Tracking the path of Hurricane Gladys, 1961

SUMMER

AUG

Onboard a Hurricane Hunter aircraft as it descends into Hurricane Flora in October 1963.

Satellite photos of a well-developed hurricane show a familiar doughnut-shaped cloud with a relatively calm open area, or eye, at the center. The hurricane is basically a deep low-pressure center encircled by thunderstorms which revolve counterclockwise around the center. I flew into Hurricane Flora with the U.S. Navy Hurricane Hunters in 1963—the first nighttime low-level penetration of a hurricane. (Hurricane reconnaissance planes fly through the less violent portion of the storm, usually the southwest quadrant.) Going in at less than a thousand feet, we were surrounded by continuous lightning.

The first stage of a developing hurricane is called a tropical depression, with sustained winds of less than 36 mph. From 36 to 74 mph the system is called a tropical storm. When winds exceed 74 mph, it is a full-fledged hurricane. There are five hurricane wind speed categories on the Saffir-Simpson scale, with Category 5 winds exceeding 155 mph.

To keep track of hurricanes and typhoons, the storms are given women's and men's names by the World Meteorological Organization in Geneva, Switzerland. There is a six-year rotating list of names, and when a storm is particularly eventful or destructive the name is retired. For that reason you will never again hear of a Janet (the only hurricane to destroy a hunter aircraft, in 1955), Agnes, Audrey, Betsy, Bob, Camille, Connie, Diana, Donna, Flora, Frederic, Hazel, Hugo, or Marilyn.

In spite of the great damage it can bring, the hurricane—like the thunderstorm—acts as earth's thermostat, regulating the climate and preventing an even more cataclysmic event.

Hurricanes begin to die as they reach land, but infrequently the remains of the storm will be able to bring gusty winds and heavy rains into Ohio as they pass near by. In October of 1916 an unnamed hurricane that made landfall along the Gulf Coast retained considerable strength as it moved rapidly northward. In near-hurricane-force winds on Lake Erie, four ships were sunk, including the *James B. Colgate* just off Ashtabula. Fifty-eight seamen drowned. Other hurricanes that affected Ohio were Hazel in October 1954, Agnes in June 1972, and Frederic in September of 1979.

SAFFIR-SIMPSON HURRICANE DAMAGE POTENTIAL SCALE

Rating	Wind speed	Damage	Impact
1	74–95	Minimal	Some damage to or destruction of shrubbery, trees, and mobile homes; roads in low-lying coastal areas flooded by storm surge tide, approximately 4 to 5 feet above normal tides.
2	96–110	Moderate	Some smaller or weaker trees blown down; damage to rooftops, windows, and mobile homes, but not structural damage; 6- to 8-foot storm surge can tear small craft from moorings and flood coastal areas, roadways, and marinas.
3	111–130	Extensive	Large trees toppled; small buildings sustain structural damage; mobile homes destroyed; coastal buildings damaged or destroyed by 9- to 12-foot storm-tide waves punctuated by large, floating debris.
4	131–155	Extreme	Roofs damaged or destroyed on smaller structures; 13- to 18-foot storm tide floods inland areas up to 6 miles, causes severe beach erosion.
5	156+	Catastrophic	Many residences and other buildings completely destroyed; small structures overturned or blown away; storm surge of 18 feet or more causes flooding up to 10 miles inland.

SUMMER

AUG

ATLANTIC HURRICANE NAMES BY YEAR
(SIX-YEAR ROTATING LIST)

1998 / 2004 / 2010

Alex, Bonnie, Charley, Danielle, Earl, Frances, Georges, Hermina, Ivan, Jeanne,
Karl, Lisa, Mitch, Nicole, Otto, Paula, Richard, Shari, Tomas, Virginia, Walter

1999 / 2005 / 2011

Arlene, Bret, Cindy, Dennis, Emily, Floyd, Gert, Harvey, Irene, José, Katrina,
Lenny, Maria, Nate, Ophelia, Philippe, Rita, Stan, Tammy, Vince, Wilma

2000 / 2006 / 2012

Alberto, Beryl, Chris, Debby, Ernesto, Florence, Gordon, Helene, Isaac, Joyce,
Keith, Leslie, Michael, Nadine, Oscar, Patty, Rafael, Sandy, Tony, Valerie, William

2001 / 2007 / 2013

Allison, Barry, Chantal, Dean, Erin, Felix, Gabrielle, Humberto, Iris, Jerry,
Karen, Lorenzo, Michelle, Noel, Olga, Pablo, Rebekah, Sebastian, Tanya, Van, Wendy

2002 / 2008 / 2014

Arthur, Bertha, Cesar, Dolly, Edouard, Fran, Gustav, Hortense, Isidore, Josephine,
Kyle, Lili, Marco, Nana, Omar, Paloma, Rene, Sally, Teddy, Vicky, Wilfred

2003 / 2009 / 2015

Ana, Bill, Claudette, Danny, Erika, Fabian, Grace, Henri, Isabel, Juan, Kate,
Larry, Mindy, Nicholas, Odetta, Peter, Rose, Sam, Teresa, Victor, Wanda

SUMMER

AUG

Lake Erie, churned up by Hurricane Agnes, pounds the Memorial Shoreway seawall, June 1972.

STARRY, STARRY NIGHTS

In our hurry to step off the daily treadmill of life in order to just sit and relax, it's easy for us to ignore the great celestial show that is there for us to see every night in the Northeast Ohio sky. True, from November into March clouds often keep the curtain closed on the performance, but when skies are clear—and you're far enough away from the glare and murky air of the cities—the stars and planets are dazzling. On an unusually clear night here we can see about 2,000 twinkling stars with the unaided eye. The stars we see at night, of course, do not simply go away during the daytime; the light from our sun is simply so blindingly bright that we can't see them.

On clear nights it's easy to believe that the heavens are carpeted with stars. But they're not, really. Scatter a couple dozen baseballs across the United States and you will have an idea of the emptiness of space.

A star is a fiery atomic furnace, and these massive balls of glowing gas shine by their own light. Stars, like humans, are born, live out their lives, and die. The ordinary star we call our sun is considered to be middle-aged, suitably bulging at the middle, with another five billion years to live before its atomic fuel runs out.

It's easy to confuse stars, which shine on their own, with planets such as earth, which shine by reflecting sunlight. (If the sun blinked out, so would all the planets.) Planets are either rocky balls, like earth, or giant balls of cold gas, like Jupiter. The thing we call our solar system is made up of the sun and all the objects that circle it: nine known planets, their moons, comets, asteroids, and meteors.

We will see different stars appear during each season of the year, and that is because our planet is revolving as it orbits the sun. During winter, for example, we will see the same stars in the same place at the same time as the previous winter.

Although stars are moving away from us at unbelievable speed, their positions in the sky will not change during the short life span of a human. (The stars you see tonight were seen by Julius Caesar). The light that reaches our eyes tonight from the supergiant star Rigel—which is 500 light years away and 20,000 times as bright as our mellow yellow sun—left that star before the birth of Columbus.

Stars are so incomprehensibly far away that astronomers calculate the distances in light years. A light year is the distance light trav-

SUMMER

AUG

els (at 186,282 miles per second) in one year. In that time, traveling at the speed of light, you would cover nearly six trillion earth miles (one trillion is a thousand billions). The nearest star to earth, aside from our sun, is Alpha Centauri, some 4.3 light years away. It would take Neil Zurcher in a One Tank Trip spaceship traveling at one million miles per hour about 2,882 earth years to reach Alpha Centauri (and the accommodations aren't that nice).

While the positions of distant stars are considered to be fixed in our sky, the relatively nearby planets continually move to new locations. (The word planet is from the Greek word meaning "wanderer.") To visualize this, imagine that you are riding a merry-go-round while eight of your friends are walking around the carousel. Each time you reach the same point in your ride the trees and buildings (stars) are exactly where they were before. Your friends (planets) have become scattered about the park (especially if they've had an argument).

Our five brother and sister planets that are visible with the naked eye are Venus, Mars, Jupiter, Saturn, and Mercury (faint, at best). At least one of the planets is visible every night; sometimes several are.

Although it seems as if the stars and planets are racing around the earth, that is an illusion. It is the earth that is turning—counterclockwise. If you face south, and are willing to invest half an hour of your time, you will notice that the stars are moving slowly from left to right (east to west). Once they have made it into the west they appear to dive toward the horizon, from upper left to lower right.

As recently as 1920, our universe was thought to be a single formation of stars. Since then, giant telescopes have shown that the cosmos is filled with cities of suns called galaxies. (Every star you see in the Northeast Ohio sky without the aid of a telescope is in the Milky Way galaxy). The Hubble Space Telescope, launched in April 1990, has revealed that there are at least 50 billion galaxies in the universe, and that each galaxy contains billions (perhaps trillions) of stars. Planet Earth is located at an obscure zip code on the edge of a spiraling arm of the Milky Way galaxy. We have no idea where the Milky Way is positioned in the firmament, because there may be no center to the universe.

The Milky Way is itself a spiral galaxy that is 100,000 light years across, which means it would take a spaceship traveling at the speed of light 100,000 years to get from one end to the other—and a light year is nearly six trillion earth miles. And that's just our galaxy. Altogether, there may be 100 billion galaxies in the universe, each containing some 100 billion stars. We are truly a mote in God's eye.

STARGAZING AT
NORTHEAST OHIO'S PLANETARIUMS

The following locations offer informative and entertaining programs on astronomy, identification of constellations, and general skywatching around Northeast Ohio. (Dates, times, and costs for programs vary, so please call ahead for information.)

Cleveland Museum of Natural History
Ralph Mueller Planetarium and Observatory
1 Wade Oval Drive (University Circle), Cleveland
(216) 231-4600; www.cmnh.org

The Cleveland Museum of Natural History offers programs each weekend throughout the year at the Mueller Planetarium, with special programs held daily during the summer and various holiday periods. The observatory is open to the public on Wednesday evenings from September through May.

Lake Erie Nature & Science Center
Schuele Planetarium
28728 Wolf Rd., Bay Village
(440) 871-2900

The Schuele Planetarium at the Lake Erie Nature & Science Center (located in the Cleveland Metroparks' Huntington Reservation) features an array of programs, usually held biweekly. Most of the shows are geared for family audiences or small children, so it's a great place to start piquing a youngster's interest in the science of astronomy and the wonders of the night sky. Special solstice programs and educational hikes for groups are also offered.

Cuyahoga Astronomical Association
Rocky River Nature Center
24000 Valley Pkwy., North Olmsted
(440) 779-9779 or (440) 734-6660

The Cuyahoga Astronomical Association, an amateur (but very active) astronomy club, meets at 8 p.m. on the second Monday of every month at the Rocky River Nature Center in the Cleveland Metroparks' Rocky River Reservation. It also hosts special programs at other Metroparks locations. All meetings and events are free and open to the public.

Astronomy Club of Akron
Portage Lakes State Park
5301 Manchester Rd., Akron
(330) 658-3125 (after 5 p.m.)

The Astronomy Club of Akron (ACA) operates out of the ACA Observatory at Portage Lakes State Park in Akron. Indoor and outdoor programs coordinated to astronomical events are held each month; bi-weekly programs are held during the summer. The observatory also holds a monthly open house in the wintertime. All events are free and open to the public.

SUMMER

AUG

SUMMER

AUG

A constellation is a grouping of stars that was given a name by ancient astronomers who believed that the star pattern resembled an animal, an object, or a mythical god or hero. Within constellations are smaller patterns that are called asterisms—the Big Dipper in the constellation Ursa Major (the Great Bear) is an example.

The most familiar cluster of them all, the Big Dipper, is the key to finding any star in the Northeast Ohio sky. For example, by drawing a line from the "pouring" side of the Dipper you are led to the North Star, Polaris. Polaris, which is also called the Pole Star, is important because it is almost always in the same place, and is almost exactly north (at our latitude the North Star appears about halfway up in the sky). All other stars revolve counterclockwise around the Pole Star once each day. While Polaris appears rather faint to us, that is only because it is four million billion miles away. Polaris is actually 1,600 times as bright as our sun, and the light we see left the star about 350 years ago.

For those who would like to learn more about the fascinating field of astronomy, there are two excellent monthly publications available at most bookstores: *Sky & Telescope* and *Astronomy*.

Don't be misled by the annual Christmastime scam that claims to—for a fee—name and certify a star for whomever you request. Grandma may be a stellar person, but stars can only be named, and authenticated, by the International Astronomical Union.

AND NOW FOR YOUR LOCAL FORECAST...

One thing that's certain about forecasting: the further ahead the forecast, the greater the chance it will be inaccurate. While temperature trends can often be deciphered up to five days in advance , detailed forecasts more than three days in advance are not reliable.

Today's forecast is the result of a never-ending series of events that begins early each morning with the liftoff of helium-filled weather (radiosonde) balloons, about five feet in circumference, across the United States and around the world. The balloon measurements are combined with surface weather observations taken every hour from nearly 300 National Weather Service sites in this country, along with reports from automated weather buoys and ships at sea, commercial airliners, satellites, and radar installations.

"LOOKS LIKE A NICE DAY."

SUMMER

AUG

Millions of bits of information are fed into Cray supercomputers at the National Meteorological Center at Camp Springs, Maryland. A master analysis of the weather across the nation will then appear. Computer-generated national and regional maps are then sent by satellite or modem to weather agencies throughout the United States.

The local weather forecaster will combine this data with current observations from his immediate locations, other "down weather" stations, knowledge of nearby ter-rain—and intuition—to come up with an estimate of what's ahead.

But even with all the exotic tools and instruments, the better weather forecasters will always take time to "look out the window." Or even open the window. The meteo-rologists at the NWS Headquarters at Silver Spring, Maryland, always knew when to take along their umbrellas. When there was a bak-ery across the street and the south-east wind filled the air with the scent of bread, fruit pies, and sticky buns, they knew that rain was on the way.

A weather balloon release.

SUMMER

AUG

GREAT BALLS OF FIRE

No reasonable scientific explanation exists for ball lightning, those fiery and rarely seen orbs that range in color from blue to purple, white, yellow, orange, and red. Because no electromagnetic, chemical, or nuclear theory explains the phenomenon, some scientists believe that when you see ball lightning you are looking into a world beyond our cosmos.

I've had a number of people ask if the ghostly illuminations that sometimes appear on the wings of aircraft in flight are ball lightning. This glow, also occasionally seen on the surfaces of airliners and sailing ships, is not ball lightning but St. Elmo's fire, a harmless electrical discharge that usually occurs before, or during the late phase of, a thunderstorm. (Although usually harmless, St. Elmo's fire may have caused the catastrophic explosion of the hydrogen-filled dirigible Hindenburg at Lakehurst, New Jersey, in 1937.)

I've never had a close encounter with ball lightning in my 40-some years of weather watching, but I have a large file of letters from those who have.

Ball lightning most often appears as a flaming sphere that ranges in size from a tennis ball to a basketball. These fireballs have the unearthly ability to pass directly through glass windows, like something out of a science fiction novel. Sometimes the fireballs disappear in a loud explosion, causing temporary deafness; at other times they silently dissipate. A strong, overpowering smell of sulfur often accompanies ball lightning.

A letter in my file from a woman in nearby Brooklyn relates an unforgettable experience. She had just inserted a macaroni casserole into the electrical oven when suddenly her eye caught the approach of a baseball-sized flaming red object on her right. She saw sparks, followed by a loud popping noise, and felt an uncomfortable pressure on her chest. There was an obvious odor of sulfur. At no time was thunder heard, and there were no electrical storms in the area. Elec-

SUMMER

AUG

tricity in the home was out for a half hour, yet no fuse was blown. The asbestos-insulated wiring to the stove had disintegrated.

Oh yes, one more thing. The macaroni casserole that had just been placed in the oven was cooked "just right" in the space of a few seconds.

With macabre humor, the pilot of a KC-97 Air Force tanker recalls one of his three encounters with ball lightning:

"We were over Elko, Nevada, and our aircraft was heavily loaded with jet fuel. St. Elmo's fire was dancing all around the windshield when a fireball, yellow-white in color, came through the glass and passed between me and my co-pilot. It went down the cabin passageway at a fast pace, skirted between the navigator and the engineer, and headed toward the rear of the aircraft. I waited for an explosion. Knowing it would be fed by a full load of JP-4 fuel onboard, I tried to concentrate on flying the aircraft.

"After approximately three seconds of amazingly quiet reaction by the crew members aft of the cabin, the boom operator in the rear compartment called on the interphone. In an excited voice he described the ball of fire that came through the cargo compartment, made a right-angle turn through the starboard window, danced out over the right wing, and rolled harmlessly off into the clouds.

"No noise accompanied the arrival or departure of the fireball."

I'm not aware of any poetry devoted to the fearsome ball lightning, but Longfellow penned this ode to St. Elmo's fire in *The Golden Legend*:

> *Last night I saw St. Elmo's stars,*
> *With their glittering lanterns all at play.*
> *On the tips of the masts and the tips of the spars,*
> *And I knew that we should have foul weather today.*

SUMMER

AUG

OHIO'S RAIN WIZARD

In 1891, 45-year-old Frank Melbourne of Canton proclaimed himself the "Rain Wizard of Ohio." The tall, dark-haired, bearded and charming Melbourne was a master psychologist and might well be called the godfather of all the rainmakers (or rain-fakers, as critics declared). Melbourne so convinced desperate and drought-stricken communities of his ability to coax rain from clouds that newspapers heralded his appearance with such banner headlines as the following: "He Is Coming!"; "The Most Wonderful Inventor Of The Century"; and "The Rain Doctor Reigns."

Melbourne, who was born in Ireland, spent 12 years in Australia and New Zealand before he showed up at his wealthy brother's doorstep in Canton in early 1891. His brother, John, refused to let him set up an experimental laboratory at his home, but a brother-in-law, who saw dollar signs dancing in the rain, allowed Frank the use of a shed. Only Frank and his brother, Will, would ever enter the shed, from which came, said witnesses, sounds like "rumbling, fluttering, and the buzzing of bees." Frank openly displayed a large revolver to preserve his privacy.

Melbourne bragged that when his technique was perfected he'd be able to make it rain in Death Valley. He said he was also working on a cold-wave machine that would bring summertime cool to large sections of the country. Melbourne added to his mystique by carrying several black satchels that never left his side, even when he dined.

Like all the meteorological confidence men, Melbourne was the consummate barnyard Barnum, using laws of averages and the realization that the longer a dry spell continued, the better the chance it would soon end.

Certain of his ability to milk the sky, in July of 1891 Melbourne assigned his brother the job of taking bets with Cantonians on whether or not it would rain on a particular day. Ohio skies are often juicy during July, and by the end of the month Melbourne had collected several thousand dollars from—as a Canton newspaper avowed—"the easily plucked, guileless gamblers."

SUMMER

AUG

After his extraordinary success in Ohio, Melbourne decided it was time to fleece the farmers in the arid Great Plains. Like all of the cloud squeezers, Melbourne offered his services on a can't-lose basis: $150 if it rains, nothing if it doesn't. Whenever Melbourne's efforts failed, he would always blame an uncooperative wind, yet he would accept credit for any rain that fell within 100 miles of his location.

> **C.W. Post, the American cereal magnate, became obsessedwith the idea that cannon firing could bring on rain.**

Melbourne's star blazed only briefly. As his increasing failures were publicized, the sky-milking offers dwindled. In 1894 the body of Frank Melbourne was found in a dingy Denver hotel room. The coroner ruled his death a suicide.

The 19th century has been called the Golden Age of Quackery. Itinerant peddlers spread out across the states in their wagons, selling their patent medicines, Kickapoo Indian elixirs, and snake-oil cures.

Standard equipment for the rainmakers was a pipe attached to an often-concealed apparatus. From the pipe would come evil-smelling gases that people guessed were a mix of muriatic acid, powdered bat's wing, eye of newt, and an assortment of chemicals. Observers said the smell often resembled Limburger cheese and that the clouds would rain out of self-defense.

"Professor" M. Smithson Ames must have been a particularly arresting sight—a lanky, Lincolnesque character with shaggy hair and tobacco-stained teeth who drove around with a huge cannon tied to the back of his wagon.

Over the centuries it had been observed that heavy rains often fell after heated battles. It was imagined that the explosion of gunpowder and the shouts of the adversaries triggered rain. C. W. Post, the American cereal magnate, became obsessed with the idea that cannon firing could bring on rain. In 1911, Post and his employees embarked on an explosive—and expensive—campaign of cannonading passing clouds, both at his sprawling 2,000-acre Texas ranch and on his estate at Battle Creek, Michigan. After one seemingly successful bombardment in Michigan, Post was crestfallen when he learned that it had rained that day all the way from the Pacific coast through the Great Lakes.

Aside from irritating his neighbors, Post succeeded only in thinning out the local bird population. In 1914, disillusioned and despondent, the multimillionaire shot himself.

The most famous of all the American rainmakers was Charles Mallory Hatfield of San Diego, who, at the age of 29, gave up selling sewing machines and announced to the world that he had solved the mystery of controlling the celestial spigot. Hatfield, who quit school after the ninth grade, had no formal weather training yet used the title "professor" when he lectured. Described as "cagey and sincere with a curious smile," Hatfield was a student of climatological averages and achieved notoriety when he claimed credit for washing out three miles of the Southern Pacific railroad track in the Mojave Desert.

In December of 1915, during a severe southern-California drought, Hatfield made what he claimed was a verbal agreement with the San Diego city council to fill the nearly dry Moreno Dam some 60 miles to the east. In January of 1916, Hatfield, assisted by his brothers, Joel and Paul, began to invoke his rain-making "expertise." So much rain fell that the Moreno reservoir burst, resulting in a flood that caused $3.5 million in damage and killed a number of people. (Rumor had it that Charley and one of his brothers were last seen riding on horseback into the desert toward Yuma, but they actually walked the 60 miles back to San Diego on foot.)

The event, forever immortalized as "Hatfield's Flood," could, of course, never be pinned on Charley. When Hatfield demanded his fee of $10,000 for filling the dam, city council responded that they would gladly pay if Hatfield would cough up the $3.5 million in damages (the last claim was not settled until 1938). Hatfield, whose story has been told—and embellished—in several movies and television presentations, retired to Glendale, California, where he died in 1958.

The "Tulsa Rainmaker" explains how he caused a million-dollar flood in Oklahoma in 1963.

Autumn

MANY OHIOANS CALL EARLY AUTUMN THEIR FAVORITE TIME OF THE YEAR. SEPTEMBER IS USUALLY A PLEASANTLY WARM MONTH WITH MILD DAYS FOLLOWED BY REFRESHINGLY COOL NIGHTS. THIS EARLY FALL PERIOD, WITH ITS LIGHT WINDS, BRINGS A SERIES OF SUNNY, OFTEN HAZY DAYS.

The first killing frosts of autumn will visit Ohio anywhere from early October to early November. Any late-September glaze is usually confined to the low-lying portions of the state, the traditional icebox locations such as Pandora in Putnam County, Vienna in Trumbull County, and Robertsville in Stark County.

The phrase "October is Ohio" has been used in praise of our first full month of autumn. Under dramatic skies the summer green steadily fades from tree leaves during October and their brilliance lights up the land.

The sumacs, as usual, make the first announcement as they change into their red-bronze autumn finery. By the end of September the maples, show-offs of the forest, are resplendent in their peacock wardrobe of yellows, oranges, and reds. The color display in Ohio usually peaks in the northern counties of the state during the second and third weeks of October, with show time in southern Ohio the following two weeks.

Ohio's Delaware Indians knew nothing of the biological time clock in trees; they attributed the change in leaf color to the slaying of the Great Bear by celestial hunters. Blood fell on some trees, went the tribal legend, turning them red.

The first snow of the season, most often in the form of hard snow grains, or soft snow pellets, falls over the northeastern counties about the third week in October. Sharp cold fronts in October are often followed by several days of

> **CLEVELAND'S WARMEST AND COLDEST AUTUMNS (MEDIAN TEMPERATURE)**
>
> Warmest: 59.8°/1931
> Coldest: 47.6°/1976

moderating temperatures and calm weather. In some years a brief period of unseasonably warm, sunny and hazy weather embraces

AUTUMN

Ohio after the first killing frosts in October. This is invariably called "Indian Summer," but there is no official rule for its occurrence. The American Indians did not recognize any such season, it was not a part of their lore.

November begins a new chapter in the Ohio weather story: the cold fronts are increasingly colder and more vigorous. November also brings the "cloud season" to the northeastern quarter of Ohio. Cold Canadian air crossing the still-warm waters of Lake Erie picks up water vapor that quickly condenses into a thick stratocumulus cloud layer upon reaching land.

When Lake Erie is ice-covered in mid- to late winter, the lake-effect cloudiness is reduced dramatically. This also reduces the potential for lake-induced snowfall, although usually unfrozen Lake Huron, just to the north, continues to supply water vapor.

The first heavy snows of the season can be expected over the extreme northeastern counties of Ohio by mid- to late November. Snow bursts of one foot or more are not uncommon under sustained and gusty west-to-northwest winds across Lake Erie. This lake-effect snow causes heavy accumulations over the high-ground snowbelt regions east and southeast of Cleveland. The primary snowbelt is in Lake, Geauga, and Ashtabula counties, and the eastern portion of Cuyahoga County.

A secondary snowbelt susceptible to a more northerly air flow across Lake Erie lies over southern Cuyahoga County, southern Lorain County, Medina County, northern Summit County, northern Portage County, and northern Trumbull County.

A term frequently used by Northeast Ohio weather forecasters is "heavier amounts in the snowbelt," because judging lake-effect snowfall is so very difficult. Even within the snowbelts, accumulations vary to wide extremes. I recall one incident when no snow fell along the shoreline just east of Cleveland in Euclid, while 19 inches piled up just one mile to the south.

Lake Erie's water temperature retreats through the 60s during September, into the 50s in October, and down to the 40s during November.

CLEVELAND'S TOP 5 WETTEST AND DRIEST AUTUMNS (LIQUID)

Wettest

1) 20.73" / 1996
2) 18.41" / 1926
3) 17.71" / 1878
4) 14.47" / 1890
5) 14.30" / 1985

Driest

1) 2.37" / 1908
2) 3.44" / 1964
3) 3.55" / 1956
4) 3.76" / 1871
5) 3.94" / 1899

AUTUMN

IN THE NORTHEAST OHIO SKY THIS SEASON

While mid-August is great for watching shooting stars (which, of course, are not really stars, but meteors), it is the poorest season for real star watching. You'll need your Clark Kent eyes; stars in the autumn sky are faint and subtle.

Mythology tells us that Queen Cassiopeia (KASS-ee-oh-PEE-ah) was punished for her vain boasting by being placed forever in the heavens. Cassiopeia makes her regal appearance (as a lazy "W") with her much fainter consort, King Cepheus (SEE-fee-us). (She wants it that way.)

If you use your imagination, the legendary winged horse of mythology, Pegasus (PEG-uh-suss), can be seen galloping across the firmament.

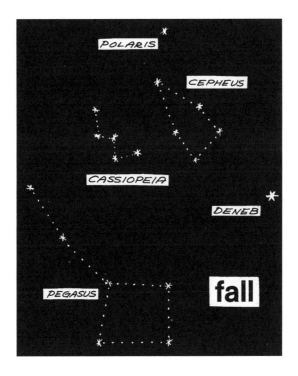

AUTUMN

AUTUMN

SUNSHINE %: 60
DRIEST MONTH: 0.48"/1908
WARMEST MONTH: 72.4°/1881
COLDEST MONTH: 58.2°/1918
LIQUID PCPN AVG.: 3.44"
RAINIEST DAY: 5.24"/1996
RAINIEST MONTH: 11.05"/1996
THUNDERY DAYS: 3
SNOWIEST DAY: Trace/1993
DAYS ONE INCH SNOW: 0

A magnificent, yet melancholy, sight as this month goes by is the southward migration of those big and beautiful orange, black, and white monarch butterflies. One of the few insects to migrate (Ohio's green darner dragonfly is another), the fragile monarchs are known to fly 50 miles every day, sometimes up to 200 miles if a blustery cold front cooperates. This incredible odyssey will take the butterflies some 3,000 miles from Ohio, to such exotic places as Mexico's Quintana Roo (on the Yucatan Peninsula), a place they have never been. The departure of the monarch and the green darner, as much as the migration of birds, foretells the early-morning frosts that are just ahead. The autumnal equinox (from Latin meaning "equal night") occurs around the 22nd. At the equinox each place on earth shares in 12 hours of darkness and 12 hours of light, and with the diminishing duration of sunlight, temperatures of 85° are seldom experienced after the 15th of the month. September did establish a Cleveland benchmark for extreme heat in 1953, when the high temperature on each of the first three days of the month hit a sizzling 101°F. September 24, 1950, will forever be remembered as Dark Sunday throughout Ohio. The cause was ash and smoke from a major forest fire in Canada's Alberta province. September 29th is St. Michael's Day; folklore says that if there has been a heavy fall of acorns (mast), a very hard, cold winter is ahead.

Day	Hi	Lo	Rec Hi	Rec Lo	Sunrise	Sunset	Lake°
1	78	58	101 / 1953	42 / 1970	6:53	8:02	73
2	78	58	101 / 1953	45 / 1970	6:54	7:59	73
3	77	58	101 / 1953	44 / 1976	6:55	7:58	73
4	77	57	95 / 1953	41 / 1946	6:56	7:56	72
5	77	57	99 / 1954	44 / 1974	6:57	7:54	72
6	77	57	98 / 1954	40 / 1976	6:58	7:53	72
7	76	57	94 / 1939	43 / 1962	6:59	7:51	72
8	76	57	95 / 1978	41 / 1951	7:00	7:49	72
9	76	56	94 / 1959	44 / 1986	7:01	7:47	72
10	75	56	93 / 1964	39 / 1883	7:02	7:45	72
11	75	56	92 / 1952	42 / 1995	7:03	7:44	72
12	75	56	98 / 1952	40 / 1943	7:04	7:42	72
13	75	55	96 / 1952	38 / 1964	7:05	7:41	72
14	74	55	94 / 1939	37 / 1975	7:06	7:39	71
15	74	55	93 / 1991	37 / 1871	7:07	7:37	71
16	74	54	96 / 1944	45 / 1979	7:08	7:36	71
17	73	54	95 / 1955	37 / 1984	7:09	7:34	70
18	73	54	94 / 1955	39 / 1959	7:10	7:32	70
19	73	53	93 / 1955	40 / 1973	7:11	7:30	70
20	72	53	92 / 1978	40 / 1956	7:12	7:29	70
21	72	53	90 / 1931	35 / 1956	7:13	7:27	69
22	72	52	92 / 1895	36 / 1904	7:14	7:25	69
23	71	52	88 / 1936	36 / 1995	7:15	7:23	69
24	71	52	87 / 1941	36 / 1995	7:16	7:22	69
25	70	51	88 / 1900	35 / 1976	7:18	7:20	68
26	70	51	89 / 1908	37 / 1947	7:19	7:18	68
27	70	51	88 / 1946	33 / 1947	7:20	7:17	68
28	69	50	89 / 1949	34 / 1984	7:21	7:15	68
29	69	50	95 / 1953	32 / 1942	7:22	7:13	67
30	69	49	86 / 1881	35 / 1963	7:23	7:12	67

*The best way to destroy an enemy
is to make him into a friend.*
– ANONYMOUS

PRESSURES OF THE JOB:
HIGH & LOW PRESSURE, WEATHER FRONTS

In an unending game of catch-me-if-you-can, high pressure chases low pressure and fronts across the weather map. Making sense out of the symbols is less difficult than it may seem.

On a weather map the letter *H* stands for high pressure, or heavy air, and might be visualized as the peak of an atmospheric air mountain. In high pressure the air gradually sinks, piles up, and warms by compression. This causes the air to dry out and clouds to disappear through evaporation.

The letter *L* represents low pressure, or light air, and can be visualized as a valley. In low pressure the air rises and cools. As the cooling continues, the invisible water vapor condenses into clouds and precipitation often occurs.

There is not any one pressure, or barometric setting, that determines what is a high- or low-pressure center. Pressure is relative. There are massive regions of high pressure and there are small high-pressure systems. There are deep caverns of atmospheric low pressure and there are slight depressions, or dimples.

A weather front —the colored line you see on weather maps—is the relatively narrow battle zone that separates air mountains (air masses) that have contrasting temperatures and moisture content. You can often pick out weather fronts by the long, curving white swirls of clouds on satellite photographs.

AUTUMN

SEP

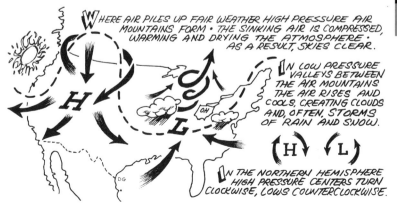

It is important to know where the air masses originate.

Three weeks ago a molecule of air you are now breathing may have floated under the Eiffel Tower in Paris. A week later it may have been swept over the Great Wall of China, before wafting past the orchid-filled Island of Hawaii on its way across the Rocky Mountains and into Ohio. It has been estimated that such a molecular globe-circling odyssey takes about 28 days.

The places where air masses form are known as source regions. The air mass itself—often more than a thousand miles across—is a body of air whose temperature and moisture at the same horizontal level are nearly uniform (homogeneous). These air masses are represented by the high-pressure regions you see wandering across the daily weather map.

An air mass can form over either land or water, and there are certain places on earth where these high-pressure cells are most likely to be born. When an air mass develops over land it is called continental and is designated with the small letter *c*. An air mass that forms over water is labeled maritime and is designated by the small letter *m*. Air whose birthplace is a polar region is classified with a capital *P,* while tropical air is identified by a capital *T.*

Air that has formed over water is milder than the air that has developed over land surfaces. That is because the energy from the sun penetrates the earth's soil surfaces to a depth of only a few inches but goes to a depth of 75 feet or more in the oceans. Places on earth that have a maritime climate experience only a moderate rise and fall of temperatures over the seasons. Locations that have a continental climate have wide extremes of heat and cold over the course of a year.

As an air mass travels across the earth, it gradually takes on the characteristics of the surface over which it is moving. For example, a frigid wintertime air mass that spirals southward from northern Canada will gradually be warmed as it crosses the United States. This is due primarily to the longer daylight at the more southern latitudes.

AUTUMN

SEP

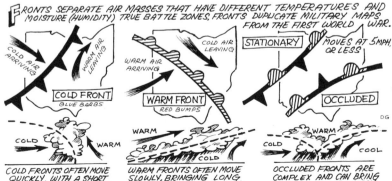

FRONTS SEPARATE AIR MASSES THAT HAVE DIFFERENT TEMPERATURES AND MOISTURE (HUMIDITY) TRUE BATTLE ZONES, FRONTS DUPLICATE MILITARY MAPS FROM THE FIRST WORLD WAR.

COLD AIR ARRIVING — WARM AIR LEAVING

STATIONARY — MOVES AT 5MPH OR LESS

COLD AIR LEAVING — WARM AIR ARRIVING

COLD FRONT BLUE BARBS

WARM FRONT RED BUMPS

OCCLUDED

COLD — WARM

WARM — COLD

WARM — COOL

DG

COLD FRONTS OFTEN MOVE QUICKLY, WITH A SHORT BURST OF RAIN OR SNOW.

WARM FRONTS OFTEN MOVE SLOWLY, BRINGING LONG PERIODS OF RAIN OR SNOW.

OCCLUDED FRONTS ARE COMPLEX AND CAN BRING HEAVY PRECIPITATION.

Conversely, a summertime air mass that forms over the Gulf of Mexico will lose its tropical personality—in terms of both temperature and moisture—as it pushes northward into the United States and eastern Canada.

The continual flow of air masses moving southward from polar regions and tropical air surging northward from the equator results in the unending formation of weather fronts between the dissimilar air masses.

Most of the continental polar air that reaches Ohio (and the rest of the United States) comes from the portion of the North American continent near the Arctic Circle and North Pole. In winter, icy air in the deep, nearly sunless valleys of Alaska and the Canadian Klondike begins to pile up and the pressure rises. Eventually the air flow aloft will pry the mountain of bitterly cold air loose and send it spiraling south and east into the United States.

Such an air mass in the heart of winter can create a blizzard along its leading edge (frontal boundary) and bring life-threatening coldness. It will be days, sometimes weeks, before the arctic air loses its original characteristics.

While the arrival of a continual polar air mass in winter is a daunting, chilling experience, the arrival of the same type of air mass in the heat of a Buckeye summer is as welcome as the first daisy of spring.

An air mass will gradually evolve into a clockwise spinning high-pressure cell in the northern hemisphere. Air flows from high pressure into low pressure, but not in a straight line, because the rotation of the earth twists the flow to the right (this is called the Coriolis force). The air being dragged across the rough surface of the earth also adds friction. The illustration shows the effect of all these factors.

Because of the clockwise flow of air around high-pressure centers, they are given the name anticyclone. High-pressure regions usually bring fair weather.

Between high-pressure systems you will find a front, a zone of discontinu-

ity, that separates the two contrasting air masses. It is along these lines of low pressure that individual low-pressure centers often develop. West of the low-pressure center, cold air is drawn southward; east of the low-pressure center, warm air is pushed northward. The weather around a low-pressure center and along a front is often unsettled and sometimes stormy. This is because the two contrasting air masses do not mix, and the rising air in low pressure foments clouds and precipitation.

The air flows counterclockwise around a low-pressure center, and this system is called a cyclone. (At one time tornadoes over parts of the Midwest were referred to as cyclones, but that is a misnomer.)

You will occasionally hear the words "ridge" and "trough" used by meteorologists. A ridge is simply an elongated, stretched-out region of high pressure. A trough is a relatively narrow, stretched-out zone of low pressure.

> **The weather around a low-pressure center and along a front is often unsettled and stormy.**

A frontal wave is an undulation, much like a wave in the ocean, that moves from west to east along a nearly stationary front.

There are two things to remember about the battle lines called fronts: (1) fronts always form between differing air masses; and (2) fronts are peripheral to adjacent high-pressure systems.

When a front is forming, the process is known as frontogenesis. A front that is weakening and breaking down is undergoing frontolysis.

The frontal surface separating air masses is not vertical but sloping. Fronts are usually several hundred miles long, and their influence extends into the upper portion of the troposphere. There are four types of weather fronts to consider: warm, cold, occluded, and stationary. With few exceptions, a front is found along a low-pressure trough or depression, and it is for that reason that pressure falls as a front approaches and rises as the front moves away.

COLD FRONT: On the weather map the cold front is drawn in dark blue with triangular points along its length. The cold front means that the air coming in is colder than the air it is replacing. The cold front can be visualized as a snowplow lifting and replacing the warmer and lighter air. The uplifting causes the warm air to cool through adiabatical expansion (the natural rate of temperature decrease with altitude), and it loses its capacity to hold its invisible water vapor. Clouds form and precipitation often follows. Precipitation along a cold front may be light or heavy, but it is usually of short duration. A rapidly moving cold front may produce thunderstorms far ahead of its intersection with the earth's surface.

AUTUMN

SEP

Cold fronts advance at speeds of 20 to 25 mph, although they are often faster in winter and slower in summer, because cold air is so much heavier and exerts more pressure. The slope of the cold front can extend for several hundred miles, and the steepness of the advancing edge usually produces clouds and precipitation in a narrow band. The more violent the uplifting of the air along a cold front, the higher the probability for storm development.

A storm complex known as a thunderstorm squall line may form 100 to 150 miles ahead of a rapidly advancing cold front, especially in spring and summer. A squall line may be continuous for 100 or more miles, but there are often quiet-weather breaks along the line. Rainfall is often heavy just behind the leading edge of the squall line.

On the United States weather map, cold fronts are almost always on a northeast-to-southwest axis and move from west to east.

Not all cold fronts (or warm fronts) bring clouds and precipitation. Some are so weak that they will go by with little noticeable change in temperature or humidity, with only a wind shift to mark their passage.

WARM FRONT: A warm front is drawn in red on weather maps, with semicircles along its length. A warm front tells you that the air coming in is warmer than the air it is replacing. Warm fronts move at about half the speed of cold fronts, often at 5 to 15 mph. Unlike the snowplow effect of the cold front, the warmer, lighter air overrides the heavier cold air with a much gentler vertical slope. This happens because the lower levels of the retreating cold air are slowed by friction with the earth's surface. A slim wedge results. Unlike the cold front, the warm front signals its approach far in advance of its intersection at the earth's surface. The first high cloudiness ahead of a warm front may precede the frontal surface boundary by hundreds of miles. Clouds and precipitation form along the line of vertical contact between the warm and cold air, and, as a result, warm frontal rain and snow can be lengthy. A slow-moving warm front can bring days of gloomy, wet weather.

OCCLUDED FRONT: An occluded front occurs when a cold front overtakes a warm front and lifts it off the ground. Rain is often heavy where this battle is waged. The occluded front is drawn in purple on maps with alternating triangles and semicircles on the same side of the line.

STATIONARY FRONT: The stationary or nearly stationary front is a battle line that has shown little or no movement in a six-hour period. On the weather map, a stationary front is drawn with alternating cold- and warm-front symbols closely spaced.

AUTUMN

SEP

DARK SUNDAY

On September 24, 1950, more than one resident of Northeast Ohio thought that the end of the world was near. The strange event seemed so supernatural that it stopped our usual Sunday afternoon pickup football game at Greensburg High. (Even back then it took a lot to impress teenagers.)

The morning dawned cool and dry, but the early brightness was soon blotted out by an increasingly dark and eerie atmosphere. It appeared that a storm of biblical proportions was about to strike— yet no storm ever came.

The clouds that stretched from one end of the horizon to the other were strikingly beautiful, streaked with yellow, orange, copper, and brassy hues. The clouds were in continual, billowing movement. A tornado was certainly coming.

As the day drew on, the sky grew darker and temperatures continued to go in reverse, chilling down through the 40s. Chickens went to roost early in the afternoon. Wild birds that are active only at night began their hooting. The afternoon baseball game between the Cleveland Indians and Detroit Tigers at Municipal Stadium became a night game as the lights blazed away. Landing lights at Cleveland Hopkins Airport were ordered on at midday.

Television was in its diaper years and local news bulletin break-ins were rare. Radio was still the primary news source, and the chief of the Weather Bureau, George Andrus, was called upon for numerous broadcast reassurances, even though the chief himself must have been whistling in the dark. Weather office phone lines were jammed.

It was the next day before any official agency was able to solve the mystery of Ohio's midnight at midday: forest fires raging across the Canadian province of Alberta had sent a gigantic cloud of fine wood ash adrift in the wind flow aloft. Canadian officials estimated the black smoke cloud to be 400 miles long, 200 miles wide, and some 3 miles in thickness. The ominous cloud moved from the upper Midwest into Ohio and then on to New York State. Several days later it drifted over England and Scotland, causing a "blue sun."

On the evening of the 24th, churches across Northeast Ohio had a sudden surge of worshipers. But by Monday morning, with the day of reckoning safely past and the meteorological mystery solved, everything was back to normal.

As the old adage goes, "Once on shore, we pray no more."

AUTUMN

SEP

WEATHER FOLKLORE

In many early religions, weather held a vital place, and it was the task of the tribal priest or wizard to determine the ideal time to plant and harvest.

It was for the same very practical reasons that American colonists and pioneers closely observed the weather and nature. Living in an agrarian society, they were constantly at the mercy of crop-killing droughts and unseasonable freezes. (Diaries from 1816 lamented the bitterly cold "Year Without a Summer.")

Visible weather events and circumstances were keenly remembered, and if they were repeated often enough, the signs became rules. Thus began the art of folklore forecasting.

Those who were most affected by the weather, especially farmers and sailors, often put their meteorological observations into easily remembered sayings or proverbs, and these adages were then handed down from generation to generation. Although no weather proverb has been given the American Meteorological Society's Seal of Approval, that is not because they have no degree of accuracy. It is that the sayings are not always true at all times in all places.

Weather lore—including sayings or adages—runs the gamut from common sense to misconception to superstition to wishful thinking. There are no infallible weather signs, and those that have a reasonably high percentage of accuracy have a scientific basis.

Sky color has long been recognized as a portent of weather change, and the most famous weather rhyme of them all is related to the color red.

This familiar proverb, which appears in the Bible (in Matthew, Chapter 16) and relates to a shepherd, is now most often heard in the following nautical couplet:

AUTUMN

SEP

> *Red sky at dawning, sailor take warning;*
> *Red sky at night, sailor delight.*

Because the wavelength of the color red is best able to penetrate a very dry and dusty atmosphere, that color has long been associated with fair weather. A red horizon in the evening tells you that a layer of dry, dusty air lies to the west. Considering the general west-to-east movement of weather at this latitude, this suggests that the air currently to the west will be overhead the next day, bringing fair skies. The other portion of the forecast is not as accurate, however, as the red sky at sunrise implies that the dry air has already passed by, which may not be so.

The color gray indicates there is a considerable quantity of water droplets suspended in the air, and there's a good chance that the tiny droplets will eventually grow large enough for gravity to pull them down:

> *Evening red and morning gray*
> *help the traveler on his way;*
> *Evening gray and morning red*
> *bring down the rain upon his head.*

There's an interesting rhyme that dates from pioneer days regarding the color of lightning in a thunderstorm:

> *Yaller gal, yaller gal, flashing*
> *through the night,*
> *Thunderstorms will pass you by, unless*
> *the color's white.*

There is some validity to the observation that yellowish lightning will never reach you, but white lightning will. The more distant the lightning, the better the chance that particles in the air will give the flash a yellow tint.

To the folklore forecaster, a golden amber sky at sunset foretells a windy day, but no rain. A pale yellow sky at sunset, however, warns of rain the next day.

On rare occasions the color green can be seen at the start of a sunrise or sunset. It is a brilliant and beautiful green ray that lasts for only an instant, and it's considered a good luck omen in many cultures. To the Scottish Highlander, just one fleeting glimpse of the green ray guarantees that you will never be deceived in love.

Winter-weather folklore forecasts are the most numerous and the most enduring. Even today these autumnal signs have their advocates and involve such disparate things as the thickness of the hair on animals and the abundance of acorns. In reality, a thick coat on a critter is most likely telling you that the animal is in good health, while a proliferation of acorns in September testifies to adequate rainfall during the growing season.

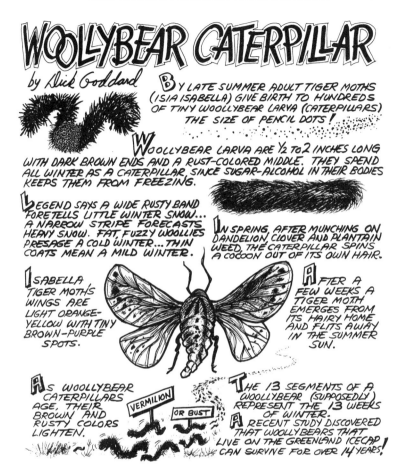

WOOLLYBEAR CATERPILLAR
by Dick Goddard

BY LATE SUMMER ADULT TIGER MOTHS (ISIA ISABELLA) GIVE BIRTH TO HUNDREDS OF TINY WOOLLYBEAR LARVA (CATERPILLARS) THE SIZE OF PENCIL DOTS!

WOOLLYBEAR LARVA ARE ½ TO 2 INCHES LONG WITH DARK BROWN ENDS AND A RUST-COLORED MIDDLE. THEY SPEND ALL WINTER AS A CATERPILLAR, SINCE SUGAR-ALCOHOL IN THEIR BODIES KEEPS THEM FROM FREEZING.

LEGEND SAYS A WIDE RUSTY BAND FORETELLS LITTLE WINTER SNOW... A NARROW STRIPE FORECASTS HEAVY SNOW. FAT, FUZZY WOOLLIES PRESAGE A COLD WINTER... THIN COATS MEAN A MILD WINTER.

IN SPRING, AFTER MUNCHING ON DANDELION, CLOVER AND PLANTAIN WEED, THE CATERPILLAR SPINS A COCOON OUT OF ITS OWN HAIR.

ISABELLA TIGER MOTH'S WINGS ARE LIGHT ORANGE-YELLOW WITH TINY BROWN-PURPLE SPOTS.

AFTER A FEW WEEKS A TIGER MOTH EMERGES FROM ITS HAIRY HOME AND FLITS AWAY IN THE SUMMER SUN.

AS WOOLLYBEAR CATERPILLARS AGE, THEIR BROWN AND RUSTY COLORS LIGHTEN.

VERMILION OR BUST

THE 13 SEGMENTS OF A WOOLLYBEAR (SUPPOSEDLY) REPRESENT THE 13 WEEKS OF WINTER. A RECENT STUDY DISCOVERED THAT WOOLLYBEARS THAT LIVE ON THE GREENLAND ICECAP CAN SURVIVE FOR OVER 14 YEARS!

It is here that I must plead guilty—and I request charitable treatment by the American Meteorological Society. Since my early days on television I have, tongue-in-cheek, publicized the woollybear caterpillar as a winter-weather forecast prophet. The woollybear is a dark-brown caterpillar with a lighter, rust-colored band around the middle. Legend says that if the dark ends crowd the rusty ring into a narrow band, a snowy winter lies ahead. If the rusty ring is wide and the dark-brown bands at each end are small, a snow-free winter is coming up.

Woollybears that are fat and fuzzy in autumn supposedly warn of a very cold winter, while the more hairless larvae presage a mild winter. The woollybear caterpillar has 13 segments, and folklorists who are true believers go so far as to say that they represent each week of the winter season.

If contemplating a caterpillar doesn't tweak your interest, here is an assortment of weather signs that legend says portend a hard and snowy winter:

Thicker than normal corn husks or onion skins

Woodpeckers sharing a tree

Early arrival of the snowy owl in autumn

Early migration of the monarch butterfly

Thick hair on the nape (back) of a cow's neck

Heavy and numerous fogs in August

Raccoons with thick tails and bright bands

Mice eating their way ravenously into the home

Early arrival of crickets on the hearth

Spiders spinning larger-than-normal webs

Pigs gathering sticks

Muskrats burrowing holes high on a river bank

Unusually abundant crop of acorns

Squirrels hyperactively gathering nuts in autumn and burying them near the surface of the soil

The weather lore of the American Indian was extensive, but much of the wisdom was recorded by pictographs on birch bark and animal hide. Unfortunately, when the bark and hide deteriorated the lore was lost to history.

Rain was welcomed by most Indians, because they preferred to hunt when the ground was wet and the tracks left by game were much easier to see. Without realizing the scientific reason, the Indian shaman often used a scalp as an indicator of rain. The shaman, or medicine man, probably knew the effect of moisture on human hair: "When locks grow (lengthen) in the scalp house, rain soon will come." Hair that shortened and curled told the shaman that dry weather would continue.

To the American Indian it was "Mother Earth" and "Father Sky," and in their continual observation of the heavens they gave names to the full moon of each month, names which often carried a meteorological significance. Each tribe had its own moon calendar, but here are some of the more common names:

January:	Snow Moon	**July:**	Thunder Moon
February:	Cold Moon	**August:**	Corn (Maize) Moon
March:	Awakening Moon	**September:**	Cool (Harvest) Moon
April:	Grass Moon	**October:**	Hunting Moon
May:	Flower Moon	**November:**	First Snow Moon
June:	Hot Moon	**December:**	Long Night Moon

The behavior of insects has long been recognized as a barometer of weather change. In the thinning air before a storm they fly lower, and, as any fisherman will tell you, they bite and sting more frequently. An hour or so before the storm arrives, they stop flying altogether. Nearly all insects become inactive and silent at temperatures under 40° F and over 105° F.

The black field cricket is an excellent summertime thermometer. Count the number of chirps in 14 seconds, add the number 40, and you'll have the temperature (in Fahrenheit, not centipede).

At a temperature of 80° the katydid sings its full song, "kay-tee-did-it." With the temperature at 74° the little green hopper will only give you a "kay-tee-didn't." At 66° the aria is reduced to "kay-didn't" and it's only "kay-tee" at 62°. Temperatures in the upper 50s will result in a timid "kay."

While we have not been able to verify the unfailing ability of flora or fauna to forecast the weather, we would be much poorer if we neglected the kernels of truth that lie within our wealth of folklore.

AUTUMN

SEP

It's often easy to confuse fact with fancy, but here are some of the more popular rhymes or jingles that have some scientific merit:

Ring around the sun or moon,
Expect the earth to puddle soon.

A ring or halo around the sun or moon is caused by sunlight or moonlight being bent, or refracted, as it passes through an ice crystal cloud called a cirrostratus. This type of cloud frequently appears in advance of a warm front, which often brings rain or snow within 12 to 18 hours after the ring appears. The larger and brighter the ring, the higher the probability for precipitation.

When the wind is in the east,
'Tis neither good for man nor beast.

South and east winds often precede a storm center that brings foul weather. North and west winds usually produce clearing skies and fair weather.

Cow's tail to the west, the weather's the best.
Cow's tail to the east, the weather's the beast.

An animal grazes with its tail to the wind. This allows it to scent a predator from one direction and see it from the other direction. Remember, easterly winds often bring foul weather, westerly winds carry fair weather.

When the glass falls low,
Prepare for a blow;
When it rises high,
Let your kites fly.

A falling barometer (glass) foretells an approaching storm. A rising barometer indicates clearing skies.

Near the surface quick to bite,
Catch your fish when rain's in sight.

Fish tend to bite more readily before a storm than after, when the water becomes roiled.

When teeth and bone and bunions ache,
Expect the clouds to fill the lake.

Within our bodies there is a certain level of pressure. When atmospheric pressure lowers (ahead of a storm) our body pressure expands, causing sensitive areas to swell and hurt.

When ditch and pond offend the nose,
Look for rain and stormy blows.

Low, or light, air pressure that accompanies a storm releases ground odors that had been held against the earth by high, heavy air pressure.

The sharper the blast,
The sooner it's past.

A sudden, unannounced storm often ends just as quickly. A storm long foretold is slow to pass.

It's a sign of rain or snow
When birds and bats fly low.

The thinning air that precedes a storm makes it more difficult for winged creatures to fly. They tend to stay nearer the ground.

When soot begins to fall,
The weather soon will squall.

AUTUMN

Chimney soot that had been held in place by high air pressure becomes loose and falls as the air pressure lowers. Chimneys were the barometers of the early American home.

SEP

When dew is on the grass,
Rain will never come to pass.

Heavy dew at night will occur under a clear sky. Rain is unlikely the following day.

Trace in the sky the painter's brush,
The winds around you soon will rush.

When wispy, featherlike cirrus clouds give way to lower and heavier clouds, rain or snow frequently follows.

When clouds appear like rocks and towers,
The earth's refreshed by frequent showers.

In summer towering cumulus (cotton ball) clouds regularly build into afternoon rain showers.

When high clouds and low clouds
do not march together,
Prepare for a blow
and a change in the weather.

Clouds moving in different directions signal the advance of a turbulent storm center or weather front.

Pimpernel, pimpernel tell me yet,
Whether the weather be dry or wet.

The pimpernel plant closes its petals when the humidity nears 80 percent. Such high, or rising, humidity often precedes rain.

When bees to distance wing their flight
Days are warm and skies are bright.
But when their flight ends near their home,
Stormy weather is sure to come.

The honeybee is an excellent forecaster. Sensing the rising humidity before a storm, the bee stays close to its hive until the threat has passed.

AUTUMN

SEP

METRICIZING AMERICA

Canada changed to the metric system of measurements in 1974 and survived. Public opinion in the United States has kept this country one of the few in the world that does not embrace the simple system based on the number 10.

Passion against the metric system runs so deep that whenever the American National Metric Council meets they are confronted by members of WAM ("We're Against Metric"). Pro-metric folks say their system is so much easier to understand; WAM counters by saying we've done just fine with what we've got.

The metric system is based on the powers of 10, and you change from one unit to another by multiplying or dividing by that number, requiring no more than a moment of mental mathematics.

Advocates of metrics are quick to point out the absurdities that conspired to determine the old English units of measurement we still accept. For example:

THE FOOT was determined by the length of King Charlemagne's foot and modified in 1305 to equal 36 barleycorns laid end to end. (How big is a barleycorn?)

THE INCH was the width of King Edgar's thumb. (His majesty evidently did not do a lot of bowling.)

THE YARD was the distance from King Henry I's nose to his fingertips.

THE MILE came to us from the Roman legion and was the distance covered by 1,000 double steps.

THE ACRE was the amount of land a pair of oxen could plow before they had to rest.

THE SIX-FOOT FATHOM equaled the span of a Viking's outstretched arms.

THE GALLON we use filled Queen Anne's wine container, which was much smaller than the ale gallon and differed entirely from the imperial gallon that was later set as the British standard.

A valid complaint of the holdouts against metrics is that the change from Fahrenheit to Celsius in the temperature scale would result in the loss of finer measurements. For example, 33° and 34° F are both 1° C, and this loss continues throughout the Celsius scale (Fahrenheit and Celsius do not meet until minus 40).

Even with the continuing public rejection, the metric system will eventually be absorbed and adopted. I just don't want to be around to pick up the pieces. Can you imagine the response to the first television weatherperson who presents this forecast:

"Winds are easterly at 20 kilometers per hour, the barometer is falling from 101 kilopascals, and there is a heavy snow warning for up to 10 centimeters of snow overnight, with 15 centimeters in the snowbelt."

I can hear the phones ringing.

"IT'S FOURTH DOWN AND FIVE CENTIMETERS FOR THE BUCKEYES, BUT IN THIS 30 DEGREE HEAT AND WITH THOSE 135 KILOGRAM LINEMEN, IT MIGHT AS WELL BE ONE POINT SIX KILOMETERS!"

AUTUMN

SEP

SUNSHINE %: 62
DRIEST MONTH: 0.47"/1886
WARMEST MONTH: 61.4°/1947
COLDEST MONTH: 45.2°/1925
LIQUID PCPN AVG.: 2.54"
RAINIEST DAY: 3.44"/1954
RAINIEST MONTH: 9.50"/1954
THUNDERY DAYS: 2
SNOWIEST DAY: 6.7"/1962
LEAST SNOWFALL: Trace (most recently in 1997)
DAYS ONE INCH SNOW: 0

October's arrival means that the season of the sun is gone in Northeast Ohio. The first three weeks of the month are usually very pleasant with comfortably mild days and cool nights. It'll turn frosty by midmonth in many nooks and crannies, and the arrival of steadily colder air over the still-warm waters of Lake Erie will often cause waterspouts and cold-air funnels to develop over the lake. Leaf color often peaks in Northeast Ohio during the third week, but it can vary if the growing season has been very wet or very dry. Most Ohioans are not aware of how lucky we are to be treated to the flaming foliage. More than 90 percent of earth's inhabitants, and three-quarters of the United States, never see the dazzling colors of autumn. October is the Woollybear Festival and the Pumpkin Festival and apple cider. Ohio groundhogs are growing fat on clover and alfalfa as they prepare to enter their winter hibernation chambers. Turtles and frogs are likewise burying themselves in muddy pond and river bottoms. Hornets will be killed by the frosts of late October, but the queens are checking out attics for the long winter to come. The return to Standard Time the last Sunday in October means we'll regain the hour of sleep we lost in early April.

AUTMN

OCT

Day	Hi	Lo	Rec Hi	Rec Lo	Sunrise*	Sunset*	Lake°
1	68	49	87 / 1952	34 / 1947	7:24	7:10	66
2	68	48	86 / 1919	32 / 1975	7:25	7:08	66
3	67	48	89 / 1953	29 / 1975	7:26	7:07	66
4	67	48	88 / 1952	33 / 1981	7:27	7:05	66
5	66	47	88 / 1951	32 / 1980	7:28	7:03	65
6	66	47	90 / 1946	34 / 1964	7:29	7:02	65
7	66	46	88 / 1946	30 / 1964	7:30	7:00	65
8	65	46	88 / 1939	31 / 1952	7:31	6:58	64
9	65	46	86 / 1947	30 / 1876	7:32	6:57	64
10	65	45	86 / 1949	30 / 1895	7:33	6:55	63
11	64	45	86 / 1928	25 / 1964	7:34	6:53	63
12	64	45	85 / 1893	26 / 1876	7:36	6:52	63
13	63	44	82 / 1969	29 / 1875	7:37	6:50	63
14	63	44	84 / 1989	30 / 1988	7:38	6:49	62
15	62	43	86 / 1947	29 / 1876	7:39	6:47	62
16	62	43	83 / 1962	29 / 1944	7:40	6:46	61
17	62	43	82 / 1953	32 / 1981	7:41	6:44	61
18	61	43	84 / 1950	28 / 1876	7:42	6:42	61
19	61	42	84 / 1953	29 / 1986	7:43	6:41	60
20	61	42	83 / 1953	27 / 1992	7:45	6:40	60
21	60	42	83 / 1953	26 / 1952	7:46	6:38	60
22	60	41	81 / 1947	27 / 1976	7:47	6:37	59
23	59	41	80 / 1963	25 / 1976	7:48	6:35	59
24	59	41	80 / 1920	22 / 1969	7:49	6:33	59
25	59	41	80 / 1963	28 / 1982	7:50	6:32	59
26	58	40	81 / 1963	24 / 1976	7:51	6:31	58
27	58	40	78 / 1927	23 / 1962	7:53	6:29	58
28	57	40	81 / 1927	24 / 1976	7:54	6:28	58
29	57	40	78 / 1946	24 / 1980	7:55	6:27	57
30	57	39	79 / 1950	23 / 1980	*6:56	5:25	57
31	56	39	82 / 1950	19 / 1988	6:58	5:24	56

* STANDARD TIME BEGINS LAST SUNDAY IN OCTOBER

*The happiest people in the world
are those who always manage to give
without remembering . . .
and to take without forgetting.*
– ANONYMOUS

OCTOBER IS OHIO

Octbober is the favorite month of many Northeast Ohioans. The first three weeks are often sunny and mild, and the splashes of leaf color that first appeared in mid-September reach a visual crescendo during mid- and late October.

With apologies to Kermit the Frog, trees find it easy being green—at least during the spring and summer. The abundant sunshine of the warm-weather months provides the energy for making the food (sugar) that allows the green pigment (chlorophyll) to overpower and mask all the other colors within a leaf. Contrary to popular belief, it is not the turn to colder temperatures in autumn that causes the leaves to change color. It's actually the steadily diminishing sunlight. As the days grow shorter the chlorophyll production line shuts down. As the green pigment fades, the other pigments (which have been present all along) begin to show through. Pigments known as carotenids produce yellow, brown, and orange. Anthocyanin pigments bring on red and purple hues.

BUCKEYE
YELLOW, ORANGE

Crimson sumacs are usually the first to announce autumn's arrival as they change into their red-bronze finery. Maples, meanwhile, stand out in a medley of woodland color: red maples become crimson; sugar maples wear mostly orange and yellow, with splashes of red; silver maples can vary from pale to luminous yellow. The Ohio state tree, the Buckeye, passes up scarlet and gray and instead dons shades of yellow and orange. Elms and hickories can become radiantly yellow, while oaks prefer scarlet and burgundy red.

The key to a colorful, or dull, autumn is the weather. If enough beneficial rain fell during the summer, all the trees need in early autumn is a series of mild, sunny days and clear, cool nights. Cloudy, wet weather will subdue the colors, while an early frost or freeze will cause the leaves to turn brown, curl up, and fall.

As the leaf nears the end of its life cycle, the cells at the base of the leaf stem divide, and the leaf is detached. The fallen leaves then form a protective covering on the forest floor and combine with fallen acorns (mast) for the benefit of small woodland animals.

The stubborn leaves of the pin oak are often the last to fall, and

AUTUMN

OCT

some may be able to hang on through the winter. As Northeast Ohioans know, the falling leaves will soon be followed by falling crystals of white snow. We go from lovely to shovely in a hurry!

Some leaf-viewing tips . . .

For weekly updates on Ohio's autumn leaf-color changes, you can call the Ohio Department of Natural Resources Fall Color Hotline at (614) 265-7000. The state's travel and tourism line also has leaf-viewing information available at (800) BUCKEYE. The Cuyahoga Valley Scenic Railroad runs special fall foliage trips through the Cuyahoga Valley National Recreation Area during autumn; call (800) 468-4070 for more information. Or, just pay a visit to a nearby Cleveland Metroparks reservation for a fine display of nature's most colorful season. Many nature centers within the reservations conduct leaf-viewing walks with staff naturalists. Call Cleveland Metroparks at (216) 351-6300 for more information.

DOGWOOD
RED-PURPLE

GINGKO
BRIGHT YELLOW

PIN OAK
YELLOW, BROWN

SASSAFRAS
RED AND PURPLE

SHAGBARK HICKORY
YELLOW, BROWN

SUGAR MAPLE
YELLOW, RED, ORANGE

RED   YELLOW PURPLE
SWEETGUM

TULIP TREE
YELLOW

AUTUMN

OCT

FROSTS & FREEZES

The cold temperatures of winter are, as a rule, preceded by autumn's frosts and freezes, which can easily arrive anytime in October. Indian summer, which can bring unseasonably warm weather in mid- or late autumn, by traditional definition cannot occur without a preliminary frost or freeze.

A frost and freeze will usually strike during the early morning hours. On nights when cold temperatures are expected, you can protect your flowers and tender plants by covering them with glass jars, boxes, or newspapers. Black plastic or anything metallic should not be used. If you ever cover your plants with clear plastic, make sure that the plastic doesn't touch the plant surface. Immediately remove the plastic or glass when the sun comes up and the temperature rises above freezing. Otherwise you'll have a parboiled petunia!

Frost forms when the temperature falls below freezing, causing moisture in the air to condense and collect on windowpanes, plants, and other objects as tiny crystals of ice. It is not the frost that kills the plant: the plant dies because the freezing temperatures cause the water inside it to freeze and expand and burst the delicate plant cells.

Ideal conditions for a visit from Jack Frost are a cool and relatively dry air cover, clear skies, little or no wind, and long nights. Under such conditions the ground and its vegetation radiate heat into space more readily than the overlying air and thus become colder than the air. The air then chills on contact with the ground.

Frost occurs more readily in low places, since cold air is heavy and drains down sloping surfaces. (You've experienced this effect even on warm summer nights if you've driven down a steep roadway and felt cool air rush in through an open car window.)

The first frost usually denotes the end of the growing season, which in Cleveland averages around 197 days.

AUTUMN

OCT

THE WOOLLYBEAR FESTIVAL

The Woollybear Festival was first held in 1973 in the little town of Birmingham, six miles south of Vermilion in southeastern Erie County.

One year earlier, I had asked my TV-8 colleague Neil Zurcher to see if there was any interest out there in starting a charity event to rival the Valley City (Medina County) Frog Jumping Contest. (It was while driving home from that unique event that I asked my daughter, Kim, what she thought of a similarly wacky festival devoted to the legendary weather-forecasting caterpillar, the woollybear. It sounded just goofy enough, so, with her seal of approval, the project was born.)

In scouting for a festival site, I told Neil, he'd probably have to find some nice folks who were just a little "off center," and who had a great sense of humor. A number of months later, Neil came by and

AUTUMN

OCT

announced that his talent search was over. The sponsor would be the Florence Elementary School Parent-Teacher Organization, and the people willing to stake their reputations on a TV weatherman and a fuzzy worm would be Maureen (Mo) Coe, Pat Zaleski, Donna Angelo, and Dottie Kudela.

The first Woollybear Festival was held on a sunny and warm Sunday in late October, and several hundred folks showed up. The miniparade consisted of the Firelands Falcons High School Marching Band, a few kids dressed up as caterpillars, and several Boy Scout troops. We seriously considered the possibility of having the parade units go around a second time. The winner of the caterpillar race was a highly suspect larva named Tommy, probably a salt marsh caterpillar. After the last woollybear caterpillar had raced, the consensus was that we had all had a very nice time. Not only that, but the local volunteer fire department and some other organizations had made a few bucks selling cider, doughnuts, pumpkins, and toy caterpillars.

So, we decided to do it again . . . and again . . . and again.

By the eighth festival in tiny Birmingham, the crowds had grown to more than 15,000. Parking was a major problem, and lawns were being trampled. When the local church appealed to us because the Sunday event was disrupting their activities, it was obvious that a new location had to be found.

In early 1980 we announced the need for a new and larger site. Thirteen towns and cities within the TV-8 viewing area soon responded with calls and letters asking us to consider their venues. Of all the offers, it was the one from Vermilion that stood out as the most attractive.

Every promise made about Vermilion's ability to sponsor the Woollybear Festival has been fulfilled. You can't hold a city hostage for a whole day without irritating some of the townsfolk, but over the years the people of Vermilion have willingly given of their time and talents. As a result, the Woollybear has grown into one of Ohio's—and the nation's—largest single-day events. (Have you ever seen a larger worm festival?) From an estimated initial attendance of about 30,000 in 1981, crowd estimates over the years have approached 100,000.

And what memories we have stockpiled! One of my most cherished is of our first "fearless folklore forecaster," the late Leon (Bad News) Bates. Leon was a shy, likable fellow who truly communed

with nature. Wearing his bib over-alls, buffalo-plaid shirt, and an engineer's cap, he was the perfect picture of a rustic—a person who shunned the everyday world and who preferred to socialize with the creatures of the forest. He added authenticity and credibility to the job of folklore forecaster.

The fact that Leon often declined a fresh shave for the festival simply added to his charm.

For years Leon was content just being Leon. Then, one incredible Woollybear Sunday, Leon arrived at the festival freshly shaven and heavily cologned, wearing a brand-new fedora and attired in a spiffy leisure suit. Leon had succumbed to the siren call of celebrity . . . and we loved him all the more for it.

Willis "Good News" Gebhardt, a much-loved centenarian, has succeeded Leon as the Woollybear Festival's fearless forecaster.

ACID RAIN

What we call "clean" rain is slightly acidic since it has mixed with naturally occurring gases in our atmosphere. Yet because of gases released by the burning of fossil fuels (especially coal) and the smelting process (melting of ore to yield metal), rain as acidic as lemon juice and vinegar has been observed. Sulfur dioxide and various oxides of nitrogen are released into the air through smokestacks and are carried great distances by the wind. These gases combine with sunlight and water vapor to become sulfuric and nitric acids that are pulled to earth when it rains.

Acid rain has been blamed for abnormally rapid corrosion and deterioration of buildings and monument stonework and the stunting, denuding, and killing of plants, trees, and whole forests. Melting snow in late winter can be extremely acidic since a whole season's worth of acid concentration is suddenly released.

Some scientists are unconvinced that there is an acid rain problem. They point out that some crops have been adversely affected while others have not.

It is believed that corrosive clouds filled with sulfur-dioxide emissions from coal-fired power plants and factories are a major cause of acid rain. The state of Ohio has been singled out as a prime producer of sulfur dioxide, much to the detriment of downwind states to our east and the Canadian province of Ontario to our north. The technology to burn coal in a "clean" manner is very expensive and, some claim, not reliable.

We should be aware that advances in science have lulled us into the belief that a technological quick fix can be found to our atmospheric pollution problems. Many scientists agree that the solution lies in the development of relatively clean sources of energy and a drastic change in lifestyles. We must learn to get more from less. Conservation is where the solution begins, and the following alternative energy sources that do not contribute to air pollution must be pursued: solar, wind, water, and safe nuclear power. The longer we pollute, the longer it will take to climb out of the environmental hole we are digging for ourselves. Ours is a forgiving planet, but there is a limit.

AUTUMN

OCT

PHOBIAS

Needing only a few hours' credit before graduation, I enrolled in Psychology 101. The professor was physically impressive, a woman with the dimensions of a medium-sized dray horse and an unkempt hairstyle that reminded one of the Gorgon Medusa. When she was in high dudgeon, which, as it turned out, was quite often, she was a daunting presence.

And she was a wonderful teacher. There was no dozing off in Psych 101.

Her special interest was in the study of phobias, defined as morbid, irrational, or excessive fears of particular objects or endeavors. (I was soon stricken with flunkophobia.)

I recall being told that humans are born with only two natural fears: the fear of heights and the fear of loud noises. All other trepidations are cultural, picked up from parents, siblings, friends, and others. It's difficult to believe that anyone can escape phobias. You can bet that if you have an excessive fear, there's a scientific name for it. You can also be assured that you are in good company.

Like so many of the world's powerful military and political leaders, Julius Caesar and Napoleon Bonaparte feared cats (ailurophobia). Both FOX sports announcer John Madden and renowned sci-fi writer Ray Bradbury travel by bus because they are afraid of flying (aerophobia). Author Graham Greene admits to two mental aberrations: fear of birds (ornithophobia) and blood (hematophobia). Glenallen Hill, the former Cleveland Indians' outfielder, suffers from arachnophobia, the dread of spiders. While Hill was with the Toronto Blue Jays he once dreamed of spiders, jumped out of bed, and injured his leg so badly that he went on the 15-day disabled list.

If you plan a career in meteorology, you should be free from the following aversions: chionophobia (snow), nephophobia (clouds), ombrophobia (rain), anemophobia (wind), heliophobia (sunlight), cheimaphobia (cold), homichlophobia (fog), and hydrophobia (water).

Potential astronomers can bag it if they have an aversion to the moon (selenophobia), or stars (siderophobia), or to dawn (eosophobia).

Those in the medical profession have taken the proverbial two strikes if they have these roadblocks: bacteriophobia (germs), gymnophobia (nakedness), nosemaphobia (illness), mysophobia (infection), and kopophobia (physical examination). At least two, however, could be an occasional ally: hypnophobia (sleep) and cathisophobia (sitting down).

> **The Roman emperor Tiberius endured keraunophobia, the fear of thunderstorms.**

One of the most famous phobias is the fear of the number 13, triskaideka-phobia. One of the most esoteric has to be arachibutyrophobia. (Just in case you're wondering, that's the fear of having peanut butter stick to the roof of your mouth—honest.) Pity those who suffer polyphobia (fear of many things), but have even more compassion for those with panophobia (fear of everything). It was President Franklin Delano Roosevelt who told us "the only thing we have to fear is fear itself!" That would be phobophobia.

The Roman emperor Tiberius endured keraunophobia, the dread of thunderstorms. Tiberius called upon his scribes and sooth-sayers to protect him from thunderbolts that were occasionally thrown his way by the great god Jupiter. Someone offered the observation that the laurel bush was never struck by lightning, so a garland of laurel leaves was made and placed upon the emperor's brow. From that day forward Roman emperors wore a wreath of laurel leaves.

"...AND A **LXV** PERCENT CHANCE OF THUNDERSTORMS TODAY, DECREASING TO **XX** PERCENT TOMORROW."

AUTUMN

OCT

WEATHER WISDOM ACCORDING TO KIDS

Today, weather is taught in most elementary schools. In fact during the school year a steady flow of mail from budding meteorologists lands on my desk.

The children usually ask weather questions or request weather maps and pictures. After 33 years I have accumulated a priceless treasure of letters from small fry, especially second and third graders.

Quite often the letter is addressed to Mr. Garter, Mr. Gutter or Mr. Gotter. Within the letter there sometimes emerges a pearl of truth and honesty that could only come from the uncomplicated mind of a child.

Whenever the isobars misbehave or six inches of partly sunny falls, I can brighten my day by thumbing through the file marked "letters from kids."

Here are a few gems:

"Our class is studying the wether, please send us
maps and things. P.S. I do not watch you.
My parents watch Channel 3."

"When the news begins I always like to watch until you come on."

"The hole 27 kids in my class are writting a letter.
I am in the second grade so if you find any mestakes
it is not my fault."

"Please send informashun on weather.
Please hurray. P.S. I got a big sister 36-40-38."

"We apresheate you coming to our school.
We were lucky. We got off gym."

"We have to watch you every night.
Even when there is a good program on."

"I would like a whether chart about tornados and hurricans.
I watch your show at 6 and 11. I am a teecher and we are
studdying the clouds. Your frinde, Mrs. Larko."

AUTUMN

OCT

Some children have offered little-known weather facts and observations:

"A January fog will freeze a hog."

"If you look at the full moon over your left shoulder you will die."

"Wind is air that gets pushy."

"A gentleman from France is called a monsoon."

Teachers always tell their students that they can determine how far away from them a thunderstorm is by counting the number of seconds between seeing the lightning flash and hearing the thunder (add one mile for every five seconds of delay . . . a 15-second delay, for example, tells you that a thunderstorm is centered three miles from you). A teacher sent me this student's explanation of the phenomenon:

"You can listen to thunder after lightning and tell how close you come to getting hit. If you don't hear it then you got hit, so never mind."

Here are a few more statements and opinions that teachers have shared with me:

"There is one good way to tell
between a high and a low pressure.
One of them makes it rain
but I can't think which one it is."

"It is so hot in some parts of the world
that the people who live there
have to live some where else."

AUTUMN

OCT

"TELL US WHY, MR. JOHNSON, YOU FEEL WE
ARE IN FOR A HARD WINTER."

AUTUMN

NOV

SUNSHINE %: 31
DRIEST MONTH: 0.41"/1904
WARMEST MONTH: 51.2°/1931
COLDEST MONTH: 31.3°/1880
LIQUID PCPN AVG.: 3.17"
RAINIEST DAY: 2.73"/1985
RAINIEST MONTH: 8.80"/1985
THUNDERY DAYS: 1
SNOWIEST DAY: 15.0"/1950
SNOWIEST MONTH: 23.4"/1996
LEAST SNOWFALL: Trace (most recently in 1994)
DAYS ONE INCH SNOW: 2

One of the electrifying sounds of November is the gabbling of Canada geese as they wing their way southward. The geese fly in their classic V formation for a reason. As each bird flaps its wings, it creates uplift for the bird immediately behind, thus allowing the flock to expand its flying range by about 70 percent. As the bird at the point of the V tires, it will drop back into the flock and another bird will become the leader. If the point bird is so worn out that it falls to the ground to rest, other birds will join their leader until he is able to return to the flock. Ohio's state animal, the white-tailed deer, is now rutting and can be very dangerous to unwary woodsmen and hunters. Motorists need to be especially alert for the next three months since deer will be constantly crossing the highways. If one deer crosses in front of you, you can expect another close behind. Lake-effect snows can be expected before the month is over. The Thanksgiving week snowstorm of 1950 dumped record amounts of snowfall around the state of Ohio, with upwards of 20 to 40 inches around Greater Cleveland and Northeast Ohio. In November of 1996, 69 inches of snow fell on Chardon in the heart of the Northeast Ohio snowbelt in Geauga county—in only five days. It was Ohio's greatest single storm snowfall. Great Lakes seamen fear the west-to-northwest gale wind of November, the "Witch."

Day	Hi	Lo	Rec Hi	Rec Lo	Sunrise	Sunset	Lake°
1	56	39	82 / 1950	25 / 1988	6:59	5:23	56
2	55	38	77 / 1938	25 / 1895	7:00	5:22	56
3	55	38	79 / 1961	19 / 1951	7:01	5:21	55
4	54	38	77 / 1935	16 / 1991	7:02	5:19	55
5	54	37	75 / 1948	16 / 1991	7:03	5:18	55
6	53	37	76 / 1977	17 / 1951	7:05	5:17	55
7	53	37	79 / 1938	23 / 1971	7:06	5:16	54
8	53	37	72 / 1945	19 / 1976	7:07	5:15	54
9	52	36	74 / 1975	22 / 1976	7:08	5:14	54
10	52	36	70 / 1991	19 / 1991	7:09	5:13	53
11	51	36	73 / 1915	21 / 1957	7:11	5:12	53
12	51	35	74 / 1949	18 / 1911	7:12	5:11	53
13	50	35	72 / 1989	15 / 1911	7:13	5:10	52
14	50	35	72 / 1994	13 / 1986	7:14	5:09	52
15	50	35	72 / 1931	14 / 1996	7:15	5:08	51
16	49	34	72 / 1931	12 / 1933	7:17	5:07	51
17	49	34	72 / 1954	14 / 1959	7:18	5:07	51
18	48	34	71 / 1954	10 / 1959	7:19	5:06	50
19	48	33	72 / 1908	4 / 1880	7:20	5:05	50
20	47	33	73 / 1931	15 / 1951	7:21	5:04	50
21	47	32	70 / 1930	3 / 1880	7:23	5:04	49
22	46	32	73 / 1934	0 / 1880	7:24	5:03	49
23	46	32	75 / 1931	7 / 1880	7:25	5:03	49
24	46	32	70 / 1931	7 / 1950	7:26	5:02	48
25	45	31	67 / 1906	15 / 1950	7:27	5:01	48
26	45	31	70 / 1896	9 / 1880	7:28	5:01	47
27	44	31	71 / 1990	7 / 1880	7:29	5:00	47
28	44	30	68 / 1990	8 / 1955	7:30	5:00	47
29	43	30	67 / 1933	6 / 1976	7:32	5:00	47
30	43	30	71 / 1934	3 / 1976	7:33	4:59	46

If you cannot find happiness
along the way,
you will not find it
at the end of the road.
– ANONYMOUS

TERROR OF THE WITCH

The Witch is coming. She always does in November.

You may recall hearing about the Witch in Gordon Lightfoot's song of tragedy on the Great Lakes, "The Wreck of the Edmund Fitzgerald." The Witch is the northwest wind, and no other wind fills the Great Lakes sailor with as much anxiety. Under a gale-force north-westerly, the Great Lakes will turn into a spuming frenzy of white water. Waves may tower over 20 feet and follow each other in rapid succession.

A streeetcar is frozen into its tracks near a downed power line, November 1913.

On November 7, 1913, the most wicked Witch of them all hit the Great Lakes, and before she rode away 235 people had drowned and 32 ships were lost. This was the most savage storm ever to strike the inland waters of the United States and Canada.

This Witch also produced the heaviest 24-hour snowfall in Cleveland weather history: 17.4 inches, during Nov. 9–10, 1913. Cleveland's total snow from the time it set in at 4:30 p.m. Sunday the 9th, until 7 a.m. Tuesday the 11th, was 22.2 inches.

Cleveland's strongest wind speed was 79 mph at 4:40 p.m. on the 9th, with an average speed of 51 mph from that Sunday afternoon through early Monday morning. For days, the Cleveland area was paralyzed under a blanket of snow and ice. Power lines went down, interurban cars were abandoned on the streets, and thousands of people were stranded.

The storm that brought this Witch to the Great Lakes began as a low-barometer center moving southeastward out of the Canadian province of Saskatchewan on Friday, November 7. At 12:15 on the afternoon of the 7th, the shore stations along Lake Superior hoisted northwest gale warnings.

The growing storm center swung south of Lake Superior and by Saturday evening, November 8, it was near Milwaukee, Wisconsin. Now a raging giant, it turned more northeasterly early Sunday morning and reentered Canada, passing just north of Lake Erie during Sunday afternoon.

AUTUMN

NOV

From there the storm center once again turned southeastward and raced to a position along the Virginia Tidewater by Monday morning, November 10.

At the time the storm began over the upper Great Lakes, there were two weeks remaining in the navigation season. In a few days, all ships would be in safe berths along the Great Lakes. But when the Witch came screaming across Lake Superior like a banshee, 44 sailors drowned. The Witch claimed 178 lives the following day on Lake Huron, while seven men perished in Lake Michigan and six in Lake Erie. The Lake Carriers Association in its annual report of 1913 stated: "No lake master can recall a storm of such violence . . . with wind gusts of such fearful speed. Storms of that velocity usually do not last over four or five hours, but this storm raged for 16 hours at an average wind speed of 80 mph with frequent spurts to 70 and over."

Testimony from those ships' masters who survived the storm told of waves that towered to 35 feet or more.

A pedestrian checks the weather kiosk on Public Square, November 10, 1913.

BACKYARD WEATHER STATION

Weather watching is fascinating, as a career or a hobby. Three of our first four presidents—Washington, Jefferson, and Madison—kept elaborate weather records. Ben Franklin enjoyed observing both human nature and nature's weather parade. (Franklin, who gave us Daylight Saving Time and discovered the Gulf Stream, was the first to determine that weather systems moved in a general west-to-east direction across the United States.)

The best part of weather watching is that it's free. Well, almost. It depends on just how dedicated you would like to become. While the human eye will always be our best weather observation tool (it even beats Doppler radar), you will need reliable equipment to make accurate measurements. It's possible to create some weather-measuring tools by hand. Just get a copy of the Boy Scout handbook. Unfortunately, homemade weather instruments suffer greatly after long exposure to the elements, and their accuracy can be suspect. Your best bet is to purchase reliable equipment, and I have included a number of sources at the conclusion of this article.

Here is a list of the basics you will need for your backyard weather station:

THERMOMETER. Most household-variety glass thermometers are filled with alcohol, or a mix of fluids, and are colored red. The more precise thermometers are filled with mercury and will cost you in the neighborhood of $20, or more. A maximum-minimum (max-min) thermometer is a nice addition, and it will automatically record the highest and lowest temperature each day (they must be reset for the next day). Thermometers should be mounted in the shade, at eye level, in an open area over a grass surface and facing true north (you want to be accurate, right?). A small wooden shelter, painted white, with louvered sides to permit easy air flow, can be made or purchased to house the thermometers.

BAROMETER. The barometer is overrated as a weather forecasting tool, but it's a nice instrument to have and it looks great hanging on a wall. This device measures air pressure—the weight of the air directly over you. The reading on a barometer will not guarantee any particular weather, but the trend of a barometer—either steadily rising or falling—will tell you if a low pressure storm system or a high-pressure fair-weather system is approaching. For centuries the elongated, classic, "stick"-style mercury-filled barometer was used as the official instrument. Extremely accurate electronic pressure sensors are now being used. The common home barometer (called an aneroid) has a metal coil enclosed that expands and contracts as air pressure changes. A barometer should never be placed out of

AUTUMN

NOV

doors at the mercy of the weather. Air pressure is identical inside and outside your home.

HYGROMETER. The instrument that measures air moisture—humidity—is called a hygrometer. Truly accurate hygrometers are very expensive and have a sensor that is exposed to the great outdoors. (A humidity indicator indoors will only tell you the air moisture inside your home.) Some of the finest humidity indicators use strands of blond human hair or spider silk for the required lengthening and shortening element.

RAIN GAUGE. Electronic self-emptying rain gauges can set you back a few bucks. Or you can use a number 10 tin can (the official rain gauge diameter is 8 inches, so this comes close). Any container you use should be flat-bottomed with straight sides. An ordinary ruler inserted straight down into the can will give a precise measurement. Place your rain gauge in an open, unsheltered area away from trees. Simple, inexpensive, wedge-shaped plastic gauges are sold in most hardware and feed stores.

SNOW. Snow depth is measured by inserting a ruler (you'll need a yardstick in the Ohio snowbelt communities) into the snow in at least three places, at least 15 yards apart, on level ground away from buildings and trees. You total the three measurements and divide by three to get your average snow depth. When snow is blowing and drifting badly you may need to take a dozen or more samplings (use your imagination). Some observers make a snowboard for taking readings. The board is about one foot by three feet, made of flat wood and painted white. An exposed wooden deck or a picnic table makes a good measuring site. Snow

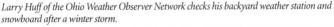

Larry Huff of the Ohio Weather Observer Network checks his backyard weather station and snowboard after a winter storm.

AUTUMN

NOV

compacts as it settles, so measuring every two hours is recommended during heavy snowfall. (Be sure to scrape off the old snow after each sampling.)

ANEMOMETER. The tool that measures wind speed is an anemometer. A wind vane is usually attached to the anemometer. While a homemade anemometer can be made using three round paper or plastic cups, there's a good chance your instrument will be on its way to the Land of Oz in the first real storm. Professionally made anemometers are another large expense, but you can also purchase the kind that automatically record peak wind gusts. Be sure to mount your anemometer on a pole, at least 10 feet above the place where it is attached. (National Weather Service anemometers are mounted at 33 feet).

WEATHER RADIO. Every weather buff should have access to the 24-hour-a-day broadcasts from the nearest National Weather Service office. A standard radio won't do this, so you will need to shell out anywhere from $20 to $80. The radios, which have an important battery-operated feature (power lines often go down in storms), can be purchased through mail or online catalogs. Radio Shack offers several models, one of which is programmable so that you can choose special codes for your county or area of concern. The automatic severe weather alert signal is guaranteed to scare the bejabbers out of you when it goes off in the middle of the night.

JOURNAL. For keeping personal weather records, you may purchase a ledger from any of the office supply stores. I have kept a weather journal for nearly 40 years, using narrow-line three-ring-notebook paper. You'll need a column for the daily high and low temperatures, sky condition, precipitation type, amount of rain or snow, and a large space for general remarks ("a nice day; wind damage; vivid lightning," etc.)

Using your computer, you can access massive amounts of weather information and plenty of statistics by calling up the Cleveland National Weather Service home page on the Internet at www.csuohio.edu/nws. The local NWS site includes links to other informative weather-data sites.

WEATHER GROUPS

For those of us who are definitely interested in weather phenomena but aren't quite ready to pack up the bags and go storm chasing, there are other local sources of information and activities that are educational and fun . . . and safer.

The Northeast Ohio Chapter of the American Meteorological Society (NEOCAMS) hosts meetings and other educational activities in order to promote meteorology and climatology. There are four meetings per year, plus a social picnic and a holiday dinner. Members include weather enthusiasts, National Weather Service personnel, and professionals working in technological and educational fields. A meteorology degree is not required in order to join the chapter. Membership is open to all ages for all residents of Northeast Ohio.

AUTUMN

NOV

Because it's a nonprofit organization, NEOCAMS members pay annual dues of $12 to help defray costs

To learn more about NEOCAMS, contact the organization at the address below, or visit them on the Internet.

Northeast Ohio Chapter of the AMS
Attn: Eric Wertz
P.O. Box 8213
Akron, OH 44320

E-mail: neocams@acorn.net
Web site: www.csuohio.edu/nws

The Ohio Weather Observer Network is another great source for local and regional weather information. It publishes a semiannual newsletter and tracks the area's widely varied weather phenomena. More information about joining the organization is available at the address below.

Ohio Weather Observer Network
Attn: Larry Huff
P.O. Box 107
Munroe Falls, OH 44262
(330) 686-1667 (fax)

AUTUMN

NOV

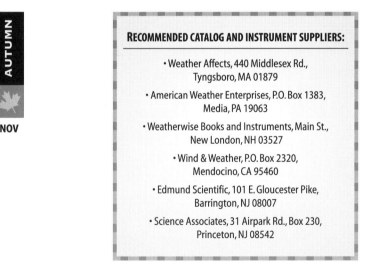

RECOMMENDED CATALOG AND INSTRUMENT SUPPLIERS:

• Weather Affects, 440 Middlesex Rd.,
Tyngsboro, MA 01879

• American Weather Enterprises, P.O. Box 1383,
Media, PA 19063

• Weatherwise Books and Instruments, Main St.,
New London, NH 03527

• Wind & Weather, P.O. Box 2320,
Mendocino, CA 95460

• Edmund Scientific, 101 E. Gloucester Pike,
Barrington, NJ 08007

• Science Associates, 31 Airpark Rd., Box 230,
Princeton, NJ 08542

THE BLIZZARD BOWL

On Saturday, November 25, 1950, bitter rivals Ohio State University and the University of Michigan met in a tragicomedy of a football game at Columbus that will be forever frozen in sports annals as the legendary Blizzard Bowl. Calling it simply a Snow Bowl would be a gross understatement.

The game was played at the height of the great Thanksgiving week snowstorm of 1950, a storm unrivaled in the state of Ohio for its duration and snowfall.

As the big Saturday approached, heavy snow had already fallen over much of Ohio since Thanksgiving night. Ralph Gurasci, the groundskeeper at Ohio Stadium, had been regularly checking with the Columbus weather bureau, which confidently predicted that the snow would end by 11 a.m. Saturday.

"That's when it really began to snow hard," recalled Gurasci.

The football field had been covered with a tarpaulin that had itself become frozen to the surface as the temperature dove to 10 above zero amid the whirling snow.

Ohio State athletic director Dick Larkin, who decreed that the

Ohio State battles the University of Michigan in the infamous "Blizzard Bowl," November 25, 1950.

AUTUMN

NOV

game would be played that afternoon, recruited spectators and a troop of Boy Scouts to help pry the tarp from the turf, but to no avail. The tarp instead came off in shreds and tatters, and several of the scouts became entangled in the canvas. (Hours after the game a rumor started that one of the scouts was missing and presumed to be still wrapped in the tarp. A frantic, fruitless search followed!)

The OSU football coach, Wes Fesler, violently protested the decision to play the game. But the contest began in blinding snow and a gale-force wind that produced a wind-chill factor close to -40°.

On a field that was a glaring sheet of ice, with no discernable yard markers, it soon became obvious to both teams that it was a disadvantage to possess the football. Players found that gloves quickly became frozen to their hands.

All afternoon the teams kept giving the ball back to each other. Chuck Ortmann, the Michigan tailback, punted the ball into the blizzard a remarkable 24 times. Vic Janowicz of Elyria, Ohio State's All-American, punted back 21 times. Michigan's longest gain came when Ortmann skidded around end for a modest six yards. Janowicz, who slid 11 yards for the Buckeyes' longest advance, equated the task with running on roller skates.

Perhaps the most incredible part of the Blizzard Bowl was that Michigan completed no passes and made no first downs, yet still won the game, 9–3.

"It was," said a beleaguered Fesler, "a game played by heroes."

The loss cost Ohio State a trip to the Rose Bowl, and Coach Fesler was heavily criticized for trying an end zone punt that was blocked. He resigned one month later. That opened the door for a young football coach from Miami of Ohio named Woody Hayes.

AUTUMN

NOV

ASTROLOGERS & PSYCHICS

If it was so, it might be;
and if it were so, it would be;
but as it isn't, it ain't.

—TWEEDLEDEE, IN LEWIS CARROLL'S *THROUGH THE LOOKING GLASS*

It has been said that we are all entitled to be a fool once each day, and our goal should be not to exceed that limit. For those who begin their day by fervently seeking out their sun-sign horoscope, that's one time. If you find it necessary to gain further personal guidance by placing a four-dollar-a-minute phone call to a faceless, anonymous psychic friend, you're over the limit.

Do not confuse the science of astronomy with the fantasy world of astrology. Consider the *Oxford English Dictionary* definitions:

"IF YOU'D BEEN BORN TWO DAYS EARLIER, YOU'D BE CHARMING, WITTY AND WISE."

ASTRONOMY: The science that deals with the material universe beyond earth's atmosphere.

ASTROLOGY: The supposed art which assumes and professes to foretell the influences of celestial objects on human affairs.

Although astrology has no basis in fact, astrologers claim that the movement and positioning of a tiny number of stars—among the trillions that exist—will determine one's destiny on earth.

Surveys in the United States have shown that one out of every four of us believes in astrology, and one-third think that sun-sign astrology is an actual science. Horoscopes are carried by two out of three newspapers. In this country there are an estimated 20,000 astrologers with millions of disciples who spend countless millions of dollars supporting the celestial nonsense.

Astrology, denounced by the early Christian church as "a disease, not a science," is the fastest-growing belief system in the United States. In France, there are more astrologers than there are members of the Roman Catholic clergy.

Astrology was born some 4,000 years ago in ancient Babylonia

AUTUMN

NOV

(now Iraq) when superstition and magic ruled and the earth was thought to be the center of the universe around which all heavenly bodies circled. Early civilizations were in awe of the objects in the nighttime sky, but they had no way of knowing the immensity of the universe and the tremendous physical distances between the stars and planets. The stars that made up the constellations were believed to be nearby neighbors and on the same horizontal plane. The ancients did not realize that those bright suns were billions and trillions of miles away from each other. (For this reason you could never take a trip to the constellation Orion, for example. As you approached the nearest star in Orion, the familiar pattern, as seen from earth, would become unrecognizable and simply disappear.)

The ancient priests, who had no calendar, laid the groundwork for astrology when they relied on observation of stars and star patterns to guide their people through the seasons. In order to keep their power and control, the priests eventually proclaimed an ability to also divine the fate of kings and the growth of crops and predict famines, war, catastrophes, and the weather. Personal predictions—individual birth horoscopes—date from after the 13th century B.C. The horoscopes were developed by the astrologer's observation of the sun, moon, and planets (technically, even the sun and moon are considered planets by astrologers) in relation to the background star constellations at the time of birth. (Wouldn't the time of conception be a more valid starting point?) The constellations were divided into 12 large regions of the heavens called the zodiac, which cover the sky like elongated tiles. (The word zodiac comes from the Greek *zodiakos kyklos,* which means "circle of animals." There are 88 constellations that are observable from earth, and the dozen that make up the signs of the zodiac were finalized in the eighth century B.C.)

The ancients saw pictures in the nighttime sky, and observing the star configurations that make up the zodiac, we must conclude that they had vivid imaginations. As you look at the random star clusters, you can make up your own zodiacal mandala of animals or mythological heroes. Connect the imaginary lines and Sagittarius could be a spider, Pisces a cat, and so forth.

While astrologers purport that stars exert a profound influence on the human body and mind, the distances from the earth to the stars are so great that any possible gravitational, vibrational, or magnetic attraction or effect is minuscule. Studies have shown not one scintilla of correlation between the positions and motions of heavenly objects and the lives of human beings. The astrologer will also impute to each planet and constellation the ability to represent a different facet of the human personality. For example, the red planet

AUTUMN

NOV

Mars, which rules the sign of Aries, supposedly exemplifies aggression and war, and, so goes the absurdity, produces the world's greatest athletes. Conversely, the watery planet Neptune governs the sign Pisces. Pisceans are considered indecisive and weak, often daydreaming away their opportunities.

A major problem with astrology—and most astrologers will not tell you this—is the scientific fact called the precession of the equinoxes. Because earth wobbles on its axis as it rotates in its orbit around the sun, the zodiacal signs have actually moved one whole sign backward over the last 2,000 years. It will be another 23,800 years before the precessional cycle returns to its original starting point. Some 2,000 years ago, at the time of the vernal equinox, the sun

> ### GENERIC
> ### (ANY DAY, ANY YEAR)
> ### HOROSCOPE
>
> You have a keen sense of humor, although it is not always appreciated by your slower-witted associates. You choose your friends carefully, but do not always approve of their behavior. While you occasionally fail to use good judgment, your basic intelligence guarantees that your decisions will be far superior to the choices of those around you. Be careful in your consumption of food and beverages, since your weight—either too much or too little—could be a problem. Be wary of strangers and do not lend them large amounts of money. Keep your doors locked and don't forget to take your shoes off before going to bed.

was "in" the constellation Aries, while today it is "in" Pisces. This means that although I was born on the 24th day of February, I'm not a weak, wishy-washy Pisces after all. Instead, I'm a militant, dominating Aries. (I know this must be so, otherwise I couldn't have written this.)

It would be too easy to say that astrology is simply a myth agreed upon, because astrologers, when presented with identical sun-sign charts, frequently disagree on what the chart forecasts. One of the most widely published astrologers has complained that at least one-half of his fellow stargazers are charlatans who have no idea what they are doing. But the business of astrology is a highly profitable enterprise, and the most advanced practitioners will run up the bill by dazzling their clients with such exotic concepts as "quincunx," "quintile," "sextile," "medium coeli," and "sesquiquad-rate."

It's easy to see why so many believe in astrology. When we find our sun sign, we compare the sign's characteristics to what we believe about ourselves. Personal traits often listed among the sun signs are: cautious, extroverted, introverted, insecure, confident, passive, aggressive, adventurous, sensitive, considerate, intuitive, authoritative, compassionate, aloof, and forthright. Who wouldn't qualify for

AUTUMN

NOV

several, if not most, of those traits, at least occasionally? We also remember the ones that we feel fit our personality and forget the rest.

Basically, astrology operates under the philosophy that if you throw enough mud (there's a better word) at a wall, some of it is going to stick.

While the science of astronomy has made gigantic progress over the millennia, the pseudoscience of astrology remains stuck in the desert sand of its birthplace. Astrology has not changed in 2,000 years. Its main contribution to humanity is that "What's your sign?" is second only to "Do you come here often?" as the classic social ice-breaker.

PSYCHICS

While astrology, if not taken seriously, can be entertaining, there can be no redemption for the fortune-telling media psychics. The phony psychic networks are raking in an estimated $400 million a year by preying upon the most gullible, most vulnerable, and least affluent among us. Fronted and promoted on television by down-on-their-luck entertainers, this scam thrives because, as in astrology, the will to believe overwhelms common sense.

In search of an accurate five-day forecast, I called a psychic pal on the four-dollars-a-minute 800 telephone number. My new best friend said that her name was "Star," and in a pleasant voice began to elicit information from me, including (curiously?) my astrological sun sign. The technique Star was using is known to professional psychologists as a "cold reading," which meant that the information I had given would soon be returned to me in such a way that I was supposed to be amazed at her clairvoyance.

Just as in astrology, pseudopsychics such as Star are schooled in the fact that people are basically more alike than different. We all share common problems and concerns, and the charlatan soothsayers are very happy to tell us what we want to hear.

The ability to keep the telephone money meter running is a prerequisite for electronic psychics, so as the 20-minute, $80 mark approached, I reluctantly informed my glib buddy that it was time that I faced the future on my own. At that point I confessed that I, too, was a prominent psychic, and that I could see a handsome and wealthy man entering her life. As she asked for details, I regretted that I had run out of time and politely hung up.

While psychic abilities may exist (haven't we all, seemingly, "been in this place before"?), there is no conclusive, decisive proof.

AUTUMN

NOV

The problem with both astrologers and psychics is that Western law regards both as simple fortune-tellers. Under our treasured freedom of speech, such hokum and flimflam are not illegal and are viewed only as entertainment, as if both were harmless. Unfortunately, too many people forfeit their free will, rationality, and sense of personal responsibility by resigning their fate to the idea that "if it's in the stars, there's nothing I can do about it."

I am personally aware of one bankruptcy that can be blamed on psychic readings, and, nationally, there has been at least one documented suicide.

"REMINDS ME OF THE BLIZZARD OF 2072!"

AUTUMN

NOV

RETIREMENT

Weather is so subjective that it is indeed an ill wind that doesn't please someone.

With that disclaimer out of the way, I'll try to answer the unanswerable question: where is the best weather for retirement? For openers, you can probably search all over the world and not find the "perfect" climate. You'll just have to settle for what comes closest to your desires. What is one person's Shangri-la is another's Tierra del Fuego. (I know I'll get nasty letters from Tierra del Fuego.)

I spent one northern hemisphere winter in the Marshall Islands of the Pacific Ocean; many believe that the island of Majuro there has the ideal, comfortable climate. Ideal in this sense is a year-round daily high temperature of 80° F with a low around 70°, steady-as-rent soothing northeast trade winds and 365 days of sunshine interrupted by afternoon cottontail cumulus clouds that drop brief and passing tropical rains.

Many would call such a monotonous climate intolerable. They find the change of seasons at a harsh northern latitude so enjoyable that they wouldn't consider swapping for warmth and wall-to-wall sunshine.

Personally, I wouldn't trade the Northeast Ohio weather from mid-May to mid-October for that anywhere else in the country. (The other seven months are negotiable.)

Surveys show that the following factors are the most important to retirees deciding where to live: 1) lack of snow and cold temperatures (the great majority of people tolerate heat better than cold); 2) uniform climate with little daily variance; 3) income potential in the area; 4) educational facilities; and 5) cost of living.

The most popular retirement areas in the United States include Florida, the Gulf coast, eastern portions of Georgia and South Carolina, southern Arizona, southern New Mexico, the California coast, and Hawaii. All feature an absence of cold, stormy weather and snow.

Florida offers mild to warm winters, especially the southern half of the state, but you'll spend your summers in a sauna. Locate near the beach and hope the sand fleas are vegetarians. Be sure your home is on pilings (stilts) if you live along the coastline, because hurricanes can threaten. Areas that ring the Gulf coast from Texas through western Florida are favored by relatively mild winters, a lack of snowfall, wilting summers, and the infrequent threat of hurricanes.

AUTUMN

NOV

A popular retirement area is the Raleigh-Chapel Hill region in the rolling Piedmont country of North Carolina. The annual temperature range is between 32° and 88° F, but is quite uniform on a day-to-day basis. Precipitation is adequate and evenly distributed, and only one or two snowfalls can be expected each winter. Just south lie the famous golf courses at Southern Pines and Pinehurst, and the Atlantic Ocean is not that far away.

California weather is consistently moderate, especially in the southern coastal regions. The Sierra Nevada mountains to the east offer excellent winter skiing. San Francisco's cool, often moist and foggy climate appeals to many, while the San Diego region can boast the most favored climate in the conterminous United States. San Diego winters are sunny and mild, while summers are warm and sunny (after the early-morning marine-layer clouds from the Pacific Ocean burn off). San Diego proper gets only 10 inches of rain each year, so irrigation is necessary (Cleveland averages 35 inches). Residents can expect to hear thunder an average of three times each year, while winds exceed 30 mph only once.

> **Personally, I wouldn't trade the Northeast Ohio weather from mid-May to mid-October for that anywhere else in the country.**

The problem with living in California, of course, is that you will face one natural calamity after another: earthquakes, wildfires, landslides, mudslides, and beach erosion. You can throw in future major water shortages and several active volcanoes, not to mention congested highway travel at speeds similar to the Indianapolis 500.

Arizona is a favored place for retirees, and there you can choose desert, valleys, or mountains. Flagstaff in the mountainous north has very cold and snowy winters and warm, pleasant summers. Prescott, an "in betweener," is preferable. Phoenix, in the south, lies in the saucer-shaped Valley of the Sun and has major pollution problems. (It is very important that the elderly escape regions of high pollution. There go Phoenix, Los Angeles, and Dallas.) Temperatures from May through October soar into the 90s and 100s on most days. Tucson, to the southeast, has slightly lower temperatures and much less pollution. Summer humidity is usually very low, and the heat is euphemistically called "dry"—but so is an oven. Las Vegas, Nevada, is experiencing a population boom, but summers there also sizzle. Water shortages will be an increasing problem throughout the southwestern United States.

In the Pacific Northwest, Seattle has a cloudy, cool, moist climate with little winter snowfall. Only 70 miles from Seattle are dormant-

°AUTUMN

NOV

to-active volcanoes on Mount Rainier and Glacier Park (there is no such thing as a dead volcano). Portland, Oregon, the City of Roses, offers an attractive climate, but Oregonians don't kowtow to strangers.

Mile-high Denver, Colorado, has a surprisingly mild Rocky Mountain climate. Denver's annual snowfall is close to Cleveland's, but the city enjoys much more winter sunshine. Denver annually receives more sunshine than Miami, San Diego, or Honolulu.

Closer to home, the Ozark Hills region of northwestern Arkansas has a little-publicized, favorable microclimate. You will be treated to a distinct change of seasons, as well.

Hawaii, our 50th state, has a moderate to warm year-round climate, and snow occasionally appears on the summit of Mauna Kea on the Big Island. Hawaii has natural air conditioning with the northeasterly trade winds, and the nighttime is cooled by down-sloping mountain winds (the mauka breeze). Only infrequently will temperatures reach 90°, and this is our only state never to experience a below-zero temperature (coldest: 14° on Mount Haleakala).

Avoid the flood plains of major rivers and streams. All coastal regions of the United States from the Gulf states through Florida and up the Atlantic seaboard will infrequently be a target for hurricanes.

Dallas and Houston rank at the top of major cities when it comes to the torrid summertime combination of temperature and humidity, while Minneapolis is our coldest major metropolitan area.

For climatological information on cities throughout the United States at a modest cost, contact the National Climate Data Center at the following address:

NOAA Federal Building
151 Patton Avenue, Room 120
Asheville, NC 28801-5001
Telephone (704) 271-4800 between 8 a.m. and 5 p.m.

The following publication will give you a nice climatological summary for 600 cities in the United States and around the world:

Pleasant Weather Ratings
Consumer Travel Publications
P.O. Box 9175
Lexington, MA 02173

CITY-BY-CITY WEATHER STATISTICS
TEMPERATURE & PRECIPITATION AVERAGES

AKRON-CANTON (Elev. 1,209 ft.)

Month	Max	Min	Pcpn	Snow
Jan	33	17	2.16	12
Feb	36	19	2.23	10
Mar	47	29	3.33	9
Apr	59	38	3.16	3
May	70	48	3.73	T
Jun	79	57	3.18	0
Jul	82	62	4.08	0
Aug	80	60	3.32	0
Sep	74	54	3.32	0
Oct	62	43	2.35	1
Nov	50	34	3.01	5
Dec	38	24	2.95	10

ASHLAND (Elev. 1,050 ft.)

Month	Max	Min	Pcpn	Snow
Jan	30	14	2.12	10
Feb	33	15	1.88	8
Mar	44	25	2.95	7
Apr	55	36	3.23	1
May	69	46	3.86	0
Jun	78	55	3.40	0
Jul	83	59	3.56	0
Aug	80	57	3.63	0
Sep	73	51	2.96	0
Oct	61	39	2.06	T
Nov	48	31	3.10	3
Dec	34	20	2.70	8

ASHTABULA (Elev. 690 ft.)

Month	Max	Min	Pcpn	Snow
Jan	31	17	2.35	20
Feb	53	19	1.78	15
Mar	43	27	2.40	11
Apr	55	36	2.98	3
May	68	48	3.41	0
Jun	78	57	3.52	0
Jul	81	61	4.07	0
Aug	80	60	3.81	0
Sep	74	54	3.63	0
Oct	63	44	3.29	T
Nov	50	25	3.48	7
Dec	38	25	2.85	17

CHARDON (Elev. 1,210 ft.)

Month	Max	Min	Pcpn	Snow
Jan	30	13	2.64	29
Feb	33	14	2.51	21
Mar	43	24	3.33	17
Apr	56	34	3.55	5
May	68	44	3.57	T
Jun	77	53	4.18	0
July	81	58	3.53	0
Aug	79	57	3.61	0
Sep	72	50	3.75	0
Oct	60	40	3.75	2
Nov	48	32	4.05	12
Dec	35	21	3.79	27

CINCINNATI (Elev. 869 ft.)

Month	Max	Min	Pcpn	Snow
Jan	37	20	2.59	7
Feb	41	23	2.69	5
Mar	53	33	4.24	4
Apr	64	42	3.75	1
May	74	52	4.28	T
Jun	82	60	3.84	0
Jul	86	65	4.24	0
Aug	84	63	3.35	0
Sep	78	57	2.88	0
Oct	66	44	2.86	T
Nov	53	35	3.46	2
Dec	42	25	3.15	4

COLUMBUS (Elev. 813 ft.)

Month	Max	Min	Pcpn	Snow
Jan	34	19	2.18	8
Feb	38	21	2.24	6
Mar	51	31	3.27	5
Apr	62	40	3.21	1
May	72	50	3.93	T
Jun	80	58	4.04	0
Jul	84	63	4.31	0
Aug	82	61	3.72	0
Sep	76	55	2.96	0
Oct	65	43	2.15	T
Nov	51	34	3.22	2
Dec	39	25	2.86	5

DAYTON (Elev. 995 ft.)

Month	Max	Min	Pcpn	Snow
Jan	34	18	2.13	8
Feb	33	21	2.17	6
Mar	50	31	3.42	5
Apr	62	41	3.46	1
May	73	51	3.88	T
Jun	82	59	3.82	0
Jul	85	63	3.54	0
Aug	83	61	3.20	0
Sep	77	55	2.54	0
Oct	65	44	2.48	T
Nov	51	34	3.07	2
Dec	39	24	2.93	6

ELYRIA (Elev. 730 ft.)

Month	Max	Min	Pcpn	Snow
Jan	36	20	1.83	11
Feb	39	21	1.85	10
Mar	50	31	2.80	8
Apr	62	41	2.82	1
May	73	50	3.51	T
Jun	82	59	3.76	0
Jul	86	63	3.39	0
Aug	84	62	3.00	0
Sep	78	56	3.03	0
Oct	67	45	2.30	0
Nov	53	37	3.14	4
Dec	40	26	3.05	10

ERIE, PA (Elev. 731 ft.)

Month	Max	Min	Pcpn	Snow
Jan	33	18	2.22	23
Feb	34	18	2.28	16
Mar	44	28	3.00	11
Apr	55	38	3.24	3
May	66	48	3.44	T
Jun	75	58	4.09	0
Jul	80	63	3.43	0
Aug	79	62	4.06	0
Sep	72	56	4.39	T
Oct	61	46	3.77	1
Nov	49	37	4.02	10
Dec	38	25	3.59	22

IRONTON (Elev. 555 ft.)

Month	Max	Min	Pcpn	Snow
Jan	41	21	2.55	7
Feb	46	24	2.78	5
Mar	58	33	3.06	3
Apr	67	42	3.50	0
May	78	51	3.98	0
Jun	85	60	3.57	0
Jul	88	64	4.58	0

Aug	87	63	3.77	0
Sep	81	56	2.59	0
Oct	70	44	2.80	0
Nov	58	35	2.93	1
Dec	46	27	3.13	3

KENT-RAVENNA (Elev. 1,150 ft.)

Month	Max	Min	Pcpn	Snow
Jan	34	17	2.30	12
Feb	38	18	2.15	11
Mar	48	28	3.21	9
Apr	59	38	3.20	2
May	71	48	3.42	T
Jun	80	57	3.33	0
Jul	82	62	3.88	0
Aug	81	60	3.38	0
Sep	75	54	3.14	0
Oct	63	43	2.39	1
Nov	49	33	2.92	5
Dec	39	24	2.59	10

LIMA (Elev. 860 ft.)

Month	Max	Min	Pcpn	Snow
Jan	31	15	1.75	7
Feb	34	17	1.59	6
Mar	45	27	2.65	5
Apr	58	37	3.03	T
May	72	49	3.79	0
Jun	81	58	3.09	0
Jul	85	63	3.44	0
Aug	82	60	2.67	0
Sep	76	54	2.95	0
Oct	63	42	1.95	0
Nov	49	33	2.51	2
Dec	37	22	2.50	4

MANSFIELD (Elev. 1,295 ft.)

Month	Max	Min	Pcpn	Snow
Jan	32	17	1.65	10
Feb	35	19	1.66	9
Mar	47	29	2.88	7
Apr	59	38	3.43	2
May	69	48	4.15	0
Jun	78	57	3.68	0
Jul	82	62	3.67	0
Aug	80	60	4.00	0
Sep	74	54	3.25	0
Oct	62	43	2.08	T
Nov	49	34	3.12	2
Dec	37	23	2.82	9

MARIETTA (Elev. 580 ft.)

Month	Max	Min	Pcpn	Snow
Jan	39	21	2.36	8
Feb	43	22	2.49	5
Mar	54	32	3.11	4
Apr	65	40	2.84	T
May	75	50	3.62	0
Jun	83	59	3.64	0
Jul	86	63	3.90	0
Aug	84	62	3.33	0
Sep	78	55	3.01	0
Oct	67	43	2.69	0
Nov	55	35	2.77	2
Dec	44	26	2.91	4

MEDINA (Elev. 1,192 ft.)

Month	Max	Min	Pcpn	Snow
Jan	31	14	2.01	12
Feb	35	15	2.13	10
Mar	46	25	3.12	7
Apr	58	35	3.25	3
May	69	46	3.86	0
Jun	78	55	3.61	0
Jul	82	59	3.86	0
Aug	80	57	3.24	0
Sep	74	51	3.39	0
Oct	62	39	2.29	1
Nov	49	31	3.33	4
Dec	36	21	3.00	10

NEW PHILA-DOVER (Elev. 890 ft.)

Month	Max	Min	Pcpn	Snow
Jan	34	16	2.37	9
Feb	38	17	2.46	7
Mar	49	27	3.49	5
Apr	61	36	3.52	1
May	72	46	3.93	T
Jun	81	55	4.06	0
Jul	85	59	4.28	0
Aug	83	58	3.35	0
Sep	76	51	3.06	0
Oct	64	39	2.48	T
Nov	51	32	2.55	2
Dec	39	23	2.94	6

NORWALK (Elev. 670 ft.)

Month	Max	Min	Pcpn	Snow
Jan	31	15	1.46	9
Feb	34	17	1.83	7
Mar	44	27	2.69	6
Apr	58	36	3.28	1
May	70	47	3.76	0
Jun	79	56	3.84	0
Jul	83	61	3.37	0
Aug	81	59	3.25	0
Sep	75	52	2.90	0
Oct	62	41	1.83	0
Nov	50	33	2.56	2
Dec	36	22	2.77	7

PAINESVILLE (Elev. 600 ft.)

Month	Max	Min	Pcpn	Snow
Jan	34	20	2.33	15
Feb	36	21	1.82	13
Mar	46	29	2.62	9
Apr	57	38	3.20	1
May	68	48	3.06	0
Jun	77	58	3.37	0
Jul	81	62	3.31	0
Aug	80	61	3.44	0
Sep	75	53	3.30	0
Oct	64	46	3.04	T
Nov	51	36	3.44	5
Dec	40	26	2.77	15

SANDUSKY (Elev. 606 ft.)

Month	Max	Min	Pcpn	Snow
Jan	31	17	1.29	9
Feb	33	19	1.71	7
Mar	43	29	2.18	S
Apr	55	39	2.80	T
May	68	50	3.68	0
Jun	78	60	3.26	0
Jul	83	65	3.27	0
Aug	80	63	3.17	0
Sep	74	56	2.53	0
Oct	61	45	2.01	0
Nov	49	35	2.50	2
Dec	37	24	2.82	7

STEUBENVILLE (Elev. 992 ft.)

Month	Max	Min	Pcpn	Snow
Jan	37	19	2.97	12
Feb	40	21	2.47	10
Mar	50	29	3.87	7
Apr	63	39	3.58	2
May	73	49	3.88	0
Jun	81	58	4.16	0
Jul	84	62	3.97	0
Aug	83	61	3.43	0
Sep	77	55	2.84	0
Oct	65	43	2.65	T
Nov	52	34	2.64	3
Dec	41	25	2.87	8

TIFFIN (Elev. 760 ft.)

Month	Max	Min	Pcpn	Snow
Jan	33	18	2.44	8
Feb	36	20	1.98	6
Mar	47	29	3.12	5
Apr	61	39	3.54	1
May	72	49	3.55	0
Jun	81	59	3.46	0
Jul	84	62	3.88	0
Aug	82	61	3.22	0
Sep	76	54	2.74	0
Oct	65	44	2.05	0
Nov	50	34	2.65	2
Dec	38	29	2.62	7

WOOSTER (Elev. 1,020 ft.)

Month	Max	Min	Pcpn	Snow
Jan	32	17	1.60	9
Feb	35	19	2.01	8
Mar	47	28	2.60	6
Apr	59	37	3.00	1
May	69	47	3.73	0
Jun	78	56	3 37	0
Jul	82	60	3.97	0
Aug	80	58	3.58	0
Sep	73	52	2.78	0
Oct	62	41	1.78	T
Nov	49	33	2.72	3
Dec	37	23	2.50	7

TOLEDO (Elev. 669 ft.)

Month	Max	Min	Pcpn	Snow
Jan	30	15	1.75	10
Feb	33	17	1.73	8
Mar	46	27	2.66	6
Apr	59	36	2.96	2
May	71	47	2.91	T
Jun	80	56	3.75	0
Jul	83	61	3.27	0
Aug	81	58	3.25	0
Sep	74	52	2.85	0
Oct	62	40	2.10	T
Nov	49	32	2.81	3
Dec	35	21	2.93	8

YOUNGSTOWN (Elev. 1,178 ft.)

Month	Max	Min	Pcpn	Snow
Jan	31	16	2.13	13
Feb	34	18	2.03	11
Mar	45	27	3.11	11
Apr	58	37	3.06	3
May	69	46	3.52	T
Jun	77	55	3.94	0
Jul	81	59	4.07	0
Aug	80	58	3.32	0
Sep	73	52	3.48	0
Oct	61	42	2.62	1
Nov	48	34	3.11	6
Dec	36	23	2.93	12

SELECTED READING LIST

GENERAL WEATHER & METEOROLOGY

How the Weather Works, by Michael Allaby (Reader's Digest Association, 1995).

Weather in Your Life, by Louis J. Battan (W. H. Freeman, 1983).

Clouds in a Glass of Beer: Simple Experiments in Atmospheric Physics, by Craig F. Bohren (Wiley, 1987).

The Nature Company Guide to Weather Watching, by William Burroughs and Robert Crowder, et. al. (Time-Life Books, 1996).

Watching the World's Weather, by William James Burroughs (Cambridge University Press, 1991).

Storms, by William R. Cotton (Aster Press Geophysical Science Series vol. 1, 1990).

Mariner's Weather, by William P. Crawford (W. W. Norton & Company, 1992).

It's Raining Frogs and Fishes: Four Seasons of Natural Phenomena and Oddities of the Sky, by Jerry Dennis (Harper Perennial, 1993).

Violent Storms, by Jon Erickson (TAB Books, 1988).

Dr. Frank Field's Weather Book, by Frank Field (Putnam, 1981).

Rainbows, Curve Balls, and Other Wonders of the Natural World Explained, by Ira Flatow (William Morrow and Company, 1988).

The Violent Face of Nature: Severe Phenomena and Natural Disasters, by Kendrick Frazier (William Morrow and Co., 1979).

Weather Proverbs, by George D. Freier (Fisher Books, 1989).

Significant Tornadoes, 1680–1995, by Thomas P. Grazulius (Tornado Project, 1996). Annual supplement available.

Winter: An Ecological Handbook, by James C. Halfpenny and Roy Douglas Ozanne (Johnson Publishing Co., 1989).

America's Favorite Backyard Wildlife, by George and Kit Harrison (Simon & Schuster, 1985).

The Basic Essentials of Weather Forecasting, by Michael Hodgson (ICS Books, 1992).

American Weather Stories, by Patrick Hughes (U.S. Department of Commerce, 1976).

Your Health, Your Moods, and the Weather, by W. S. Kals (Doubleday, 1982).

Skywatch East: A Weather Guide, by Richard A. Keen (Fulcrum Publishing, 1992).

Weather Wisdom: Facts and Folklore of Weather Forecasting, by Albert Lee (Congdon and Weed, 1976).

The Weather Companion: An Album of Meteorological History, Science, Legend, and Folklore, by Gary Lockhart (John Wiley & Sons, 1988).

The National Audubon Society Field Guide to North American Weather, by David L. Ludlum (Alfred A. Knopf, 1995).

The Weather Factor. by David McWilliams Ludlum (Houghton Mifflin, 1984).

Sunsets, Twilights, and Evening Skies, by Aden and Marjorie Meinel (Cambridge University Press, 1983).

Awake to Wildlife: A Great Lakes Wildlife Almanac, by Tom Nowicki (Glovebox Guidebooks Publishing Co., 1994).

A Field Guide to the Atmosphere, by Vincent J. Schaefer and John A. Day (Houghton Mifflin Co., 1981).

Thunder in the Heartland : A Chronicle of Outstanding Weather Events in Ohio, by Thomas W. and Jeanne Schmidlin (Kent State University Press, 1996).

Wandering Through Winter, by Edwin Way Teale (Dodd, Mead & Company, 1981).

Journey Into Summer, by Edwin Way Teale (Dodd, Mead & Company, 1981).

Autumn Across America, by Edwin Way Teale (Dodd, Mead & Company, 1981).

North with the Spring, by Edwin Way Teale (Dodd, Mead & Company, 1981).

Meditations at Sunset : A Scientist Looks at the Sky, by James Trefil (Scribner, 1987).

Rainbows, Snowflakes, and Quarks, by Hans C. von Baeyer (McGraw-Hill, 1984).

The Weather Sourcebook : Your One-Stop Resource for Everything You Need to Know to Feed Your Weather Habit, 2nd ed., by Ronald L. Wagner and Bill Adler, Jr. (Globe Pequot Press, 1997).

Heaven's Breath: A Natural History of the Wind, by Lyall Watson (William Morrow and Co., 1984).

The Weather Handbook, by Alan Watts (Sheridan House, 1994).

The Weather Book, by Jack Williams (Vintage Books, 1997).

ASTRONOMY & SKYWATCHING

Asimov's Chronology of Science and Discovery, by Isaac Asimov (Harper and Row, 1989).

Star and Planet Spotting: A Field Guide to the Night Sky, by Peter Lancaster Brown (Sterling Publishing Co., 1990).

The Nature Company Guide to Advanced Skywatching, by Robert Burnham and Alan Dyer, et. al. (Time-Life Books, 1997).

Thunderstones and Shooting Stars: The Meaning of Meteorites, by Robert T. Dodd (Harvard University Press, 1986).

Touring the Universe through Binoculars, by Philip S. Harrington (John Wiley & Sons, 1990).

Beyond the Blue Horizon: Myths and Legends of the Sun, Moon, Stars, and Planets, by E. C. Krupp (HarperCollins, 1991).

The Lunar Effect: Biological Tides and Human Emotions, by Arnold L. Leiber, M.D., (Anchor Press/Doubleday, 1988).

A Field Guide to the Stars and Planets, by Donald H. Menzel and Jay M. Pasachoff (Peterson Field Guide Series, 1983).

The Moon Observer's Handbook, by Fred W. Price (Cambridge University Press, 1988).

The Skywatcher's Handbook, by Colin A. Ronan (Crown Publishers, 1985).

Cosmos, by Carl Sagan (Random House, 1980).

Wonders of the Sky: Observing Rainbows, Comets, Eclipses, the Stars, and Other Phenomena, by Fred Schaaf (Dover Publications, 1983).

Comets: A Chronological History of Observation, Science, Myth, and Folklore, by Donald K. Yeomans (John Wiley & Sons, 1998).

ACKNOWLEDGMENTS

I'd like to express my sincere thanks to the many kind people who helped me put this book together.

As a weather forecaster and meteorologist, I rely heavily on the resources of the National Weather Service (NWS) and the National Oceanic and Atmospheric Agency (NOAA). Many thanks to the following weather professionals for their help with the collection of many of the book's charts, images, and statistical data: Larry Gabric and the Cleveland office of the NWS, technician Jennifer Offutt and her colleagues at the Cleveland NOAA office, and Carla Wallace at the NOAA's Central Library in Washington, D.C.

Thanks also to the folks at FOX 8 who put in considerable time and effort providing technical assistance, especially fellow meteorologist André Bernier, producer Bob Levkulich, graphics coordinator Kay Filla, and Mark Neumayer, head of the FOX 8 Graphics Unit.

A blizzard of special thanks to Larry Huff at the Ohio Weather Observer Network, CWRU Earth Sciences Professor Peter Whiting and student researchers Jeff Shaw and Janice Poling, Cleveland State University archivist Bill Becker, and photo contributors Bob Steharsky and Ruth Calain. Thanks also to the many FOX 8 viewers who over the years have sent in photos and information about our dynamic Northeast Ohio weather.

Finally, my grateful appreciation to those who helped me compile and organize the many articles, charts, statistics, photos, and other illustrations that comprise this weather guide and almanac: transcriber Erica Moehring, designer Larry Nozik, my editors at Gray & Company, and, most of all, to my wife, Amber, and my daughter, Kim, for their love and support.

And to all FOX 8 weather watchers, thanks for your continued support of charitable causes. Part of the proceeds from this book will go to animal welfare organizations around Northeast Ohio.

PHOTO CREDITS

All illustrations by the author unless otherwise noted. Individual photos credited where applicable.

Key to Photo Credits:
Auth—Author's Collection
CSU—Cleveland Press Collection, Cleveland State University Archives
FOX 8—FOX 8/WJW-TV Graphics Unit
NOAA—National Oceanic and Atmospheric Agency
OWON—Ohio Weather Observer Network

Winter
Page 10, NOAA; 18, CSU/Photo by Jim Fiedler; 27, FOX 8; 32, Auth; 33, FOX 8; 34, FOX 8; 35, CSU/Photo by Timothy Culek; 37, FOX 8; 38, NOAA; 43, FOX 8; 50, CSU; 51, CSU; 54, CSU; 69, CSU; 71, CSU; 73, Auth; 74, CSU; 76, Auth; 81, NOAA; 82, NOAA.

Spring
Page 88, Auth; 90, Auth; 91, CSU; 102, NOAA; 105, FOX 8; 117–118, NOAA (all); 125, photo by Ruth Calain; 127, Auth; 128, Auth; 131, NOAA; 138, photos by Bob Steharsky; 141, CSU; 145, NOAA.

Summer
Page 148, NOAA; 151, Auth; 153, CSU; 157, Courtesy of Joe Williams, Jr.; 159, NOAA; 162, Auth; 163, Auth; 168, NOAA; 173, CSU; 174, CSU; 176, Auth; 179, Auth; 187, Auth; 188, Auth; 190, CSU; 195, Auth; 196, NOAA; 201, Auth.

Autumn
202, CSU/Photo by Fred Bottomer; 218, Auth; 230, Auth; 231–232, Auth; 232, Auth; 241, Auth; 242, CSU; 244, OWON (both); 247, Auth.

INDEX